Legislative Entrepreneurship in the U.S. House of Representatives

Michigan Studies in Political Analysis

Michigan Studies in Political Analysis promotes the development and dissemination of innovative scholarship in the field of methodology in political science and the social sciences in general. Methodology is defined to include statistical methods, mathematical modeling, measurement, research design, and other topics related to the conduct and development of analytical work. The series includes works that develop a new model or method applicable to social sciences, as well as those that, through innovative combination and presentation of current analytical tools, substantially extend the use of these tools by other researchers.

GENERAL EDITORS: John E. Jackson and Christopher H. Achen

Keith Krehbiel
Information and Legislative Organization

Donald R. Kinder and Thomas R. Palfrey, Editors
Experimental Foundations of Political Science

John Brehm
The Phantom Respondents: Opinion Surveys and Political Representation

William T. Bianco
Trust: Representatives and Constituents

Melvin J. Hinich and Michael C. Munger
Ideology and the Theory of Political Choice

John Brehm and Scott Gates
Working, Shirking, and Sabotage: Bureaucratic Response to a Democratic Public

R. Michael Alvarez
Information and Elections

David Austen-Smith and Jeffrey S. Banks
Positive Political Theory I: Collective Preference

Gregory Wawro
Legislative Entrepreneurship in the U.S. House of Representatives

Legislative Entrepreneurship in the U.S. House of Representatives

Gregory Wawro

Ann Arbor

THE UNIVERSITY OF MICHIGAN PRESS

Copyright © by the University of Michigan 2000
All rights reserved
Published in the United States of America by
The University of Michigan Press
Manufactured in the United States of America
♾ Printed on acid-free paper

2003 2002 2001 2000 4 3 2 1

No part of this publication may be reproduced,
stored in a retrieval system, or transmitted in any form
or by any means, electronic, mechanical, or otherwise,
without the written permission of the publisher.

*A CIP catalog record for this book is available
from the British Library.*

Library of Congress Cataloging-in-Publication Data

Wawro, Gregory J. (Gregory John)
Legislative entrepreneurship in the U.S. House of Representatives / Gregory Wawro.
p. cm. — (Michigan studies in political analysis)
Includes bibliographical references and index.
ISBN 0-472-11153-1 (cloth : alk. paper)
1. United States. Congress. House. 2. Legislators—United States. 3. Bills, Legislative—United States. 4. Legislation—United States. 5. Entrepreneurship—United States. I. Title. II. Series.

JK1319 .W38 2000
328.73′077—dc21 00-023486

For Mom, Dad, and Thad

Contents

Figures

Tables

Acknowledgments

One of the first things I do when I buy a new album is read the acknowledgments in the liner notes. Reading the names that appear there I get a better understanding of the music by learning about the artist's influences, family, friends, mentors, and fellow travelers who play an indispensable role in the production of the music. It is always interesting to see the wide array of individuals who contributed to the production of the work and to consider how they helped shape the final product. I hope these acknowledgments give additional insight into the production of this book and convey my deep gratitude to the wide array of individuals who have helped make it much better than it would have been without their assistance, encouragement, and support. They are quite an eclectic bunch, including academics from different disciplines and from very different camps within the different disciplines, as well as nonacademics. I am grateful that so many people have taken an interest in me and my work and thought enough of it to spend some of their scarce time and resources to help me improve it. I hope you agree that their efforts were worthwhile, and that, to the best of my limited abilities, I have done them justice.

Most thank you lists on albums start with family, so I don't see why this list should be any different. My parents, Patricia and Thaddeus K. Wawro, and my brother, Thaddeus W. Wawro, provided love, encouragement, and support to me throughout this project and throughout my life. I dedicate this book to them.

This project began as my dissertation, and I am indebted to many people who helped me during my graduate school days at Cornell University. My dissertation committee members, Ted Lowi, Walter Mebane, and Andy Rutten, indelibly shaped the early development of the project and my development as a scholar. Their comments, criticism, and encouragement have been crucial to this project. Several other Cornell professors provided support, including Richard Bensel, Jonathan Cowden, Robert Gibbons, Sidney Tarrow, and Marty Wells. Ann Gray and Carol Murphree of the Cornell Institute for Social and Economic Research and the staff at Cornell's Olin Library were invaluable in my data collection efforts.

I am indebted to several individuals who provided scholarly support. Gary

Jacobson, Garrison Nelson, and David Rohde provided me with data that made much of the empirical research possible. Many individuals discussed chapters of this book in paper form at conferences over the years, and their comments have helped to vastly improve the work. Members of the political methodology section of the American Political Science Association helped with this project from its earliest stages, and I am indebted to them for letting me present my work in various forms at several of the group's summer meetings. I am also grateful to the faculties of the various universities that invited me to give job talks or participate in workshops where I could discuss this work. I am especially thankful to members of the faculty at Columbia University, who not only invited me to present my work but gave me a job where I could continue it! Present and former professors at Columbia who have provided comments, encouragement, and assistance in transforming my work from a dissertation to a published book are Charles Cameron, David Epstein, Ira Katznelson, Nolan McCarty, Sharyn O'Halloran, Sunita Parikh, and Bob Shapiro. Matt Atlas and Dan Fisher at Columbia provided excellent research assistance. Gary Cox, Bill Bianco, Sarah Binder, Forrest Maltzman, Eric Schickler, and Wendy Schiller all provided helpful comments on the manuscript.

Others were especially helpful in the concluding phases of the project. Michael Alvarez was invaluable in dealing with the publication process, from initial submission of the manuscript to typesetting. Gary King offered me a very generous leave at Harvard, which helped me complete the project, and he helped at crucial points with the manuscript. Jim Alt and the Center for Basic Research in the Social Sciences at Harvard provided me with office space and resources during the completion of the book (and, most importantly, tolerated the presence of my dog and sine qua non, Bristol, at the center). A first-time author could not ask for a better editor than Chuck Myers, whose patience, professionalism, enthusiasm, and encouragement made the arduous process of publishing a book as smooth as possibly imaginable.

Several friends helped and supported me while I worked on this project. They are Paul Apostolidis, Steve Carter, Tony Elmquist, Sophie Gee, Bill Hamilton, Orit Kedar, Chuck Kroll, Cathy Layton, Jeannie Moorefield, Jennifer Reardon, Jeff Turlik, Doug Usher, Jeremy Varon, and Juliet Williams. Two dear friends who deserve special recognition are Libbie Rifkin and Lynn MacKenzie. In addition to their friendship and support, they read and commented on the manuscript, giving me the confidence I needed to advance to the next stages in the production of this book.

CHAPTER 1

The Puzzle of Legislative Entrepreneurship

In the first session of the 100th Congress, Representative Richard Armey (R–TX) introduced H.R. 1583, which was a bill that offered a solution to the perennially contentious issue of military base closings. Armey's bill provided for the establishment of a 12-member, bipartisan panel to recommend to the secretary of defense a list of military bases that it deemed superfluous. The secretary would then take the necessary steps to close or scale back the bases on the list.

It is surprising that Armey would have taken on such a difficult issue. Between 1977 and 1987, when Armey introduced his bill, not one U.S. military base had been closed, despite potential savings of hundreds of millions of dollars and Pentagon support for base closures. At the time, Armey was a member of the minority party who was only in his second term. He did not occupy a position in the House of Representatives that endowed him with resources that he could have used to get his bill out of committee, much less enacted into law. He was not even a member of the Armed Services Committee, the key committee of jurisdiction.

It is even more surprising, then, that Armey realized the success that he did with his proposal, considering that "base-closing proposals usually don't make it past bureaucratic red tape or committee markups" (Mills 1988a, 1145). To mix metaphors, military bases have traditionally been a sacred cow in the congressional pork barrel, making base closures one of the most difficult issues around which to build a winning coalition.

But Armey was not just tilting at windmills. As part of his strategy for pushing his bill through the legislative process, Armey attempted to attach his bill as an amendment to the fiscal 1988 defense authorization bill. To the surprise to the Democratic leadership, the proposal almost passed, with the House barely rejecting the proposal on a vote of 192 to 199.

Armey reintroduced his base closing bill as H.R. 4481 in the second session of the 100th Congress. Even though the new bill was cosponsored by the chair and ranking minority member of the Armed Services Committee, it faced more of an uphill battle the second time around as members of Congress mobilized to protect the bases in their districts. Armey again attempted to attach his legislation to a defense authorization bill, which would have put the bill on a fast track to passage. After complaints from the chairs of the Government Operations and Merchant Marine and Fisheries Committees, the Rules Committee refused to let Armey offer his legislation as an amendment to the authorization bill. Instead, the measure was multiply referred for consideration as a piece of freestanding legislation. Four separate committees reported the version of the bill that made it to the floor. Many new provisions had been added to the bill, diluting its effectiveness and leading to fears that it would die a "death by pinpricks" (Mills 1988b).

On the floor, Armey proposed an amendment in the nature of a substitute for the reported bill. The substitute largely restored the bill to its original form, although it included important compromises to widen its appeal. The House agreed to Armey's substitute on a vote of 223 to 186. With the acceptance of his proposal, Armey won a major, though by no means easy, legislative victory on an issue that had been extremely vexing to members of Congress.

What explains Armey's efforts on his base-closing bill? Why did he invest the time and resources to draft, introduce, and push his legislation?

Understanding Armey's behavior is key to understanding how the U.S. House of Representatives satisfies its constitutionally designated role as a governing institution. In order to perform this role, individual members of the House must work to pass legislation. Since it is a majoritarian institution, any legislation that passes the House is by definition a group effort. However, individual members, such as Dick Armey, who engage in *legislative entrepreneurship* perform a function that is crucial to the policy-making process because they bear much of the burden of the production of legislation. Members engage in legislative entrepreneurship when they invest time, staff, and other resources to acquire knowledge of particular policy areas, draft legislation addressing issues in those areas, and shepherd their proposals through the legislative process by building and maintaining coalitions.

The purpose of this book is to explain why members of the House engage in legislative entrepreneurship.[1] The key puzzle I try to solve is why *individual* members bear the costs of engaging in legislative entrepreneurship instead of free riding on the entrepreneurial efforts of others.

Solving this puzzle and explaining this behavior are crucial to understanding how the House functions as a policy-making body and performs its role in the federal government. Without individuals who devote time and effort to entrepreneurial activity, it is doubtful that the House could pass legislation. If its members did not engage in legislative entrepreneurship, the House cer-

1. While many of the arguments I make in this book apply to the Senate, a separate analysis of legislative entrepreneurship in that body is necessary. The structure, rules, and norms of the Senate create a very different environment from the one in which House members operate. An analysis of legislative entrepreneurship in the Senate is beyond the scope of this study, however.

tainly could not be a source of legislative initiative, nor could the institution be much more than a rubber stamp of Senate and executive branch proposals. The House would cease to be a full partner in the separation of powers system, which would prevent this system from serving as the bulwark against tyranny that the Framers designed it to be.

Yet the Framers did not see a need to establish formal requirements that members become legislative entrepreneurs (LEs).[2] Other than delineating the general powers of Congress, the Constitution says nothing about what *individuals* who are elected to the House are supposed to do. House rules pertaining to the duties of members (rule VIII) require only that members "vote on each question put" unless they are prevented from doing so or have a conflict of interest. Members have a wide variety of activities that they can undertake as elected officials, but they have a limited amount of resources that they can allocate to different activities. Assuming that members are goal-oriented, rational actors (as most studies of Congress do), members will choose to allocate resources only to activities that they believe will help them achieve their goals. Explaining why members would engage in legislative entrepreneurship entails explaining how this activity contributes to the attainment of these goals.

One of the first obstacles we face in explaining this activity is that the literature on Congress lacks a coherent, explicit definition of *legislative entrepreneurship*. Though the term *entrepreneurship* appears regularly in this literature, the concept of entrepreneurship as it pertains to legislative activity remains inchoate. Price's in-depth analysis (1972, 297) of the lawmaking process mentions members of Congress who operate as policy entrepreneurs, but it does not define what these individuals do beyond saying that they stimulate more than they respond to pressure groups. Hall (1996, 233) identifies legislative entrepreneurship as "a special case of [legislative] participation, one where the individual ranks at the high end of the formal and informal participation scales." But Hall does not go into much more detail regarding the specific activities that members engage in when they participate as LEs.

Some studies identify LEs simply as members of legislatures who fit a general definition of entrepreneurs. For example, Kingdon (1984, 188) defines policy entrepreneurs as "advocates who are willing to invest their resources—time, energy, reputation, money—to promote a position in return for anticipated future gain in the form of material, purposive, or solidary benefits." LEs for Kingdon, then, are simply members of a legislature who become policy entrepreneurs. But this definition is not very useful because it means that almost every member of Congress engages in entrepreneurship almost every day that

2. Although I will often refer to members as legislative entrepreneurs, I am sacrificing conceptual clarity for ease of exposition. The House cannot be divided into LEs and non-LEs because members engage in entrepreneurial activity to different degrees at different times.

Congress is in session. That is, every member casts votes (a very important resource) that promote a position (for or against legislative proposals) in ways that they presumably benefit from. A more discriminating definition that captures the important aspects of the behavior of individuals like Dick Armey is called for.

To build such a definition, I start with the basics. An individual engages in *entrepreneurship,* generically speaking, when he or she coordinates the actions and resources of other individuals so that they can realize gains that would not be possible without such coordination. *Economic entrepreneurs* coordinate the activities of buyers and sellers so that the parties involved can supply themselves with private goods.[3] Entrepreneurs in political settings work to coordinate the resources of individuals to produce political outcomes that can be obtained only if the individuals act as a group (Fiorina and Shepsle 1989, 32–33). *Political entrepreneurs* provide a mechanism for the pooling of resources so that individuals can act effectively as a group and supply themselves with collective goods (Frohlich and Oppenheimer 1978; Frohlich, Oppenheimer, and Young 1971).

It is important to distinguish entrepreneurship in legislatures as a special case of political entrepreneurship. Legislators are in privileged positions as political entrepreneurs. They have resources and access to the policy-making process that others do not. They also are in danger of losing these resources and their access if they do not allocate them properly because misallocation of resources can lead to electoral defeat.[4]

The definition I use in this study is as follows: legislative entrepreneurship is a set of activities that a legislator engages in, which involves working to form coalitions of other members for the purpose of passing legislation by combining various legislative inputs and issues in order to affect legislative outcomes. LEs invest time and effort to become aware of existing opportunities for enacting legislation that others have failed to notice and gather information about how to combine various legislative inputs to exploit these opportunities. They use this information to supply a *legislative package* that has the potential to attract a winning coalition. A legislative package includes the text of

3. For a review of the relationship between economic and political entrepreneurs, see Schneider and Teske 1992. In the development of the concept of the legislative entrepreneur I draw heavily on Kirzner's concept (1973) of the economic entrepreneur.

4. Frohlich and Oppenheimer's discussion (1978) of members of Congress as political entrepreneurs pertains to building coalitions of voters in districts so that the members will be elected and then will use their offices to bestow collective goods on their constituents. The concept of legislative entrepreneurship that I develop here pertains to members building coalitions among other members within the legislature. However, one of the most important issues that I consider is how building coalitions within the legislature affects members' abilities to build coalitions in their districts.

the proposal as well as information about its chances of becoming law and the consequences if the legislature passes it. Thus, the legislative package reduces uncertainty about the consequences of different legislative alternatives and uncertainty about what other legislators want to enact.

Legislative packages are the mechanisms LEs use to pool the resources of other legislators. The most important resources that LEs pool are legislators' votes. Legislative packages can pool other resources such as those associated with a member's position in the institution. For example, an LE might draw on a committee chair's authority to schedule hearings to inform others of his or her proposal. However, these other resources are useful to LEs only if they can use the resources to attract votes.

The central goal of LEs is to gather enough votes to pass legislation (or at least to make credible threats of passing it). In order to pass legislation, LEs must convince a majority in the chamber as well as other key players involved in the legislative process that the LEs' proposals will benefit them.

The concept of the LE that I employ is similar to Arnold's concept (1990) of the *coalition leader.* Coalition leaders are those who "design policy proposals and select strategies for enacting them" (5). Coalition leaders engage in activities similar to those in which LEs engage. Yet I develop the concept of the LE rather than simply employing Arnold's terminology because using the term *entrepreneur* more closely ties my analysis to the extensive work on political and economic entrepreneurs. The latter is especially important because of its focus on risk (Kirzner's 1973; Knight 1921). As I will discuss in more detail later, legislative entrepreneurship is a potentially risky activity with respect to reelection. Given the central role that the reelection goal has played in the literature on Congress, it is especially important to consider the electoral risks associated with engaging in entrepreneurial activities. Arnold claims that the strategies coalition leaders devise recognize the electoral necessity of those whom they seek to bring into the coalition. But it is not clear how the activities of coalition leaders relate to their own electoral necessities. By Arnold's (1990, 8, n. 7) own admission, the activities of those who build coalitions do not appear to satisfy their electoral needs. This is an issue that I will explore in more theoretical and empirical detail.

In order to fully develop the concept of legislative entrepreneurship, it is necessary to consider in more detail the four main activities that constitute legislative entrepreneurship: acquiring information, bill drafting, coalition building, and pushing legislation. Although these activities are intertwined, in the following sections I disentangle them in order to elucidate the part that each plays in legislative entrepreneurship. To put some flesh on this conceptual skeleton, I give examples of how members of the House have engaged in these activities.

Acquiring Information

The acquisition of policy-relevant information is central to the concept of legislative entrepreneurship. One of the first activities that legislators undertake when they assume the role of LE is to gather information about a particular policy area, learning about existing policy and salient issues in that area. As budding LEs, legislators learn which policies can produce which outcomes and which outcomes are potentially desirable to themselves and other legislators.

LEs gather essentially two types of information. First, they learn about the relationship between policy proposals and policy effects. The acquisition of this type of information provides the motivation for informational theories of legislative organization (Gilligan and Krehbiel 1987, 1989a, 1989b, 1990; Krehbiel 1991). Informational theories use the term *specialization* to refer to learning about policies and outcomes. This use of the term differs somewhat from how it has been used traditionally in studies of Congress. According to the literature on congressional norms, specialization is a norm that induces legislators to focus on a few issues under the jurisdiction of the committee(s) on which they sit (Asher 1973). "They become expert, or at least facile, in a particular field, earn the respect of their colleagues for their diligence and command of the subject matter, and eventually come to be recognized as one of the congressional authorities in that area, a ready source of information and advice" (Clapp 1963, 110). Legislators become specialists, gaining in-depth knowledge of a narrow policy area, as opposed to becoming generalists who gain a superficial understanding of several policy areas.

LEs are not necessarily specialists in this sense. While focusing on a narrow set of issues should be sufficient for acquiring adequate levels of knowledge, it is not clear that it is necessary. In fact, LEs might want to avoid being so narrowly focused. While it is important for legislators to acquire some substantive knowledge of the policy areas in which they are operating as LEs, it is not necessary for them to focus on these areas exclusively. The degree to which legislators must concentrate on a particular area to be successful entrepreneurs depends to a significant degree on the complexity of the issues in that area.

The second type of information that LEs need to acquire is what Hall (1996, 91) refers to as *political intelligence.* This type of information concerns the policy preferences of an LE's fellow legislators, especially the preferences of those in formal leadership positions, who possess additional resources that they can deploy to help or hinder the LE's cause. In order to affect legislative outcomes, an LE must gain some sense of what other legislators are willing to enact into law. Thus, an LE needs to acquire knowledge not only of the relationship between policy alternatives and their consequences but about what other legislators want and what stands a chance of making it to and passing on the floor.

Les Aspin: Expert on Defense Issues

Representative Les Aspin (D–WI) represents a paradigmatic case of the importance of the acquisition and use of policy knowledge in legislative entrepreneurship. During his tenure in the House from the 92d through the 102d Congresses, Aspin cultivated a reputation for being an LE on defense issues. Even though he had no military bases or contractors in his district, he became a specialist in the traditional sense, confining his attention to the work of the Armed Services Committee and rarely introducing legislation that was not related to defense. As a result of this focus, Aspin obtained a technical knowledge of military issues that was unequaled in the House. His expertise concerning military issues "forced administrations of both parties to use him as a source of information, even if they disagree[d] with him" (Ehrenhalt 1983, 1643). In addition to knowing the technical details of military issues, Aspin was keenly aware of members' preferences on these issues, which enabled him to "tailor his policies to the political marketplace" (Towell 1985, 102).

Aspin's extensive knowledge of policy and preferences played a key role in his entrepreneurial efforts. Early in his career, Aspin won an impressive legislative victory by putting together a coalition to pass an amendment that reduced defense expenditures by about 4 percent—a major coup for a junior member ("House Votes" 1973). After becoming chair of Armed Services, Aspin used his expertise to produce overwhelming majorities on defense authorization proposals, something that previous chairs had been unable to do (Ehrenhalt 1987, 1638).

Drafting Legislation

When legislators gather information about a policy area, they learn how to attain certain ends through legislative means as well as what kinds of proposals other legislators will support. Once they acquire this information, they can draft the actual text of the legislation. Legislators not only must draft the legislation so that they can credibly claim that their proposals will accomplish certain ends, but they must also draft it in such a way that it will be attractive to a majority in the legislature. For example, a legislator might try to widen the appeal of a proposal by using vague wording that leaves others room for interpreting the bill differently.

Through bill drafting, an LE provides the basic legislative vehicle for debate and action on some issue or set of issues. The LE must draft the legislation

Fig. 1.1. No opportunity for new legislation

so that it conveys a core idea or set of ideas about problems or issues that the member thinks Congress should address. Though the proposal as originally introduced is likely to change, a member needs to provide an initial piece of legislation that other legislators will recognize as something worthy of their attention. As legislation progresses through the House, more information about the preferences of legislators and other key players in the process will become available. The legislation as initially drafted needs to be flexible enough so that legislators can modify it to incorporate this new information.

A Spatial Illustration of Bill Drafting and Innovation

Some simple spatial models of a three-person legislature are useful for illustrating how entrepreneurs draft bills to take advantage of opportunities for enacting new legislation.[5] Figure 1.1 is a hypothetical, one-dimensional policy space with each point along the continuum representing a policy addressing a particular issue. H_i represents the ideal point of the ith legislator on this issue, and *sq* represents the status quo policy. I that assume that these actors have quadratic utility functions, so they prefer points along the continuum that are closer to their ideal points than to ones that are farther away. I also assume that the preferences of the legislators are common knowledge. In order to enact a statute, a majority of the legislators must vote for it, and to vote for it they must prefer it to the status quo point.

Suppose a budding LE (who could be any one of the H_i) can make a proposal anywhere along the continuum and the legislators have a single, up or down vote for the proposal. If the legislators' preferences are fixed, no proposal along this continuum can beat *sq*. Any proposal would move the policy away from the ideal point of the median voter, making him or her worse off, and so no proposal can attract the votes necessary for passage. Since no proposal can beat the status quo, I refer to *sq* as an "equilibrium" outcome in the sense that it is stable (cf. Shepsle 1979). With this array of preferences, there are no opportunities for new legislation on this dimension.

5. Spatial models have become an essential part of the legislative scholar's tool kit. For those readers who are unfamiliar with spatial models, Enelow and Hinich 1984 is a very accessible introduction. 1988 provides an excellent review of the use of spatial models in legislative studies.

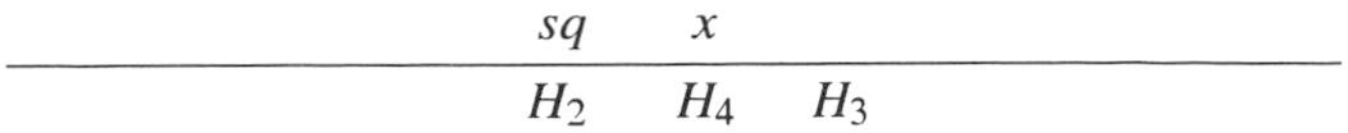

$sq \quad x$

$H_2 \quad H_4 \quad H_3$

Fig. 1.2. Opportunity exists for new legislation

If the preferences of one or more of the actors were to shift, this might create the opportunity to enact legislation at points other than sq. Suppose that an election takes place and H_4 defeats H_1, replacing him or her in the legislature. Figure 1.2 represents the new configuration of ideal points. H_4 is now the median voter on this dimension. The role of the LE is to propose new legislation, x, such that $sq < x \leq sq + 2(H_4 - sq)$. To establish a new equilibrium outcome, the LE should propose $x = H_4$.

In this example, the LE does not cause the shift in preferences; he or she only takes advantage of it after it has occurred. To use Kingdon's terminology (1984, 174), the change in the array of preferences in the legislature has opened up a "policy window"—an opportunity for action on particular initiatives. This opportunity arises because the composition of the legislature has changed. When they gather information, LEs can discover those dimensions on which a "disequilibrium" similar to that in figure 1.2 exists and can draft proposals with the ability to defeat the status quo on those dimensions.

LEs do not necessarily have to wait for shifts in preferences in the legislature to alter policy on a particular dimension. Opportunities for legislative entrepreneurship exist even in the absence of dimensions in disequilibrium because LEs can combine issue dimensions in their proposals. William Riker's work on *heresthetics* is key here (cf. Schneider and Teske 1992). Riker (1986, ix) defines *heresthetics* as the art of "structuring the world so you can win." Heresthetícians exploit certain features of collective decision-making institutions in order to produce outcomes they desire. According to Riker (147), one of the most important activities that constitute the art of heresthetics is the manipulation of issue dimensions. The manipulation of dimensions is also a central part of legislative entrepreneurship. LEs engage in heresthetics by selecting and combining different issue dimensions through bill drafting, making it possible for majorities to enact new legislation.

Figure 1.3 illustrates this type of heresthetical maneuver.[6] In the figure, H_{ij} represents the ideal point of member i on dimension j. Although the relative locations of the ideal points and status quo on both the horizontal and vertical dimensions in figure 1.3 are the same as the locations in figure 1.1, an

6. The concluding chapter of Riker 1986 contains an example similar to that of figure 1.3. In other chapters of the book, Riker presents accounts of dimension manipulation, some of which occur in legislative settings.

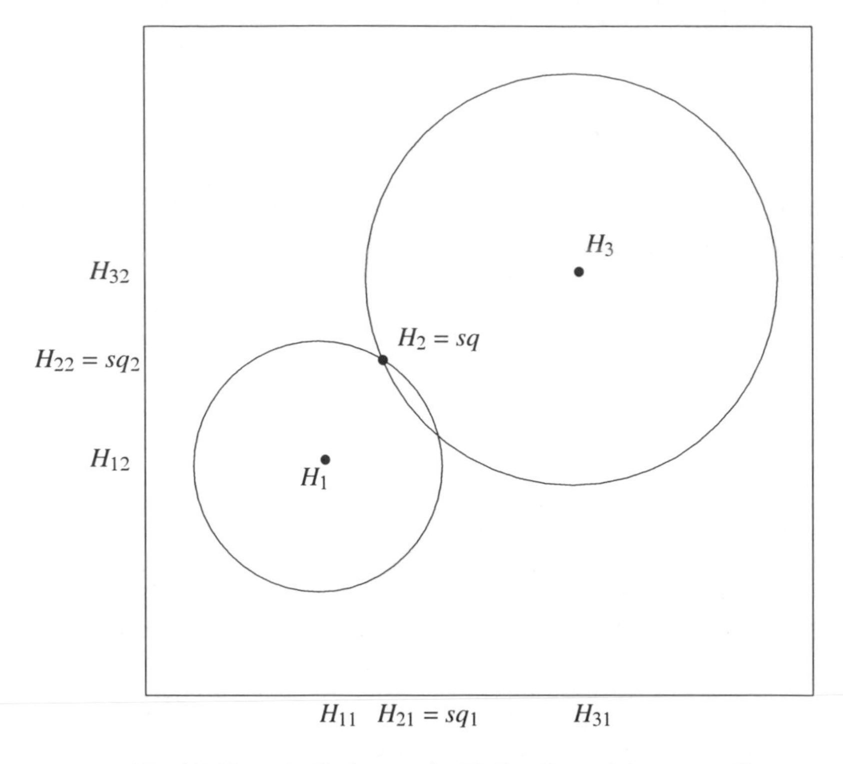

Fig. 1.3. Opportunity for new legislation through issue coupling

opportunity exists for enacting new legislation. The opportunity arises through the coupling of issue dimensions. If the legislators consider the horizontal and vertical issue dimensions separately, no proposal can be made that would beat sq_1 or sq_2. The role of the LE is to draft and introduce legislation that couples these dimensions as in figure 1.3 and locates the legislative outcome in the "win set"—i.e., the intersection of the indifference curves of H_1 and H_3—where there is the potential for a winning coalition to form in support of the proposal.[7]

When LEs engage in activities like those illustrated with the spatial model, they engage in *legislative innovation.* That is, they pursue legislative activities on issues Congress has not addressed previously, introducing new dimensions

---

7. If the status quo is located at the median's ideal point and the locations of ideal points are identical on all dimensions, then it is not possible to make a proposal that would beat the status quo. Opportunities for new legislation exist in multiple dimensions as long as the locations of legislators' ideal points differ across dimensions.

into the political debate, or they combine issues previously addressed in new ways.

George Miller and the Garrison Diversion Water Project

The efforts of George Miller (D–CA) to revive the Garrison Diversion water project in the 99th Congress provide a good example of entrepreneurial bill drafting and issue grouping. The Garrison project was a system of canals and reservoirs for irrigation and water supply in North Dakota with a billion dollar price tag. Controversy had surrounded the project since Congress first authorized it in 1965, making it difficult to follow through with the project. Fiscally conservative legislators opposed it because of its cost, and environmentalist legislators feared that it would damage wetlands.

We can think of the Garrison project in terms of the spatial model in figure 1.3. Suppose the two relevant issue dimensions for this bill were the project's cost (represented by the vertical dimension in fig. 1.3) and the protection of wetlands (represented by the horizontal dimension). Miller was able to draft a bill that attracted majority support on these two dimensions. Miller's bill reduced the cost and acreage of the project and set up a trust fund for wetlands preservation. In terms of figure 1.3, since it reduced the project's cost and increased protection for wetlands, Miller's bill was located in the win set to the southeast of *sq*. Miller's bill set up a logroll between fiscal conservatives and environmentalists that resulted in the passage of the legislation. This compromise satisfied the different factions and even drew vocal support from those who had previously opposed the project ("Modified Irrigation" 1986; Davis 1986).

Coalition Building and Pushing Legislation

According to Riker (1986, 151), manipulation of dimensions is the "preferred heresthetical maneuver" because "once performed it does its work without further exertion by the heresthetician." However, once an LE drafts legislation that groups dimensions in a way that will attract a winning coalition, his or her work has only just begun.

As Miller's efforts on the Garrison Diversion water project illustrate, coalition building begins when legislators draft legislation. But the text of the proposal provides only a base on which the LE will build the supporting coalition. Legislative entrepreneurship involves more than just drafting and introducing legislation. As Kirzner's (1973, 136) emphasizes in his discussion of economic entrepreneurship, entrepreneurial activity does not end with the production of a commodity. Entrepreneurs must alert consumers to the availability and desirability of their products. Just as entrepreneurs have to perceive the potential gain from producing particular commodities, they must make others aware of the opportunity to consume the commodities they have made available.

Advertising is thus a crucial part of coalition building. When they advertise, LEs make others aware of the opportunity for addressing some issue or set of issues through legislation and try to draw their colleagues into the supporting coalition. LEs must communicate information about opportunities for new legislation in ways that those unfamiliar with the issues can understand. An LE faces competition from others engaging in entrepreneurial activity and must convince legislators that his or her proposal deserves some of the limited time that the House has to consider the thousands of proposals that are introduced each year. One way in which legislators advertise is by circulating "Dear Colleague" letters that inform others of the "desirable features of their proposals" (Campbell 1982, 415). LEs also spend resources on activities like distributing press releases, making speeches on the floor, and testifying before committees to inform others of their legislation. Press releases, speeches, and testimony are all part of the legislative packages that LEs offer.

The goal of advertising is to convince key legislators at different stages in the legislative process that a proposal should advance to the next stage and ultimately should achieve passage. An important first step in the process is hearings on the legislation. An LE, if he or she does not hold such a position, may need to convince the relevant committee or subcommittee chairs that a particular bill is worthy of a hearing. Committee hearings give important exposure to the issues that a bill addresses and what it proposes to do about them. After hearings are held, the LE may have to fight to try to maintain the proposal's integrity during markup and may have to convince subcommittee members to forward the proposal to the full committee. The LE may have to endure a similar process in the full committee, including more hearings and markups, while attempting to convince a majority on the committee to which the bill was referred (or majorities on different committees in the case of multiple referral) that it should report the legislation to the floor.

Once the bill makes it out of committee, the LE tries to create propitious circumstances for floor consideration. For example, the LE may testify before the Rules Committee in an attempt to secure a "friendly rule" for the legislation that will help it to gain passage on the floor (Smith 1989, 44). The LE may need to convince party leaders to schedule the bill for floor consideration and seek support from the whip organization in building and maintaining a winning coalition. Once the bill reaches the floor, the LE lobbies rank and file legislators to cast their votes in favor of the legislation. If the LE is the floor manager for the bill, he or she must take responsibility for controlling time during the debate as well as designing the parliamentary strategy for securing passage (Oleszek 1989, 150).

If the legislation passes the House, then the LE must pursue similar activities with respect to the other chamber, perhaps working to maintain the integrity of the bill in the conference committee. Entrepreneurial activity requires legislators to pay attention to what members of the Senate and the president want since their approval is necessary if the legislation is to be enacted into law. As they are pushing their legislation through the House, members will often work with senators to ensure that a companion bill progresses through the other chamber. Working with senators and the executive helps push legislation through the House. For example, House members may be reluctant to take action on a bill if there is little chance that the Senate will also pass the legislation.

In making others aware of and pushing their legislation, it is especially important that LEs exert effort to get legislators who occupy pivotal positions to support the legislation. Whether it be convincing a subcommittee or full committee chair to schedule hearingscommittee hierarchy or planning strategy with the party leadership, an integral part of coalition building involves drawing on the resources of these leaders.[8]

Henry Waxman and the Omnibus Health Bill of 1986

H.R. 5546 would not have gotten very far in the legislative process without Representative Henry Waxman's (D–CA) tenacity and coalition-building efforts. H.R. 5546 addressed the issue of childhood vaccinations. In the mid-1980s, the costs of some vaccinations had soared and shortages of vaccines that prevent common childhood diseases such as measles and mumps became a concern. Waxman's bill included a provision that would require the Department of Health and Human Services to maintain an adequate stockpile of these vaccines. Waxman's bill also addressed the cause of the price increases and shortages. Manufacturers had dramatically cut back the production of certain vaccines because they had suffered financial losses from lawsuits by the families of children who had been injured by the vaccines. The manufacturers wanted protection from massive jury awards before they would resume full-scale production. Parents' groups wanted to preserve the right to sue to

8. An LE can try to do an end run around key players in pushing legislation. For example, legislators may try to circumvent the committee system altogether and attach their proposals as amendments to other pieces of legislation on the floor (Bach and Smith 1988). This can be a dangerous strategy, as legislators risk alienating those who might be able to contribute their own resources to pushing the legislation. While parliamentary maneuvering is an important part of legislative entrepreneurship, there are limits to the extent to which legislators can exploit rules and procedures to advance their proposals.

provide incentives for the manufacturers to produce safer vaccines. Waxman's proposal set up a no-fault compensation fund for families of children who suffered injury or death as a result of adverse reactions to childhood vaccinations. Waxman's proposal embodied a compromise that made both manufacturers and parents happy: parents could still sue manufacturers, but if they did they would not be able to claim any compensation from the fund.

Despite the fact that both of the main interests involved supported this compromise, the prospects for the bill becoming law remained in doubt. It had taken Waxman two years to build a coalition that would pass the bill in the House, and prospects for enactment grew dim as the adjournment of the 99th Congress rapidly approached. The Senate's version of the bill had stalled. Even if the bill did pass the Senate, the Reagan administration strongly opposed the provisions for the compensation fund, raising the possibility of a veto. An aide to Paula Hawkins (R–FL), the sponsor of the companion bill in the Senate, claimed that "it would take a miracle" for the legislation to pass before the end of the session (quoted in Rovner 1986a).

In fact, what it really took was some concerted coalition building efforts by Waxman. Pharmaceuticals were a hot issue in the 99th Congress. Democrats had successfully used the threat of vaccine shortages and the adverse effects of some vaccines as an issue against the Reagan administration (Hook 1985). To prevent the Democrats from scoring additional political points, the administration favored some kind of bill addressing these issues. In the Senate, Orrin Hatch (R–UT), then chairman of the Labor and Human Resources Committee, was pushing a bill that would allow companies to export drugs that had not been approved for use in the United States. Waxman sought to bring Hatch and Reagan into the coalition supporting the vaccine legislation. Together with Hatch, Waxman crafted a package that included his vaccine provisions, Hatch's export drug provisions, and several other pieces of legislation that were favored by the administration and Senate Republicans. Through his efforts, Waxman was able to build a majority coalition in the House and win the approval from the other chamber and the president that was necessary to enact his proposal into law (Rovner 1986b).

Member Goals and Motivations

Why do members engage in the activities discussed in the previous sections? The literature on chaos in collective decision-making bodies suggests that an unlimited number of opportunities for enacting new legislation exists. As long as legislators can make proposals in multidimensional policy spaces, as in the spatial model discussed earlier, and there are no limits on proposals, legislators will always have opportunities to alter the status quo (Plott 1967; McKelvey

1976). However, taking advantage of legislative opportunities is costly (Sloss 1973). Members must devote time and resources to learning about the preferences of members on various dimensions, drafting legislation that is consistent with those preferences, and encouraging others involved at different points in the legislative process to support the legislation. What motivates legislators to incur such costs to take advantage of these opportunities and engage in legislative entrepreneurship?

As readers will probably have surmised by now, this book adopts a rational choice approach in order to answer this question. This approach entails figuring out how the benefits of engaging in legislative entrepreneurship outweigh the costs by examining how this activity helps members of Congress achieve their goals. Fenno (1973) argues that members have three basic goals: enacting "good public policy," getting reelected, and obtaining influence within the institution. In order to understand why members would engage in legislative entrepreneurship, we need to understand how this activity contributes to the attainment of these goals.

An important consideration is that these three goals are not independent of each other. The attainment of one goal can help or hinder the attainment of the others. The relationships among the goals depend on what activities members engage in to accomplish the goals and the ways they must allocate their resources to engage in these activities. While certain activities may help accomplish one goal, resource constraints mean that members may not be able to undertake activities to accomplish other goals. In terms of activities and the deployment of resources, members operate in two essentially distinct arenas—the district arena and the Washington arena (Fenno 1978; Cavanaugh 1981).[9] The amount of resources that members spend on activities in one arena reduces the amount that they have to spend in the other, so members face tradeoffs when making their resource allocation decisions. These tradeoffs are important because resources spent in the different arenas vary in the amount they contribute to the attainment of members' goals. Legislative entrepreneurship requires members to concentrate resources in the Washington arena. How does this particular allocation of resources contribute to the achievement of Fenno's triumvirate of goals?

Legislative entrepreneurship clearly helps members accomplish the goal of enacting their conception of good public policy. By engaging in activities that are necessary for passing legislation, LEs play a central role in enacting what they presumably believe to be good public policy. Hall (1996) has found evidence that members' policy goals in part motivate them to participate in the legislative process. However, it is not clear that their policy goals will motivate

9. The two arenas are not necessarily distinct in geographic terms. Members and their staff often perform district-oriented activities inside the Beltway.

members to participate to the degree that legislative entrepreneurship entails (233). Members will have different beliefs about the amount of effort they need to exert to produce good public policy. Instead of drafting and pushing proposals themselves, members could achieve this goal simply by showing up on the floor and voting for what they perceive to be good public policy.

Entrepreneurial activity involves much more than just voting and hence is much more costly in terms of time and resources. Achieving the goal of enacting good public policy by engaging in legislative entrepreneurship can conflict with the other goals because of constraints on members' resources. A member who wants to enact good public policy can do so without exerting the amount of effort that legislative entrepreneurship entails. While a desire to enact good public policy will provide some motivation for members to engage in legislative entrepreneurship, there are plenty of other activities that are less costly but can help them achieve this goal. Members might want to substitute these activities for entrepreneurship in pursuit of their goals.

Since legislative entrepreneurship requires members to focus their resources on the Washington arena, they will have fewer resources to allocate to activities in the district arena. Some have argued that resources spent in the district arena on casework and constituency service are crucial for achieving the reelection goal, while resources spent on legislative activity in the Washington arena do little (Fiorina 1989; Cain, Ferejohn, and Fiorina 1987). Casework involves helping constituents deal with government bureaucracies, for example, by helping constituents cut through bureaucratic red tape so that they can receive disability or social security checks. Arnold (1990, 8, n. 7) claims that "it is generally true that investing time and energy in other activities (casework, newsletters, trips home, personal appearances, fund raising, and the like) produces larger and more secure [electoral] dividends than building policy coalitions." Most works on Congress published since Mayhew's *Congress: The Electoral Connection* (1974) adopt some variant of the assumption that members are *primarily* concerned with getting reelected. The reelection goal stands apart from the other goals because the others cannot be achieved if members are not reelected. The primacy of reelection forces members to give priority to activities that help them achieve this goal (Mayhew 1974, 16–17). Even though legislative entrepreneurship advances the goal of enacting good public policy, if it does not enhance members' reelection prospects they will be strongly discouraged from devoting resources to this activity.

In order to determine how entrepreneurship relates to reelection it is important to determine how electorally relevant actors respond to this activity. Electorally relevant actors are those individuals who can contribute resources to a member's reelection effort. These range from constituents who can simply vote for an incumbent to more politically active individuals who can contribute other resources such as time and money to promote reelection campaigns. If constituents respond to legislative entrepreneurship by casting their votes for the incumbent, then there is a direct, positive relationship between the reelection goal and this activity. If this were the case, then we would have a straightforward explanation for legislative entrepreneurship and this would be a very short book.

Some have argued that a direct relationship between reelection and entrepreneurial activity existed during the period under analysis. According to this argument, legislative entrepreneurship has become an important part of members' reelection strategies because of changes that occurred in the electoral environment in the 1960s and 1970s. As the role that party organizations play in mobilizing grassroots support for members has declined and television has become "the dominant news and campaign medium," members have sought to mobilize support from their constituents by engaging in entrepreneurial activity on issues that are salient to their constituents (Price 1989, 425; Davidson 1981). The higher profile that members obtain through legislative entrepreneurship enables them to attract voters who are less inclined to vote simply on the basis of partisan identification.

But in order for there to exist a direct, positive relationship between legislative entrepreneurship and constituents' responses, constituents must, first, be aware of their members' entrepreneurial efforts and, second, approve of these efforts. It is possible that neither of these conditions will be met. Constituents generally know very little about their members of Congress and might not possess much information about their activities inside the Beltway (Miller and Stokes 1963). Even if constituents are aware of their members' entrepreneurial activities, constituents will not necessarily respond favorably to them. Constituents will respond negatively if they do not like the positions that members have taken through their "entrepreneuring" of certain issues (Fiorina 1989). If the above two conditions are not met, then the net effect of entrepreneurial activity on reelection could be negative as far as constituents' responses are concerned. As stated above, legislative entrepreneurship requires members to focus their attention on the Washington arena at the expense of their districts, requiring members to allocate resources away from activities to which constituents are more attuned, such as casework and constituency service. Even if constituents do not respond unfavorably to entrepreneurial activity directly, they may punish the incumbent if he or she does not do enough to meet casework and constituency service demands.

In chapter 3, I assess these alternative views regarding entrepreneurial activity and the electoral connection by conducting an empirical analysis using data on legislative entrepreneurship and individual-level survey data. I find that entrepreneurial activity does not positively affect members' reelection prospects in terms of direct constituent response, but I do not find strong evidence of a direct negative effect either.

Yet this does not mean that entrepreneurial behavior is unrelated to the reelection goal. Although constituents' votes are ultimately what members need in order to achieve reelection, other, subsidiary factors that can help achieve this goal might be connected to legislative entrepreneurship. Campaign funds are a crucial part of successful reelection campaigns. Political organizations may pay attention to members' legislative activities and take legislative entrepreneurship into consideration when making campaign contributions. In chapter 4, I explore this possibility by examining the relationship between legislative entrepreneurship and contributions from political action committees (PACs). Extending the work on service-induced campaign contributions and campaign contributions as investments (Baron 1989a, 1989b; Snyder 1990, 1992), I consider that PACs may want to "invest" in legislative entrepreneurs by contributing campaign funds to them with the expectation that the PACs will benefit from the members' future entrepreneurial efforts. If this is the case, reelection-seeking members have a strong incentive to engage in legislative entrepreneurship in order to attract campaign contributions.

An assumption that underlies the analysis of the relationship between legislative entrepreneurship and campaign contributions is that members can use their authority as lawmakers to create an institutional environment that promotes the achievement of individual and collective goals. Although the proper unit of analysis for explaining entrepreneurial behavior is the individual member rather than, say, committees or parties, we would not make much progress if we did not consider the institutional environment in which members operate. Though the focus in this book is primarily on individual members and their motivations, in order to understand this behavior we must look at the ways members have structured their institution. Since the Constitution grants members almost unlimited discretion to determine the rules, proceedings, organization, and general institutional environment of the House, its members are in the unique occupational situation of having the authority to determine the conditions under which they work and remain employed as legislators. Many important works on Congress have sought to understand how members have used this authority to organize their institution in ways that facilitate the attainment of their goals. This book builds on these institutional analyses by looking at the institutional features that provide incentives for members to engage in legislative entrepreneurship.

The campaign finance laws that members have enacted for themselves are an important determinant of whether or not incumbents keep their jobs. Campaign finance laws may provide an institutional link between members' reelection interests and legislative entrepreneurship. But, for members to go through the trouble of establishing such an institutional link, they would have to benefit generally from entrepreneurial activity.[10]

I argue that the key part that legislative entrepreneurship plays in legislative production implies that members benefit generally from this activity and therefore it makes sense that they would devise institutional features that provide incentives for each other to engage in entrepreneurship. On the one hand, the production of legislation promotes the reelection chances of House members who do not engage in entrepreneurial activity. Passing legislation is crucial to enhancing party labels, which affect individual members' reelection chances (Cox and McCubbins 1993). Legislation is also a vehicle for providing district-specific benefits, which members find valuable for reelection (Sinclair 1995, 240). Even if members prefer the status quo to a piece of legislation that passes, they can appeal to their constituents by taking positions on the legislation that their constituents favor and by claiming to have "fought the good fight" against the legislation (Mayhew 1974).

On the other hand, the *failure* to pass legislation can hurt members' reelection prospects. Quality challengers who can mount serious campaigns against incumbents are most likely to enter races when national political conditions are unfavorable to incumbents (Jacobson and Kernell 1983). Such unfavorable conditions can arise if the electorate perceives that Congress has failed to address pressing national problems through legislation. For example, the failure of the 104th Congress to pass some of the appropriations bills for fiscal year 1996 and the resulting shutdown of the federal government negatively affected the approval ratings of congressional Republicans, sending members of the GOP scrambling to solve the crisis (Koszczuk 1995c). Hibbing and Theiss-Morse (1995) found that Congress's failure to solve "the budget deficit problem" substantially contributed to the public's negative feelings about Congress. However, Durr, Gilmour, and Wolbrecht (1997) argue that the passage of major legislation decreases public approval of Congress as an institution, which in turn can hurt individual members' reelection prospects. But this does not mean that legislative entrepreneurship will lead to lower public approval of Congress. Members engage in some form of entrepreneurial activity on any piece of legislation that passes, not just the major ones. Durr et al. contend that public approval declines because people do not like the way the legislative process works for major pieces of legislation. But it is hard to believe that public approval would increase if Congress passed no major legislation.[11]

---

10. Campaign finance laws might also provide a link between the reelection goal and the goal of enacting good public policy. However, the policies that members have to entrepreneur in order to attract campaign contributions may not be consistent with their ideas of good public policy.

11. Previous studies have conceived of legislative entrepreneurship as involving major na-

Although constituents may not respond to their particular member's entrepreneurial efforts, a lack of entrepreneurship on the part of any member can hurt them collectively. Thus, members have an interest in providing each other with incentives to engage in entrepreneurial activity, which helps to ensure that members do not free ride on each others' entrepreneurial activity.

An important part of the recent literature on congressional organization attempts to explain how members have organized the institution to link their behavior within it—which constituents for the most part do not observe—to the external responses of constituents. The laws that govern campaign finance are one feature of the institution that can link behavior inside the legislature to a member's performance back in the district. However, the empirical analysis in chapter 4 indicates that campaign finance and the laws that govern it do not provide much incentive for entrepreneurial activity. I find no relationship between entrepreneurial activity and contributions from PACs.

In chapter 5, I continue to pursue an institution-based explanation for legislative entrepreneurship by examining how members exploit the internal structure of their institution to provide incentives for legislative entrepreneurship. One of the key features of the institutional organization of the House is the division of labor among different subunits in committee and party hierarchies. A by-product of this division of labor has been the creation of various prestigious positions. These positions are prestigious because they confer on their occupants special parliamentary rights and resources. I argue that members can provide incentives for each other to engage in legislative entrepreneurship by making appointments to these positions contingent on a member's entrepreneurial activity. I develop a theory of intrainstitutional mobility that explains how this incentive scheme works not only to encourage members to become LEs but to ensure that qualified members occupy positions of influence in the House.

Advancing to prestigious positions can help satisfy all three of the goals that Fenno argues members have. Obtaining a prestigious position directly satisfies members' influence-seeking goals. The increased influence over the legislative process that these positions give members puts them in a better position to enact their visions of "good public policy."[12] This influence can also

tional policies. The concept that I employ does not explicitly make reference to the national importance of the legislation involved. However, the concept implies that entrepreneurial efforts involve issues that are not purely local. While the concept does not exclude from consideration entrepreneurial efforts that involve minor legislation, the measures of this activity that I develop are sensitive to the importance of the legislation members entrepreneur in terms of the complexity of the legislation and the amount of interest it generates.

12. For example, for his bill on the Garrison Diversion project George Miller used his authority as a subcommittee chair to push the bill through the legislative process. He waived a markup session, which prevented subcommittee members from making amendments that would

help with reelection. Members in these positions can deploy the additional resources associated with them to secure distributive benefits for their districts. They may also have an easier time securing campaign contributions because their influence makes them more attractive investments for interest groups seeking to affect policy outcomes (Hall and Wayman 1990; Snyder 1992).

The empirical analysis in chapter 5 indicates that members have organized the House to reward each other for entrepreneurship. I find that the more entrepreneurial activity a member of the majority party engages in, the more likely it is that he or she will advance to a committee or party leadership position. Thus, the most compelling explanation for why members of Congress engage in legislative entrepreneurship is that it increases the probability of advancing to a prestigious position within the House, which helps to satisfy the three main goals that members have.

In chapter 6, I consider how the findings in chapter 5 extend to the Republican-controlled Congress. Although the analysis in this chapter is more qualitative, I find evidence that Republicans are using prestigious positions in a way that will promote legislative entrepreneurship.

Summary

By gathering information, drafting legislation, and pushing legislation through the legislative process, members who assume the role of LEs help the House to satisfy its policy-making role. The House would have great difficulty producing any legislation without LEs, who coordinate the efforts and resources of other members. Thus, all members are generally better off when some members engage in these activities.

An LE contributes his or her own resources and coordinates the resources of others to supply collective goods. The legislative package that an LE supplies is itself a collective good. An LE cannot prevent others from using the information contained in the package. For example, other members can use the information to determine how alternative policies will affect their constituents. Nor can the LE prevent others from taking different positions on the legislation, which may help them in their districts. Even if members do not support the legislation an LE proposes, they still value the legislative package. They can use the information in it to figure out whether they should support the proposal in the first place, and it gives them something on which they can stake an opposing position. The legislative package is also a resource-pooling mechanism. Through the legislative package, an LE coordinates the resources

---

have unraveled the delicate compromise before it reached the floor.

of others so that they can form coalitions and enact legislation.

LEs provide valuable services to other members. Without the policy information that LEs provide, members risk voting for legislation that could be detrimental to their constituents. Without the coordination of resources, members of Congress cannot enact legislation. If members do not enact legislation, they will not be able to meet the demands the electorate places upon them. At the individual level, failure to meet these demands will lead to defeat at the polls for some members. At the institutional level, failure to meet these demands will lead "to net losses in the scope of Congress's policy control and in its ability to make its own decisions" (Cooper 1977, 144). Such losses would make service in the House much less attractive. Careerist members of the House "have a stake in maintaining its prestige as an institution" as well as "a stake in maintaining congressional control over resources that are useful in electoral quests" (Mayhew 1974, 145). Members work hard to obtain and maintain their seats in the House, yet those seats would be worth very little if the House could not function as a governing body (Polsby 1968, 166).

Although all members are better off if some members engage in legislative entrepreneurship, it is not clear how LEs benefit individually from this activity. The costs associated with legislative entrepreneurship present members of the House with a standard collective dilemma: although all members benefit when some members acquire policy expertise, draft legislation, build coalitions and push their proposals through the legislative process, individual members are tempted to free ride on the entrepreneurial activity of others (cf. Hall 1996, 50–52).

Yet it appears that members have resolved this dilemma. In any given Congress, we observe members who do not free ride on others' entrepreneurial activities. How do members of the House overcome the collective dilemma associated with legislative entrepreneurship? Unlike other productive groups such as firms, legislators cannot dismiss those who do not engage in entrepreneurial activity (cf. Weingast and Marshall 1988), nor does it seem that they can provide each other with salary bonuses if they do engage in entrepreneurship. Such bonuses would be ethically suspect and politically infeasible given the controversy that perennially surrounds the issue of congressional salaries.

Recent works on Congress have focused on how its members have organized the institution to resolve similar dilemmas.[13] Since members benefit

---

13. For example, Cox and McCubbins (1993) focus on how congressional parties solve a collective dilemma to get party members to vote for legislation that enhances the party's reputation. The collective action problem with legislative entrepreneurship lies not in getting members to vote for proposals but in getting members to make proposals in the first place. When LEs manipulate issue dimensions in the appropriate fashion, in a sense they make a majority an offer it can't refuse. The problem lies in getting members to do the work necessary to draft the legislation and see that

from legislative entrepreneurship, they should try to organize their institution to promote this activity. I argue that members have used their authority to shape the rules that govern their institution in order to promote entrepreneurial efforts. The conclusion that I reach is that members have established committee and party hierarchies that contain prestigious positions and have made advancement to these positions partly contingent on a member's entrepreneurial activity. Members of the majority party will engage in legislative entrepreneurship with the expectation that they will be rewarded with "promotions" to these positions.

The layout of the book is as follows. Since my analysis has a strong empirical focus, it is necessary to develop measures of legislative entrepreneurship. Few studies have attempted systematic empirical analysis of the behavior that I define as legislative entrepreneurship, so reliable quantitative measures of this behavior remain to be developed. In chapter 2, I develop the measures of legislative entrepreneurship that I use in the empirical analyses in subsequent chapters. Chapters 3 through 5 constitute the heart of the analysis. Instead of concentrating all of the theoretical development in one chapter, in each of these chapters I develop the theory behind a particular explanation of legislative entrepreneurship and then present empirical tests of the theory. This structure helps to ensure that readers will see the strong connection between the rational-choice-based theories I develop and the empirical tests. In chapter 3, I examine the relationship between entrepreneurial activity and the reelection imperative. I look at how this activity affects various aspects of support for members in their districts and how it ultimately affects votes for the incumbent. I confirm the results of previous studies that indicate that entrepreneurial activity does not directly help members at the polls. I look at the relationship between entrepreneurship and PAC contributions in chapter 4. I find no relationship between entrepreneurship and campaign contributions. I then look to see what incentives for this activity exist within the institution. In chapter 5, I argue that the House is organized to exploit members' career concerns—that is, their desires to advance to more influential positions within the institution—in order to promote legislative entrepreneurship. I find that entrepreneurial activity positively affects the probability that members of the majority party will advance through the committee and party hierarchies in the House. In chapter 6, I discuss the implications of my analysis for the Republican-controlled Congress. Although one of the features that sets this book apart from previous works on legislative entrepreneurship is its emphasis on quantitative analysis, such analysis is premature for the Republican majority at this time. The more qualitatively oriented analysis in chapter 6 indicates that the key explanation

---

it gets to the points in the legislative process where members can cast votes for or against it.

for legislative entrepreneurship holds for Republicans now that they are in the majority. Evidence from the 104th and 105th Congresses indicates that Republicans are using prestigious positions to provide incentives for legislative entrepreneurship. In chapter 7, I conclude by discussing how this analysis can be improved and extended and by examining its implications of this analysis for our understanding of Congress and American political institutions in general.

CHAPTER 2

Measuring Legislative Entrepreneurship

Although previous studies have broached the topic of legislative entrepreneurship, none has been devoted to explaining this behavior explicitly and in a systematic fashion. Prior studies of entrepreneurial activity have been largely anecdotal or have employed case study methods.[1] This book seeks to improve on these studies by undertaking a systematic analysis of legislative entrepreneurship using quantitative methods in order to answer the questions posed in chapter 1. The proper unit of observation for this analysis is the individual member, making it necessary to develop measures of legislative entrepreneurship for individual members. I draw on the qualitative studies of legislative entrepreneurship because they provide some guidance as to what activities we should look at when developing measures appropriate for a quantitative analysis of individuals. In this chapter, I discuss the measures I use in my analysis. The measures capture the theoretically important aspects of this activity that were discussed in chapter 1, including a member's legislation-drafting efforts, coalition-building efforts, and level of policy knowledge. Given that the quantitative nature of this book is what sets it apart from previous studies, I do not relegate the discussion of the measures to a data appendix. Rather, I include this discussion in the text so that the description of the data serves to explicate more fully the behavior of legislative entrepreneurship and its theoretically interesting aspects.

Approaches to Measuring Legislative Entrepreneurship

How exactly does one measure legislative entrepreneurship? One obstacle to moving beyond case studies to a broad range of members of Congress is to come up with indicators that are not too costly to collect for large number of members yet reasonably capture the behavior of interest. Hall's study (1996) of participation in the legislative process suggests one method. Using detailed records of committee deliberations, staff interviews, and floor activity as reported in the *Congressional Record,* Hall collected data on the level of partici-

1. For example, see Fenno 1989, 1991; Loomis 1988; and Reid 1980.

pation of members on a sample of bills from the 99th Congress for three different committees.[2] From this data, he produced an ordinal scale of participation in the committee and floor stages of the legislative process, where members' levels of participation range from doing nothing to engaging in "agenda action." While some of the activities that Hall examines are certainly related to legislative entrepreneurship, the measures do not specifically measure the theoretically relevant aspects of this activity that were discussed in the previous chapter.

Another approach involves developing measures of legislative entrepreneurship from the products of entrepreneurs: the legislation that they sponsor. From the different characteristics of legislation, one can determine its "entrepreneurial qualities" and credit its primary sponsor accordingly.[3]

While assigning entrepreneurship measures on the basis of primary sponsorship is a reasonable method, it does have some shortcomings. A member who is the primary sponsor of a piece of legislation is not necessarily its author. Members can sign their names to legislation drafted by interest groups or executive branch bureaucrats. Since there are no copyright restrictions on legislation, members can and often do introduce legislation that is identical to what another member has drafted (Schneier and Gross 1993, 95). It is questionable, then, whether members should be credited for the characteristics of bills that they do not draft themselves. Alternatively, members may contribute entrepreneurial effort to legislation that they have not sponsored.[4]

While Hall's approach enables one to obtain information about authorship and the effort that members put into legislation that others have sponsored, this kind of data is incredibly costly to obtain—prohibitively so if we want to obtain data for a large number of members over several Congresses. The empirical analysis that I undertake in later chapters requires data for individuals over several Congresses. Thus, it would be too costly to adopt Hall's method to develop entrepreneurship measures for a longitudinal analysis, which, as will become clear in later chapters, is necessary for explaining legislative entre-

2. Hall supplemented the data from this Congress with data for the same committees in the 103d Congress and data for one of them—Education and Labor—for the 87th.

3. While there have been a few systematic studies of primary sponsorship (e.g., see Schiller 1995), these studies do not use measures based on the characteristics of bills. Hibbing (1991) examines legislative activity over members' careers using some characteristics of bills. Some of the measures that I develop draw on Hibbing's measures.

4. Another potential problem with assigning credit to primary sponsors of bills is that *clean bills* will inflate the entrepreneurship measures for full committee and subcommittee chairs. Whenever a committee amends a bill, the relevant chair will often introduce a new bill "by request" that incorporates the committee's modifications to the original piece of legislation (Oleszek 1989, 104–5). Using primary sponsorship for computing the entrepreneurship measures will credit the chairs for these bills even though it is difficult to determine how much credit they deserve.

preneurship.[5] Instead, I sacrifice richness for breadth and rely on the primary sponsorship method for computing measures of entrepreneurship. This method enables me to build measures of entrepreneurial activity for every member of the 94th through the 103d Congresses.

Despite its shortcomings for assigning credit for entrepreneurial activity, primary sponsorship *does* convey very important information about individuals' legislative behavior. Primary sponsorship of legislation gives members an opportunity to identify themselves formally with a particular set of issues and build reputations as entrepreneurs (Schiller 1995). The legislation that a member chooses to put his or her name on "is a strong indicator of which issues he or she wants to be associated with and the reputation he or she wants to acquire among colleagues" (187). Although members will not take an immense interest in every piece of legislation they introduce, they will not put much effort into bills that they do not want to be an important part of their legislative portfolios.

Primary sponsorship typically involves more than just signing one's name to a piece of legislation and dropping it in the "hopper"—the mahogany box at the front of the chamber that serves as a depository for all bills introduced in the House. The tasks and responsibilities of the primary sponsor typically involve entrepreneurial activities such as gathering and communicating information, coalition building, and shepherding legislation through the House. A primary sponsor is responsible for "answering correspondence on the bill, defending it before colleagues, seeking clearance from the appropriate administrative agencies, and discussing it with proponents and opponents" (Schneier and Gross 1993, 96). Although a primary sponsor may not be the sole or even the most important author of a piece of legislation, he or she must be able to handle these public relations tasks, which require substantial knowledge about the content of the legislation.

A primary sponsor also has important responsibilities as the legislation wends it way through the legislative process: "It is the congressional sponsor . . . who is counted on to be there at the right time to defend the bill in committee, protect it on the floor, handle relationships with the president, and conduct (but not necessarily devise) parliamentary maneuvers" (Schneier and Gross 1993, 97). Leaders in the House usually consult the primary sponsor when they determine a favorable time for floor consideration of legislation (114).

Assigning entrepreneurial credit to primary sponsors and not to cospon-

5. As Hall notes, the proliferation of online services providing information about Congress has substantially reduced these costs and may make this data-collecting task much easier. Indeed, I collected many of the data I use in this analysis from online sources including *Congressional Quarterly*'s Washington Alert, Legi-Slate, and the Library of Congress.

sors is conservative since some cosponsors help draft and push the legislation and hence deserve some of the credit for "entrepreneuring" it. However, it is often impossible to determine the degree to which cosponsors have been active. The more restrictive rule of assigning entrepreneurship scores only to primary sponsors makes more sense than attributing the scores to members who, as cosponsors, are not likely to engage in the kinds of activities we would like to explain (cf. Hibbing 1991, 112). However, as we will see, cosponsorship is useful for measuring a primary sponsor's coalition-building efforts.

While using primary sponsorship of legislation as the criterion for determining an individual's level of entrepreneurial activity is an important decision that has implications for the validity of the empirical analysis, an equally important decision concerns what types of legislation to use to compute the measures. In the House, there are four legislative vehicles: simple resolutions, concurrent resolutions, joint resolutions, and bills.[6] The wide variety of uses for some of the vehicles compromises their usefulness in measuring legislative entrepreneurship. Simple and concurrent resolutions do not have any legislative impact outside of Congress. The uses of these resolutions include establishing matters of structure, such as the number and size of committees, and procedure, such as special rules for floor consideration of legislation in the House, as well as establishing budgets for the federal government. Simple and concurrent resolutions can have a tremendous impact on the kinds of policies that come out of Congress through their effects on the policy-making and budgeting processes. However, it is doubtful that simple and concurrent resolutions are useful for tapping a member's entrepreneurial activity. House members often use these types of resolutions for "expressing" the support, opposition, or "sense" of Congress regarding an issue. Members of Congress often use simple and concurrent resolutions to encourage actions they want government officials (domestic and foreign) to take, although the officials are under no legal obligation to comply. These types of resolutions primarily serve as vehicles not for legislative entrepreneurship but for pure position taking (Mayhew 1974).

Joint resolutions do have the force of law and can be important pieces of legislation, especially when used to amend the Constitution. However, joint resolutions also are typically used for position-taking. Members often use them to declare commemorations such as "Working Dog Awareness Week" (H.J. Res. 578, 99th Congress, by Representative Molinari [R–NY]) or "National Holstein Day" (H.J. Res. 278, 99th Congress, by Representative Coelho [D–CA]). Rather than making difficult and highly subjective decisions to sep-

6. See Filson 1992, 351–56, for details on the different types of congressional legislative vehicles.

arate substantive from nonsubstantive resolutions, I do not use these pieces of legislation when computing the legislative entrepreneurship measures.

Instead I compute the entrepreneurship scores from bills—that is, legislation designated by an "H.R." number—although I exclude private bills. I do not include private bills because they are essentially vehicles for constituency service. Members use private bills to provide relief for a specific individual or group. For example, private bills often admit individuals to the United States for permanent residence under the Immigration and Nationality Act. Bills have the force of law and are the primary vehicles for members' legislative efforts, and so computing measures from the characteristics of bills that members sponsor is suitable for tapping their entrepreneurial efforts.

Legislative Data

The data on bills that I use for computing all but one of the measures of legislative entrepreneurship come from the Congressional Research Service's (CRS) Legislative Information Files. The CRS files contain detailed information on every piece of federal legislation introduced from the 93d through the current Congress, although this analysis will use data from only the 94th through the 103d.[7] Scholarly researchers have for the most part overlooked these data, even though they contain a wealth of information about legislation and the legislative activity of members of Congress. CRS employees extract information about the contents of every piece of legislation introduced and enter it into a data base on CRS computers. They then keep track of the various actions taken on the legislation and add this to the information on content. These files can be searched for various types of information using the Library of Congress's Subject Content Oriented Retriever for Processing Information Online (SCORPIO) software.

Members of Congress created this data base to provide accurate information on legislation concisely and quickly so that they can keep abreast of the institution's voluminous workload (Frantzich 1982). Given that members of Congress and their staffs rely on this data base for information about the content and progress of legislation, the CRS files are a reliable source of the kinds of data required for an empirical analysis of legislative entrepreneurship.[8] In

---

7. The data for the 93d Congress differs in important ways from the data for the others, making it highly questionable whether it should be combined with the other data.

8. I obtained access to the CRS files via Telnet through the Library of Congress (locis.loc.gov). I collected the data between 24 May and 6 June 1995, using *expect* software. *Expect* enables one to automate the search and retrieval process that can be done manually over the Internet. I retrieved the data by searching for bills sponsored by each member of Congress. I then downloaded the raw text files and used text-processing programs to cull the relevant infor-

the sections that follow, I discuss several indicators of legislative entrepreneurship developed from the data on bill characteristics contained in the CRS files.

Cosponsorship as a Measure of Coalition Building

One of the most important aspects of legislative entrepreneurship is coalition building. One obvious indicator of a member's coalition-building skills is the number of members who vote for legislation that he or she sponsors. However, using roll call votes to measure this aspect of legislative entrepreneurship is problematic because only a tiny fraction of bills that are introduced come up for a vote. Whether a member's bill comes up for a vote depends on his or her coalition-building skills, but many other factors are involved that are beyond the member's control. The main problem with using roll call votes for legislation as an indicator of a member's coalition-building skills is that other members do not get the opportunity to express their support for legislation by voting for it. This essentially amounts to a censoring problem that would lead us to underestimate a member's coalition-building skills.

A way to measure a member's coalition-building skills that is not plagued by this censoring problem is to look at the number of cosponsors a member gets to sign onto his or her legislation. Although members do not get the opportunity to vote for every piece of legislation they might want to, once a piece of legislation is introduced they have the opportunity to cosponsor it.[9]

The number of cosponsors a member can get to sign onto a bill is indicative of the member's ability to convince others that the bill is worthy of their support. Members exert "significant effort to recruit members as cosponsors" and use the number and diversity of cosponsors to make claims about the support for the legislation (Campbell 1982, 415). If many legislators sign onto a proposal, the primary sponsor can argue that the bill has a good chance of passing and encourage others to "jump on the bandwagon" in support of it.[10] Attracting numerous cosponsors can keep a bill moving through the legisla-

---

mation from the files. Professor Walter Mebane deserves special recognition for his assistance in collecting and processing these data.

9. A different kind of censoring problem could occur if primary sponsors refuse to allow others to sign on as cosponsors. Under rule 22 of the House, a member must have the primary sponsor submit to the Speaker a signed request to be added as a cosponsor. While a primary sponsor could always simply refuse to submit these requests to the Speaker, it is not clear what would motivate him or her to do so, especially given the potential advantageous effect that accumulating cosponsors can have on a bill's progress. Even if primary sponsors refuse to allow others to cosponsor their legislation, others can express support for it by introducing duplicate bills on their own.

10. Wilson and Young (1997) find that the more cosponsors there are for a piece of legislation the more likely a bill will receive some action in committee. However, they do not find a bandwagon effect for later stages of the legislative process.

tive process. For example, Schneier and Gross (1993, 99) contend that "the aggressive pursuit of numerous cosponsors sometimes serves as the functional equivalent of a discharge petition," which would force a committee to report a bill to the floor.[11]

Some might argue that it is not difficult to convince others to sign onto proposals and that cosponsorship is simply position taking that has little to do with coalition building. Members might simply sign onto proposals so they can claim to have done something on a particular issue when they return to their districts. However, empirical evidence indicates that cosponsorship is more than just position taking. Krehbiel (1995) finds that variations in cosponsorship activity lead to a rejection of the hypothesis that position taking is the sole motivation for cosponsoring bills.[12] Gilligan and Krehbiel (1997) find that cosponsorship is an indicator (albeit imperfect) of policy expertise, which is consistent with the argument that recruiting cosponsors is an important element of coalition building. Legislative entrepreneurs should want to line up experts in support of their bills so that they can convince others of the "worthiness" of the bills.[13]

Thus, one indicator of the coalition-building aspects of legislative entrepreneurship is the number of cosponsors of members' proposals. The CRS data contain lists of cosponsors for each bill. For each member, I add up the number of cosponsors for each bill sponsored by the member.

One problem with computing the cosponsorship and the other entrepreneurship scores is that members often introduce multiple copies of the same bill, typically to get around caps on cosponsors or to try to reinvigorate bills that have stalled in the process.[14] Each copy is assigned a different bill number and so appears in the data as a different bill. Not accounting for identical bills introduced by the same member would result in grossly underestimating the degree of support through cosponsorship.

---

11. But Krehbiel (1995) finds that some members may not be willing to sign onto a petition to discharge a bill they have cosponsored.

12. See also and Kessler Krehbiel 1996.

13. Wilson and Young (1997) find that having the support of purported experts through cosponsorship increases the probability that a bill will receive some committee action, but they also find that such support has negligible affects on final passage.

14. Prior to the 96th Congress, House rules capped the number of cosponsors for bills at 24 and required cosponsors to sign on at the time of introduction. If a member could get more than 25 cosponsors for a bill or could convince more members to sign on after introduction, he or she would have to introduce another bill identical to the original. The House changed the cosponsorship rules in the 95th Congress, allowing an unlimited number of cosponsors to be added until the bill was reported out of committee (Thomas and Grofman 1993). Under the current rules, members must introduce identical bills if more cosponsors want to sign on after committees report the original bills.

Fortunately, each bill entry in the legislative data lists other bills that are identical. When a member sponsors identical bills, I determine which one was the original bill. I then merge the information for the identical bills, treating them as if they were one bill. For the cosponsorship measure, this entails adding the number of cosponsors of the identical bill(s) to the number of cosponsors of the original bill.

As a complement to the general cosponsorship measure, I compute a leadership cosponsorship measure. While a majority of members in the House must support a bill for it to pass, having the support of members in leadership positions in the institution can greatly enhance a bill's prospects of making it through the legislative process. The committee chair who supports a bill is more likely to schedule the committee meetings necessary for the bill to advance to the later stages of the process. If the Speaker supports a bill, then it is more likely that he or she will schedule it for consideration on the floor.

Yet leaders should be more selective when making cosponsorship decisions than rank and file members are if the leaders want to use cosponsorship as a meaningful signal of support. Cosponsorship is a meaningful symbol of support only if cosponsors are willing to use their resources to increase the probability of passage. Others will be less likely to believe leaders' signals of support if they cosponsor large numbers of bills. The more bills leaders cosponsor the fewer resources they have to devote to each one. In the extreme, if the number of bills that a leader endorses through cosponsorship exceeds the number of bills that have a realistic chance of passing, or even making it to the floor, then leadership cosponsorship is not likely to be a credible signal of support. Obtaining leaders as cosponsors, then, should be an indicator of superior coalition-building skills.

The leader cosponsorship measure taps these skills. To compute this measure, I determine the number of times that party and committee leaders signed onto a member's proposals. For Democrats, party leaders include the Speaker, majority leader, majority whip, chief deputy and deputy whip, and the chair and secretary of the Democratic Caucus. For Republicans, party leaders include the minority leader, minority whip, chief deputy and deputy whips, and the chair, vice chair, and secretary of the Republican Conference. Committee leaders are full committee chairs for members of the majority party and ranking minority members on full committees for members of the minority party.[15]

15. The data on party leaders are from *Congressional Quarterly* special reports. The data on committee chairs are from the *Congressional Directory* and Legi-Slate.

Issue Grouping

Another important aspect of legislative entrepreneurship is the grouping of issues to attract a majority coalition. In chapter 1, I used a simple spatial model to show how entrepreneurs can create opportunities for enacting new legislation by drafting bills that group issues. The CRS data contain information that can be used to measure how members group issues in the legislation they introduce. For each piece of legislation a member introduces, the CRS staff assigns index terms to the legislation using the CRS Legislative Indexing Vocabulary Thesaurus (see U.S. House 1987). The index terms indicate the issues that a piece of legislation addresses and can be used to locate bills that deal with particular subjects of interest.

As a measure of issue grouping, I count the number of index terms in the lists for each bill. Admittedly, this is a very crude measure of the phenomenon in which I am interested. When drafting bills, legislative entrepreneurs do not necessarily try to maximize the number of issues their bills address. They combine issues in certain ways. Still, it may be that the higher the "dimensionality" of a bill—that is, the larger the number of issues it addresses—the greater the probability that it will attract support. In an attempt to broaden a coalition, a member may draft a bill that addresses a range of issues that many members care about so that they will become interested in the legislation.

Bill Drafting

Another measure of legislative entrepreneurship is the number of titles in a particular bill. A bill with multiple titles typically addresses a broad range of issues. As I discussed in the previous section, drafting a bill that addresses a range of issues can interest more members and attract them into the supporting coalition. Also, bills that include multiple titles are likely to be very complex pieces of legislation that only members with extensive knowledge and well-developed parliamentary skills can draft and push through the legislative process.[16]

One difficulty with this measure is that bills with multiple titles are typically omnibus bills that are the result of many different members' legislative efforts. Senior members, especially those in the party or committee leadership, typically sponsor such major legislation. Some may argue that this measure might be just another way to measure seniority or formal leadership. However,

16. Though I have not emphasized the "importance" of legislation in the development of the concept of legislative entrepreneurship, the bill titles and index term measures give us some idea of the national significance of legislation. Bills that concern narrow, local matters will not have multiple titles or a large number of index terms.

it is not uncommon for junior members to draft and push these kinds of complicated bills. Junior members who sponsor bills with multiple titles can send a strong signal to others about their entrepreneurial abilities. this with trellis?

Information on titles can be obtained from digests that are part of the CRS data. A team of lawyers in the CRS Bill Digest Section puts together the digests, which concisely describe the contents of each bill. As part of this description, the digest lists the number of titles included in the bill if there are any. To compute this measure, I simply count the number of titles in each bill's digest.

Knowledge of Policy

One could argue that, following Gilligan and Krehbiel 1997, we could also use cosponsorship as a measure of policy knowledge. Yet, as Gilligan and Krehbiel demonstrate, cosponsorship is an imperfect measure, and although they develop a method for correcting for the imperfection, their method would be difficult to use for the analysis presented in the later chapters of this book. While any measure will be imperfect, I use one that more directly measures a member's knowledge of policy than does cosponsorship. Instead of using cosponsorship, I compute a measure of policy knowledge using data on committee hearings.[17] Members often testify before committees regarding legislation that concerns them. They even testify before their own committees. In some instances, members testify before committees when they are the primary sponsor or a cosponsor of a bill.[18] The fact that members appear as witnesses rather than assuming their usual role of asking questions of witnesses during hearings is a signal about their knowledge of and engagement with a particular topic.[19]

To compute this measure, I count the number of times that members testified before committees in the House in each Congress, excluding testimonies before the Appropriations Committee. Members typically testify before Appropriations regarding the merits of public works projects that are of interest to their districts. Such testimonies do not appear to be signaling the kind of policy knowledge that I am interested in, but rather they indicate members'

---

17. The data on committee hearings are from the Congressional Information Service's *Congressional Masterfile 2* CD-ROM.

18. For example, in the 100th Congress members testified before committees 1,723 times. In 197 cases, the members were the primary sponsors of the bills that were the subject of the hearings. In 320 cases, the members who testified were cosponsors.

19. Legislators do not have to appear as witnesses to participate in hearings held by committees on which they do not sit. Members often sit in on other committees' hearings and participate in the questioning of witnesses.

attempts to secure pork for their districts.[20] I then sum the testimonies for each member and divide by the total number of hearings that were held during the Congress.

Summary Measures of Legislative Entrepreneurship

The measures discussed in the previous section (with the exception of the measure based on hearings) give scores for each bill sponsored by each member. The next step is to use the scores for each bill to compute summary scores for each member. One option would be to sum over the scores for each bill. This summary measure is problematic, however. Suppose that Representative A sponsors 100 bills with one cosponsor for each while Representative B sponsors one bill with 100 cosponsors. Though Representatives A and B would have the same summary score, it would seem that B has been more successful in his or her coalition-building efforts than A and hence should have a higher score to indicate superior entrepreneurial efforts. This problem could be eliminated if we divided the total by the number of bills sponsored—that is, computed the average over bills. Yet taking the average over bills sponsored is not without its problems. Suppose Representative C introduces 10 bills and obtains 100 cosponsors for one of the bills but no cosponsors for the others. Representative C would have an average cosponsorship score of 10, which would equal the score of a representative who sponsors just one bill and obtains 10 cosponsors. Thus, if members tend to concentrate their entrepreneurial efforts on a few bills but introduce many bills that they do nothing with, taking the average of their raw scores for their bills might underestimate their entrepreneurial efforts.

Another option, which would avoid some of the problems of averaging, would be to assign members the maximum of the scores from their bills to compute a measure of the member's "best effort." However, this measure might also be misleading. Suppose Representative D sponsors five bills that have 100 cosponsors each while Representative E sponsors five bills but obtains 100 cosponsors for one of them and no cosponsors for the others. Although these individuals have the same "best effort" score, Representative D has clearly been more entrepreneurial than Representative E, who appears to be a "one-hit wonder."

It is not clear which of these measures best captures a member's entrepreneurial activity. Fortunately, it does not seem to make much difference which of the measures we employ. The measures are all highly correlated and the empirical results described in subsequent chapters are essentially the same for the

20. The results do not change much when I include testimonies before Appropriations.

three measures just described. The empirical results that I report are obtained by using the average of the entrepreneurship scores.

Tables 2.1 and 2.2 contain descriptive statistics for each of the average entrepreneurship measures for the 94th through the 103d Congresses. Figure 2.1 contains time series plots of the means of members' average general cosponsorship, leadership cosponsorship, bill titles, index terms, and policy knowledge measures over this period. The mean scores for Democrats and Republicans are plotted separately since I will differentiate by party in the empirical analysis that follows. Not surprisingly, the mean scores for Democrats (the majority party during this period) generally exceed those of Republicans. Except for the policy knowledge measure, the means follow a general upward trend beginning with the 94th Congress. The mean of the general cosponsorship measure peaks in the 101st Congress and declines in the 102d and 103d for Democrats, with the value for Republicans exceeding the value for Democrats in the 103d. The leadership cosponsorship measure follows a similar pattern, but it begins its descent in the 100th Congress for Democrats. The mean of the policy knowledge measure is essentially flat for Democrats, showing a slight decrease between the 94th and the 100th Congresses. This measure is more erratic for Republicans, increasing from the 94th to the 95th, falling in the 96th and 97th, and then trending upward slightly for the remaining Congresses. The different pattern for the policy knowledge measure may have something to do with the norm of specialization in Congress having "fallen upon difficult times" (cf. Hibbing 1991, 122).

Legislative Entrepreneurship Scale Score

The five measures of legislative entrepreneurship that I have developed are all proxy measures of the same behavior.[21] Including each of these measures as a separate explanatory variable in a regression equation is likely to cause collinearity issues and can lead to more serious problems in making inferences about legislative entrepreneurship.[22]

To avoid these problems, we can can compute a single measure by taking some combination of the separate measures. I compute an *entrepreneurship scale score,* which is measured in terms of the same units as the general cosponsorship measure. For member *i*, I divide each of the five measures by its

---

21. One might argue that the measure of policy knowledge is unique and perhaps even in conflict with the other measures and therefore should not be included in the scale. However, the results of the empirical analysis are essentially the same when I treat the measure of policy knowledge separately from the rest of the measures.

22. See Achen 1985 for details about the problems in regression analysis when one uses two or more proxy variables to measure the same underlying variable.

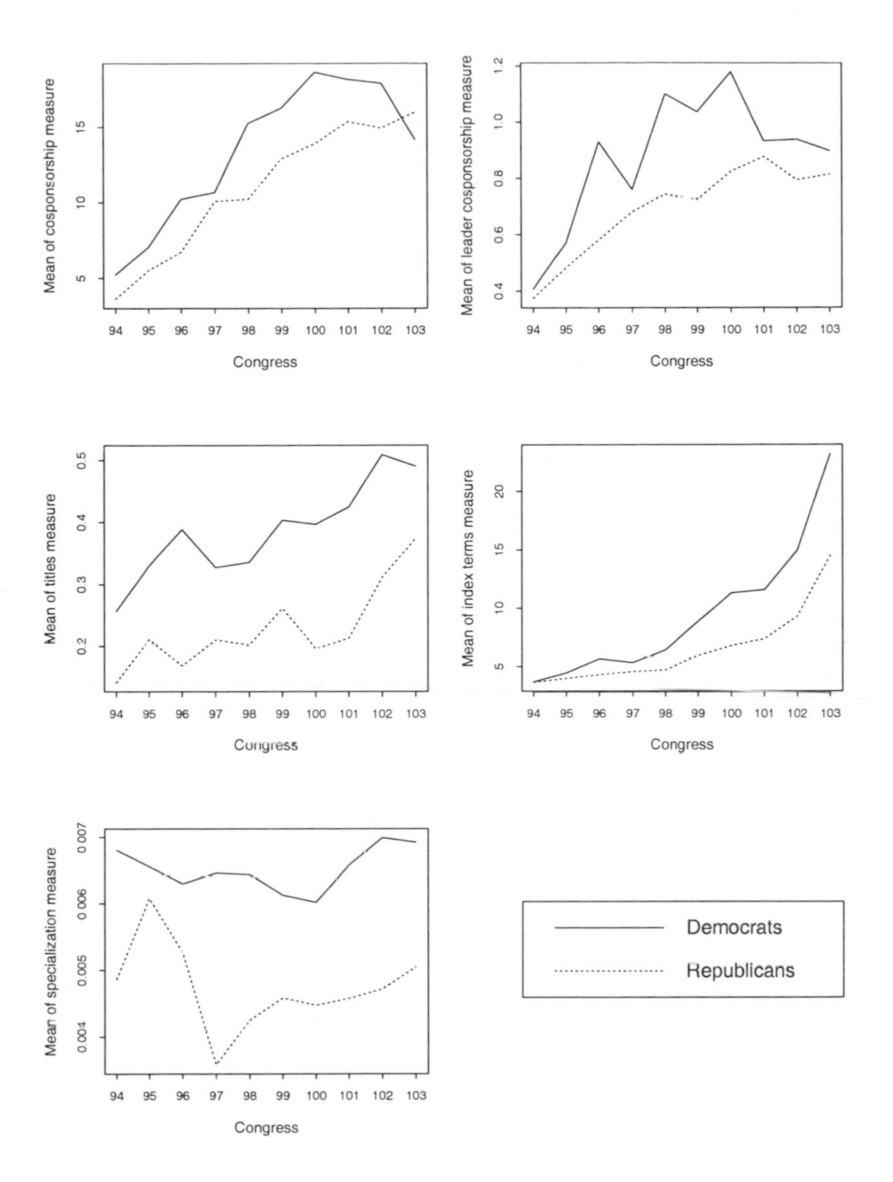

Fig. 2.1. Time-series plots of the means of the averages of the legislative entrepreneurship measures, 94th through the 103d Congresses

TABLE 2.1. Descriptive Statistics of the Averages of the Legislative Entrepreneurship Measures: 94th through the 98th Congresses

Entrepreneurship Variable	Mean	SD	Median	Minimum	Maximum
	94th Congress ($N = 441$)				
Avg. no. of general cosponsors per bill	4.696	5.584	2.870	0	39
Avg. no. of leadership cosponsors per bill	.397	.507	.235	0	4
Avg. no. of titles per bill	.219	.349	.08	0	3
Avg. no. of index terms per bill	3.685	.826	3.636	0	10.750
Policy knowledge score	.006	.006	.006	0	.037
	95th Congress ($N = 441$)				
Avg. no. of general cosponsors per bill	6.548	7.862	4.105	0	66
Avg. no. of leadership cosponsors per bill	.542	.700	.319	0	7
Avg. no. of titles per bill	.291	.454	.132	0	4
Avg. no. of index terms per bill	4.300	2.407	3.833	0	27.286
Policy knowledge score	.006	.006	.0051	0	.039
	96th Congress ($N = 441$)				
Avg. no. of general cosponsors per bill	8.956	11.107	6.046	0	127
Avg. no. of leadership cosponsors per bill	.804	1.466	.464	0	24
Avg. no. of titles per bill	.309	.513	.068	0	4
Avg. no. of index terms per bill	5.176	2.819	4.512	0	28
Policy knowledge score	.006	.006	.005	0	.031
	97th Congress ($N = 443$)				
Avg. no. of general cosponsors per bill	10.416	13.777	6.917	0	154
Avg. no. of leadership cosponsors per bill	.726	.848	.5	0	9.333
Avg. no. of titles per bill	.276	.520	0	0	5
Avg. no. of index terms per bill	5.014	3.135	4.333	0	36
Policy knowledge score	.005	.006	.003	0	.033
	98th Congress ($N = 440$)				
Avg. no. of general cosponsors per bill	13.339	14.006	9.201	0	74
Avg. no. of leadership cosponsors per bill	.965	.927	.8	0	6.667
Avg. no. of titles per bill	.285	.558	0	0	5
Avg. no. of index terms per bill	5.780	4.108	4.643	0	41.200
Policy knowledge score	.006	.006	.003	0	.037

TABLE 2.2. Descriptive Statistics of the Averages of the Legislative Entrepreneurship Measures: 99th through the 103d Congresses

Entrepreneurship variable	Mean	SD	Median	Minimum	Maximum
	99th Congress ($N = 441$)				
Avg. no. of general cosponsors per bill	14.866	14.645	11	0	105
Avg. no. of leadership cosponsors per bill	.906	.928	.667	0	7
Avg. no. of titles per bill	.345	.655	0	0	6.556
Avg. no. of index terms per bill	7.663	8.892	6	0	135.667
Policy knowledge score	.006	.006	.004	0	.035
	100th Congress ($N = 442$)				
Avg. no. of general cosponsors per bill	16.736	15.092	13	0	94
Avg. no. of leadership cosponsors per bill	1.036	.949	.828	0	8
Avg. no. of titles per bill	.316	.601	0	0	3.833
Avg. no. of index terms per bill	9.500	11.730	7	0	113.667
Policy knowledge score	.005	.005	.004	0	.036
	101st Congress ($N = 446$)				
Avg. no. of general cosponsors per bill	17.045	15.600	12.576	0	144.250
Avg. no. of leadership cosponsors per bill	.910	.890	.688	0	7.500
Avg. no. of titles per bill	.340	.561	0	0	3.750
Avg. no. of index terms per bill	9.896	11.739	7.537	0	172.250
Policy knowledge score	.006	.006	.004	0	.034
	102d Congress ($N = 441$)				
Avg. no. of general cosponsors per bill	16.769	17.639	11.353	0	175
Avg. no. of leadership cosponsors per bill	.883	.806	.75	0	5.500
Avg. no. of titles per bill	.433	.808	.111	0	5.882
Avg. no. of index terms per bill	12.811	16.678	9	0	197.600
Policy knowledge score	.006	.006	.004	0	.045
	103d Congress ($N = 439$)				
Avg. no. of general cosponsors per bill	14.925	13.160	11.786	0	90.750
Avg. no. of leadership cosponsors per bill	.865	.818	.667	0	6.333
Avg. no. of titles per bill	.445	.756	0	0	4.556
Avg. no. of index terms per bill	19.755	22.585	13.417	0	192.556
Policy knowledge score	.006	.006	.003	0	.043

TABLE 2.3. Descriptive Statistics of the Scaled Entrepreneurship Score

Congress	Mean	SD	Median	Minimum	Maximum
94th	43.483	16.342	40.805	0	112.664
95th	40.238	23.666	35.443	0	154.983
96th	53.970	32.004	48.309	0	320.616
97th	63.935	42.386	56.249	0	321.181
98th	68.976	42.430	61.514	0	281.902
99th	63.713	46.815	56.662	0	494.509
100th	68.458	44.993	61.196	0	334.310
101st	71.812	46.649	64.255	0	336.065
102d	76.771	50.099	67.185	0	296.316
103d	60.767	39.222	56.444	0	253.261

standard error in Congress t and then multiply by the standard error of the general cosponsorship measure. These scaled measures are then added together to get the entrepreneurship scale score for each member. Another way to produce a single measure from multiple measures would be to compute principal component scores. The entrepreneurship scale score is highly correlated with the principle component scores of the entrepreneurship measures, so I opt for the simpler additive scale in this analysis.[23]

Table 2.3 contains descriptive statistics of the entrepreneurship scale score. As one would expect, figure 2.2 shows that this measure follows the same upward trend as do most of the individual measures for Democrats and Republicans, although it falls sharply in the 103d Congress.

As a reality check I have plotted in figure 2.3 the entrepreneurship scale scores for the four House members discussed in chapter 1 against the 90th and 80th percentile scores (by party) in the Congresses for which data are available. Dick Armey, Les Aspin, George Miller, and Henry Waxman all have reputations as top-notch legislators (Loomis 1988), and these reputations should be reflected in their entrepreneurship scores. The scores for George Miller most accurately represent his entrepreneurial reputation. In eight out of the 10 Congresses in this analysis, his scores exceed the 80th percentile score, and in five Congresses his scores place him in the 90th percentile. In the 99th Congress, during which Miller entrepreneured the legislation concerning the Garrison water project, his score puts him in the 95th percentile. Waxman's scores place him in the 80th percentile in five of the Congresses and in the 90th percentile in two of them. Armey's scores place him in the 80th percentile in four out of the five Congresses in which he has served and in the 90th per-

23. The way I compute the scaled entrepreneurship score should also help reduce any inflation in the scores that might occur over time.

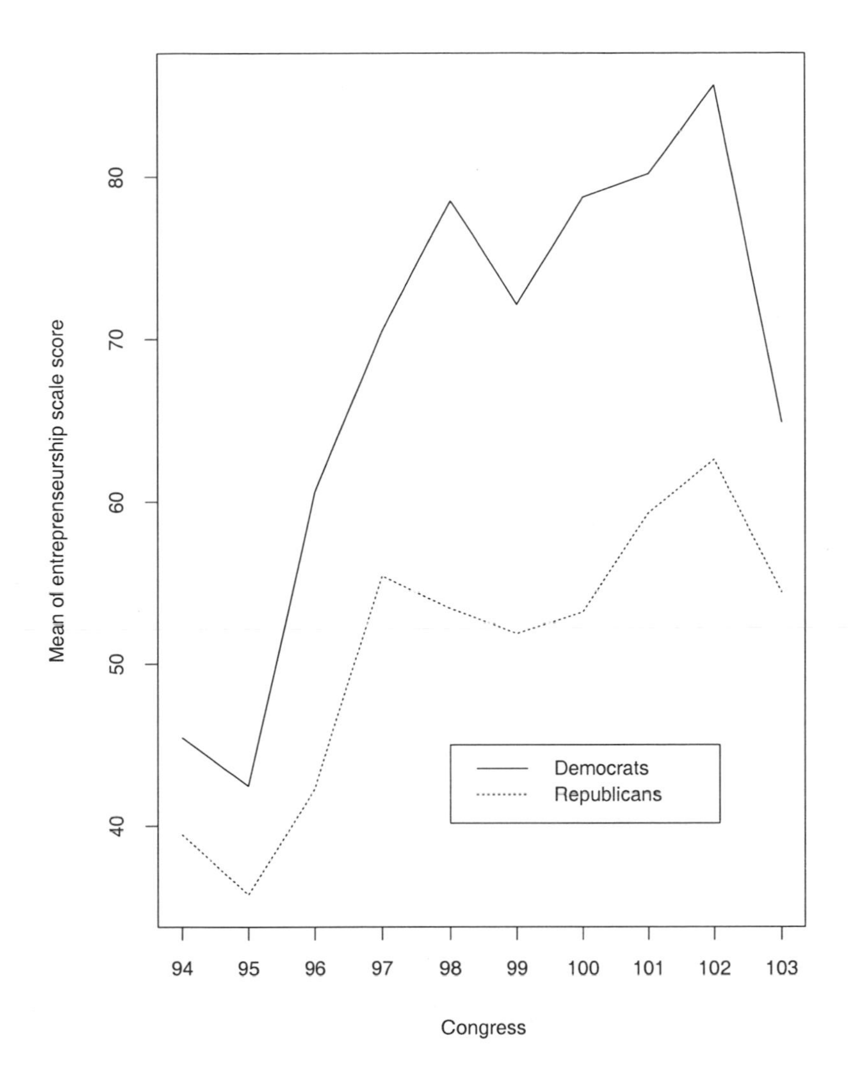

Fig. 2.2. Time-series plot of the mean of the scaled entrepreneurship score, 94th through the 103d Congresses

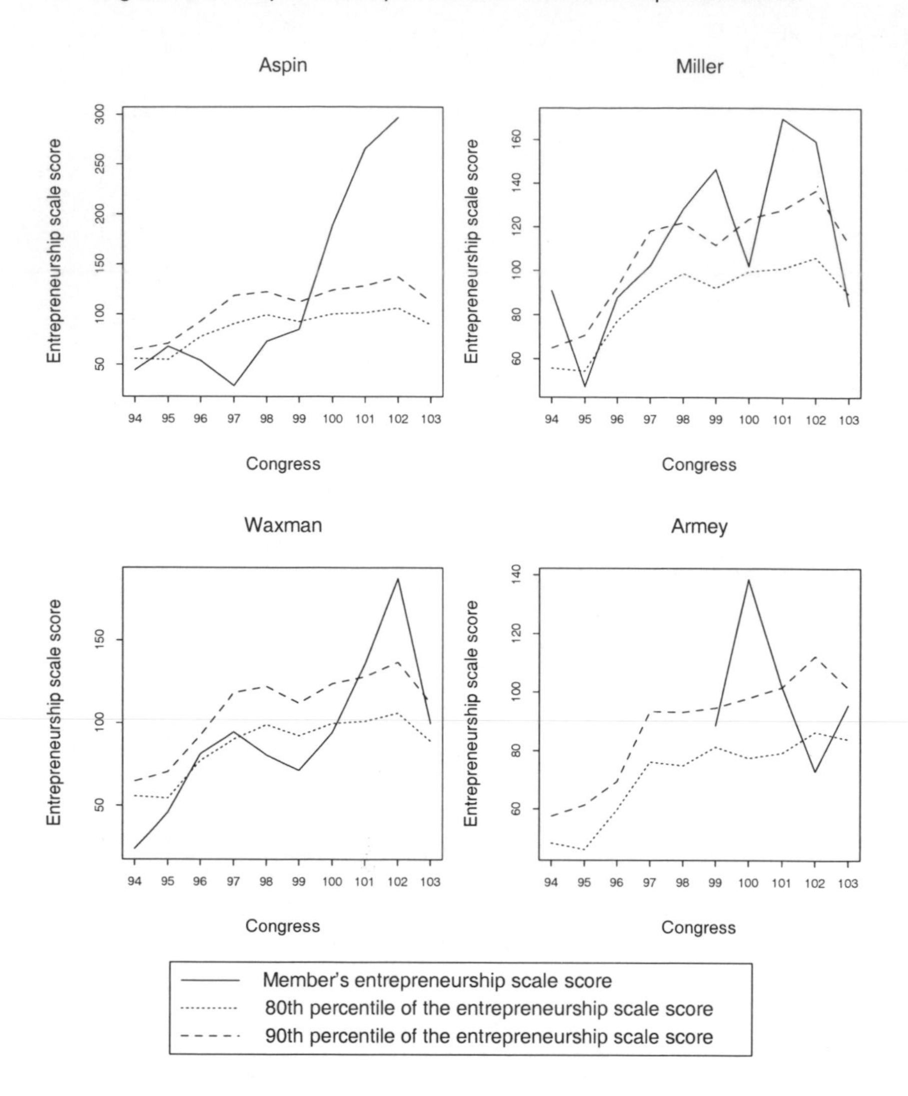

Fig. 2.3. Time-series plots of entrepreneurship scale scores for selected members, 94th through the 103d Congresses

centile in two out of these five. Armey's highest score, which places him in the 95th percentile, occurs in the Congress in which he entrepreneured his base-closings bill. Aspin's scores are surprisingly low given his reputation, although they shoot up after he assumes the chair of the Armed Services Committee. In fact, Aspin had the highest entrepreneurship score of all members in the 102d Congress. Although the scores of these members do not perfectly match qualitative assessments of their entrepreneurial activities, they do reasonably reflect the reputations of members who have been identified as LEs.

As an additional reality check on the legislative entrepreneurship measures, I compared the entrepreneurship scale scores with profiles of members in *Politics in America.* These profiles describe in some detail the legislative efforts of members of Congress. There is substantial variation in the profiles concerning legislative activity. Some profiles mention no legislative activities by members who have very modest to nonexistent legislative agendas, while other profiles have several pages devoted to describing their activities with regard to acquiring policy knowledge, drafting and pushing bills, and building coalitions. I drew a random sample of 20 members each from the 96th, 98th, 100th, and 102d Congresses, and based on the description of their legislative efforts in their profiles I assigned them a number from one to three (lowest to highest) depending on the degree to which they engaged in activities that constitute legislative entrepreneurship in these Congresses. Appendix A lists the legislative entrepreneurship scores and the legislative profile scores for the members in the sample. The legislative entrepreneurship scale scores fair well in this reality check. The legislative entrepreneurship scale scores and the scores coded from the profiles are correlated at .70 for Democrats and .66 for Republicans.[24]

Summary and Caveats

Although previous studies of legislative entrepreneurship have typically used case study methods, the empirical analysis that I undertake is more general and systematic. A more general analysis requires measures of entrepreneurship that are appropriate for quantitative methods. In this chapter, I have described the measures that I use in the empirical analysis in subsequent chapters.

Legislative entrepreneurship is a very difficult activity to quantify, and I do not claim to have measured it perfectly. However, the measures that I have developed capture the important aspects of entrepreneurship, namely, bill drafting, coalition building, and acquiring policy knowledge. The measures are much more detailed than those used in previous quantitative analyses of legislative activity and are essential to explaining entrepreneurial behavior.

---

24. Readers who wish to perform their own reality checks or use the data on legislative entrepreneurship can download the data from http://www.columbia.edu/~gjw10. All of the data and computer programs used for the analyses reported in this book are available from the author on request.

I should note that, although the goal of this book is to explain legislative entrepreneurship, the entrepreneurship scale score I discuss in this chapter appears as an explanatory rather than a dependent variable in the equations in the statistical analysis that follows. The logic behind this is that we can determine whether entrepreneurship positively affects the achievement of members' goals such as obtaining the support of constituents, attracting campaign contributions, or advancing within the institution. If entrepreneurship does help members achieve these goals, then it is easy to see why they would engage in this activity. If entrepreneurship has positive effects on variables related to these goals—for example, the probability that constituents will recognize their names, the amount of money they receive from PACs, or their position in the institution—then it makes sense for rational, self-interested legislators to engage in this activity.

A more accurate empirical model might involve a system of equations that treats the legislative entrepreneurship variable as endogenous. Indeed, many of the variables used in this analysis in addition to the entrepreneurship variable could justifiably appear on both the right- and left-hand sides of regression equations. Although an argument could be made that the variables in this analysis should be treated as part of a complex system of equations, such a system would be impossible to identify and estimate. Unfortunately, available data and methods do not allow us to do much about this endogeneity problem. Although I do adopt a system of equations approach where feasible, it would be foolish to believe that we could eliminate the problems associated with endogeneity completely. I cannot claim to have solved all of the problems, and indeed many of these problems may be unsolvable. Certain parts of the analysis presented in later chapters are perhaps best thought of as being of the "reduced form" variety and should be interpreted with appropriate caution. While I acknowledge the limits of quantitative analysis, I hope to convince the reader that, despite its shortcomings, this kind of analysis is more useful for understanding legislative entrepreneurship than are the less systematic, qualitative methods employed by previous studies of this behavior.

CHAPTER 3

Legislative Entrepreneurship and Constituency Response

A member of Congress can choose to engage in a variety of activities. A key determinant of the activities a member chooses is the response that constituents have to these activities. A member seeks to engage in the kinds of activities that his constituents favor so that they will return him to office. An important issue for this analysis to examine, then, is how constituents respond to legislative entrepreneurship. Does this response affect their overall perception of their representatives and their willingness to grant them additional terms in office? To what degree does constituent response provide incentives to engage in legislative entrepreneurship?

The purpose of this chapter is to develop and test hypotheses about the relationship between legislative entrepreneurship and members' efforts to build winning electoral coalitions in their districts. Congressional scholars have been preoccupied with how the reelection imperative affects members' behavior. Any study that sought to explain legislative behavior would be negligent if it did not thoroughly explore the relationship between the behavior of interest and the reelection motive. If constituents respond favorably to entrepreneurial activity, then we have a relatively straightforward explanation of this activity.

I examine two opposing arguments concerning how entrepreneurial activity directly affects members' reelection prospects. The first argument contends that changes in the electoral environment during the 1960s and 1970s have led members to become LEs as part of their reelection strategies. The decline of political parties has shifted the burden of building and maintaining winning coalitions in the district onto individual members. Members have adapted their campaign styles in response to the decline of parties in part by taking advantage of technological advances. In particular, the increasing importance of electronic media in campaigns has led members to engage in activities that give them exposure through this medium. Rather than reaching out to voters through the party apparatus, members reach out through the electronic media. Entrepreneurial activity and the exposure it brings can presumably help members build support, for example, by increasing name recognition among their constituents.

The second argument contends that constituents *do not* respond to legislative activity in ways that help reelection. The weak form of this argument is that constituents are largely oblivious to the legislative efforts of their representatives and so these efforts do not enter into constituents' evaluations of their representatives. The strong form of this argument is that entrepreneurial activity actually hurts members' reelection chances. Any legislative activity that is salient to a member's district can evoke negative as well as positive responses (Fiorina 1974). An LE can alienate constituents who disagree with the issue positions he or she adopts when engaging in this activity. Furthermore, entrepreneurial activity can hurt members' reelection chances because it draws resources away from other activities—such as casework and constituency service—to which constituents respond favorably (Fiorina 1989).

In this chapter, I assess these two competing arguments. A key consideration in the theoretical development in this chapter is the tradeoffs that members face in allocating resources between activities in the Washington and district arenas. Although the total amount of resources that are available to members has grown, the demands on members in the postreform era have also grown. Members still face "the omnipresent and severe" strain "between the need to attend to Washington business and the need to attend to district business" (Fenno 1978, 33). The more resources members allocate to the Washington arena the fewer they have to devote to district-oriented activities. These tradeoffs have bite if resources allocated to one arena evoke a more favorable constituent response than do resources allocated to the other arena.

The empirical analysis in this chapter uses data on entrepreneurial activity and individual-level survey data to analyze the effects that legislative entrepreneurship has on constituents' evaluations of their members of Congress and in particular how entrepreneurial activity affects the probability that constituents will vote for the incumbent. I find little support for the argument that constituents respond positively to legislative entrepreneurship. While I do find some negative effects of entrepreneurship, including a negative effect on the vote for Democratic incumbents, this activity generally does not have a substantively significant impact on the relationship between constituents and their representatives. Thus, direct constituent response does not seem to provide members with much incentive to engage in legislative entrepreneurship.

Demands on Members

During the postreform era, members have faced increasing demands in both the Washington and district arenas. Ornstein, Mann, and Malbin (1996) report steady increases in the number of recorded votes, the number of pages of public bills enacted, the number of hours spent in session, and an increase in committee and subcommittee meetings from the 80th through the 102d Congresses. In addition to increased legislative demands in Washington, members have also had to cope with high levels of demand for constituency service and other district-oriented activities (Cain, Ferejohn, and Fiorina 1987).

To be sure, members themselves bear some of the responsibility for the expansion in these demands, for they have ventured into new policy areas as well as encouraging constituents to demand more from them in terms of casework (Fiorina 1989). Members have allocated more resources to themselves to help them cope with the growing volume of work, including dramatically increasing the number of personal, committee, and auxiliary staff (Thurber 1981; Rieselbach 1986; Fox and Hammond 1977, 20–26). Increases in staff have helped members cope with expanding workloads both in Washington and with district-oriented activities. The expansion of staff resources has at least made it possible for all members to draft and push their own proposals (Smith 1989, 10). Yet research on the allocation of staff indicates that members have devoted most of the additional resources to district-oriented service, not Washington-oriented legislative activity (Malbin 1981; Schiff and Smith 1983; Ornstein, Mann, and Malbin 1996). This calls into question the degree to which the expansion of staff resources has promoted legislative activities.

Though the expansion of resources can certainly ease the strain members feel in satisfying district and Washington demands, there are limits to the palliative powers of having more staff because the most precious resource that members have—their time—remains severely limited. While technological advances can make it easier for members to perform different activities, they are still limited by the amount of time they can spend on any given activity. Even though a legislator can delegate many tasks to staff, he or she has to monitor to verify that the staff does what he or she wants. Just as a member can claim credit for the activities of his or her staff that constituents favor, he or she can also be blamed for poor staff performance: "That the individual member may not always personally perform each and every function does not diminish the impact of the work, or the member's ultimate responsibility for what is done in his or her name" (Salisbury and Shepsle 1981, 565). But monitoring staff activities takes time, and the more tasks a member delegates the more time he or she must devote to monitoring.

Members cannot delegate tasks such as giving speeches on the floor of the House or making personal appearances in the district. Personal appearances are especially important because it is crucial that reelection-seeking members make themselves accessible by presenting themselves to their constituents in the district (Fenno 1978, 131–32). Members must decide how to allocate their time between monitoring activities and activities that only they can perform (Davidson and Oleszek 1985, 436). The benefits of the expansion of staff resources are limited, then, by members' abilities to monitor staff activities effectively.

Building and Maintaining the Personal Vote

Constraints on resources and time affect members' decisions concerning which goals to pursue and how to pursue them. One of the primary goals of members is to build and maintain the support of their constituents so that they will be reelected. Members have little or no control over many of the factors that affect the degree to which their constituents support them. Such factors include district demographics, economic and social conditions, and support for other political leaders, especially the president (Fiorina 1981a; Kiewiet 1983). One important component of support over which members do have some control is the *personal vote*—"that portion of a candidate's electoral support which originates in his or her personal qualities, qualifications, activities, and record" (Cain, Ferejohn, and Fiorina 1987, 9). Cain et al. argue that members exert significant effort to cultivate the personal vote in order to promote electoral success. In the short run, there is little that members can do about their personal qualities and qualifications apart from attempting to shape constituents' perceptions by adopting a particular "home style" (Fenno 1978). However, members can do a great deal to establish a favorable record through their activities.

Members can choose from a variety of activities in order to cultivate the personal vote. These activities are essentially divided between the two arenas in which legislators operate. Activities in the district arena include giving speeches, attending constituent functions, holding "office hours," and performing general constituency service activities. Activities in the Washington arena include roll call voting, giving speeches on the floor, participating in committee oversight, and engaging in general legislative activities. While there is some overlap between these two arenas (e.g., constituents often visit their member's office in the capital or caseworkers in the Washington office will help constituents with agencies there), they are for the most part distinct in terms of the allocation of resources between them. How does the allocation of resources to entrepreneurial activity in the Washington arena affect a member's efforts to build support in the district?

Legislative Entrepreneurship, Increased Visibility, and Reelection

Devoting resources to legislative activity in Washington might have a direct positive effect on district support, mainly through the media attention that this activity can bring. In fact, some would argue that the conditions under which members of the postreform Congress seek reelection may even compel members to engage in some form of legislative entrepreneurship. One of the most important conditions that has changed is the role that parties play in congressional elections. "Grassroots party organizations [have] declined, in most localities forfeiting their historic roles as sponsors and anchors for political careers" (Davidson 1981, 107). With the decline of parties, "members [have] faced voters less inclined to support them on partisan grounds alone, and party organizations [have become] less effective in communicating with and mobilizing the electorate" (Price 1989, 425). Members can no longer rely on parties to provide them with the resources they typically need to get reelected. The decline of parties, "together with the rise of television as the dominant news and campaign medium, [has given] members incentives to seek a higher public profile" (425). Davidson (1981, 107) contends that members "necessarily [have become] individual entrepreneurs, relying upon their own resources for building and nurturing supportive constituencies," though it is not clear that they have become entrepreneurs of the legislative variety for this purpose.

Legislative entrepreneurship is one possible way that members can attain a high public profile. The activities that constitute legislative entrepreneurship have traditionally been associated with members of Congress who are *workhorses*. Workhorses are those members who take on the onerous, often behind the scenes tasks of legislating. These individuals stand in contrast to *show horses,* members who seek the limelight but avoid legislative travail (Clapp 1963). However, in a study of the allocation of legislators' time, Langbein and Sigelman (1989) found that the traditional workhorse/show horse distinction between types of legislators no longer seems to hold. They argue that workhorses have become show horses in the sense that those who work the hardest legislatively receive the most attention from the media (82).

If this argument is correct, then legislative entrepreneurship can directly promote reelection by attracting media attention and increasing a member's visibility with his or her constituents. Members seek increased visibility with constituents because, according to Stokes and Miller (1966, 205), "to be perceived at all [by them] is to be perceived favorably." Members engage in legislative entrepreneurship because this type of "legislative activism itself will garner attention and credit" (Johannes 1983, 541).

The evidence supporting this argument is mixed, however. Johannes and McAdams (1981) find that, while the number of appearances a member makes on the House floor increases his or her vote share, the number of bills introduced or cosponsored does not have a statistically significant impact. Ragsdale and Cook (1987) also fail to find a statistically significant relationship between the number of bills sponsored and the incumbent's vote share.[1]

---

1. Hall (1996) finds that constituency interests have a positive impact on the degree to which

One possible explanation for these null findings is simply that bill sponsorship does not accurately measure legislative entrepreneurship. Though Mayhew (1974, 61–63) claims that *position taking*—"the public enunciation of a judgmental statement on anything likely to be of interest to political actors"—through bill sponsorship can be "electorally useful," it may be that in modern, media-dominated elections members must do more than introduce bills in order to attract attention. Sponsoring bills and doing nothing with them is tantamount to show horse activity. Members might attract media and constituent attention only if they take sponsoring more seriously and are actively involved with their bills after introduction. Hence, the null findings of previous studies may be due to inadequate measures rather than the lack of constituent response to entrepreneurial activity. The measures of legislative entrepreneurship that I employ should overcome this problem and give us a much better understanding of the relationship between legislative activity and constituent response.

Past studies might also have produced null findings because legislative activity does not positively affect constituents' willingness to vote for incumbents. If this is the case, then legislative entrepreneurship may not enter into the voting calculus in a positive way. In the next section, I explore the issue of how legislative entrepreneurship and the visibility that it may bring might not help—and could even hurt—members' reelection chances.

Costs, Uncertainty, and Legislative Entrepreneurship

Pursuing the limelight through legislative entrepreneurship is one strategy members can adopt in order to achieve reelection. However, some would argue that this is a risky strategy. One argument is that legislative entrepreneurship will not help reelection efforts simply because constituents do not pay much attention to this kind of activity when deciding whom to vote for. Individual members seem to have difficulty claiming credit with their constituents for legislative accomplishments because legislation is the product of a large collectivity (i.e., at least a majority of the House) and it is very costly for constituents to verify the validity of these claims (Mayhew 1974, 59–60; Fiorina 1989, 43).

Members often express frustration at the difficulty of receiving credit from constituents for their legislative efforts. Consider the following comments by members regarding constituents' responses to their legislative work:

---

members participate in the legislative process, though he does not examine directly how constituents respond to legislative participation. While it appears that members act as if constituents respond to their legislative activities, it is important to determine whether there is a direct link between these activities and constituent response.

> In the minds of many people those things don't count. Number one they are not aware of them. And number two, what's important is what I can do for them on a personal basis . . . (quoted in Fiorina 1989, 79)

> I'd hate to think of the reasons why people vote for me. But none of them has anything to do with what I do in Washington or how I vote on the issues. (quoted in Fenno 1978, 133)

> The footwork of Congress may be important to people in Washington, but residents of communities in my state don't appreciate the footwork at all. (quoted in Clapp 1963, 108)[2]

Even though members may make their constituents better off through legislative entrepreneurship, it is difficult for them to turn these accomplishments into votes. "In the short run, making good public policy is rewarded no better than merely talking about it, and it consumes a good deal more time, energy, and staff resources" (Jacobson 1997, 191).

Jacobson's quote suggests a stronger form of this argument: if constituents do not respond to legislative entrepreneurship, then this activity can hurt reelection efforts because it consumes resources that could be spent on activities to which constituents do respond. In terms of constituent response, Fiorina (1989, 49) argues that pork barreling—the delivery of federal benefits to constituents—and constituency service are "both safe and profitable." That is, members have an easier time claiming credit for the delivery of tangible benefits in the form of pork and constituency service than they do for their legislative efforts, and thus they receive positive returns at the polls from delivering tangible benefits.[3] If Fiorina's argument is true, the opportunity costs of engaging in legislative entrepreneurship should discourage members from engaging in it.[4]

---

2. Indeed, the evidence presented in chapter 5 indicates that the "footwork of Congress" with respect to legislative entrepreneurship is important to people in Washington (namely, members of Congress), and its importance to them provides the most compelling solution to the puzzle of legislative entrepreneurship.

3. Johannes and McAdams (1981) and McAdams and Johannes (1988) dispute the claim that casework and constituency service promotes reelection, and, as previously discussed, they find evidence that legislative activity in the form of speaking on the floor promotes reelection.

4. Existing evidence about the resource tradeoffs between the Washington and district arenas is mixed. In his analysis of congressional careers, Hibbing (1991, 164) finds a strong negative correlation between members' attentiveness to their constituencies (measured by trips home and the number of staff persons assigned to the district) and their involvement in legislative activity (measured by bill sponsorship and cosponsorship, speaking on the floor, legislative focus, and progress of members' bills through the legislative process). Johannes (1983), however, does not

If constituents do pay attention to legislative entrepreneurship, this activity may still hurt reelection efforts because it can alienate constituents who do not agree with the policies that members are entrepreneuring. Fiorina argues that legislative activity is "dangerous" in terms of reelection strategies because any policy position that a member stakes out through this type of activity will inevitably alienate some constituents. This stands in contrast to Mayhew's arguments (1974, 61–63) about the electoral benefits of position taking through legislative activity. How can we reconcile these apparently contradictory arguments?

One possible reconciliation concerns the type of legislative activity that members engage in and the amount of resources that this activity takes away from other activities geared toward learning about district preferences and satisfying district demands. A member's perception of his or her *reelection constituency*—those individuals in a district who vote for the member—is characterized by uncertainty (Fenno 1978, 10–11). Arnold (1990) argues that reelection-seeking members must consider more than just *attentive publics,* those constituents who are mobilized and pay relatively close attention to members' Washington behavior. Members must also worry about *inattentive publics,* who may be mobilized in response to members' activities. The heterogeneity of constituencies requires members to devote substantial amounts of resources to learning about policy preferences in their districts so they can anticipate adequately how constituents will react to different legislative activities.

Certain types of legislative activities, however, will force members to allocate large amounts of resources to the Washington arena, which leaves fewer resources for the district arena. According to Mayhew, members can take positions simply by introducing bills; they need not do anything beyond introduction. Introducing bills requires a minimal amount of resources. Legislative entrepreneurship requires a much larger amount. When LEs acquire policy knowledge, they gather information about the preferences of key players in the Washington arena but not necessarily information about the preferences of voters in the district arena. If a member focuses his or her attention on the Washington arena—as members must do when they engage in legislative entrepreneurship—he or she has fewer resources with which to learn about and satisfy district preferences. Legislative activity might only become dangerous when members engage in activities like legislative entrepreneurship, which requires a larger allocation of resources to the Washington arena and makes it

---

find a negative relationship between "legislative activism" and either time spent on casework or the size of casework-related staffs. Though he concludes that members do not face a tradeoff between legislative and casework activities, his findings should be interpreted with caution because his measure of legislative activism is simply the number of bills sponsored or cosponsored, which, as I have argued, is not a very good measure of the amount of resources devoted to legislative activity.

difficult to learn about district policy preferences. Although these activities may bring visibility, that visibility may work against members because they are seen as entrepreneuring policies that are not adequately in tune with district preferences.

Evidence exists indicating that, contrary to the long-standing notion that if constituents perceive their member at all they perceive him or her favorably, familiarity with the incumbent may in fact breed some contempt. Jacobson (1997, 96) finds that as their familiarity with the incumbent increases, survey respondents mention more things they dislike about the incumbent. Furthermore, "ideology/policy" are always more commonly mentioned as things disliked rather than liked about candidates (Jacobson 1997, table 5.15). Thus, entrepreneuring policy proposals may increase visibility, but in a way that is detrimental to building a majority coalition in the district.

While one might argue that LEs could entrepreneur policies that address only "safe" issues to avoid alienating constituents, it is hard to imagine how any issue could be "safe" under all circumstances. There is always some degree of uncertainty regarding how constituents will respond because by definition LEs are combining issues in ways not seen before. Even though members of the House might know the makeup of their districts well enough to conclude that a certain issue or set of issues is safe, when they stake out a clear position and take action on those issues they may decrease their future political viability. Shifts in the political climate, changes in district population, the entrance of new voting cohorts, and redistricting may force them to run for reelection with different constituencies that might disapprove of their legislative records. For example, the entrepreneurial efforts of several Democrats in the service of liberal causes in the 1970s contributed to their defeat in the 1980 Reagan landslide. Although their entrepreneurial activities made them "highly visible," it also made them highly vulnerable (Loomis 1988, 202–3). Previous entrepreneurial efforts may come back to haunt members later in their careers.[5]

In sum, there are essentially three arguments about how entrepreneurial activity might not help reelection chances. The first is simply that there is no relationship between this activity and reelection. The second is that there is an indirect, negative relationship because resource tradeoffs force members to neglect activities to which constituents do respond. The more resources mem-

---

5. One might argue that members can devote enough resources to constituency service to "keep their heads above water," electorally speaking, and devote the rest to entrepreneurial activity. However, the entrepreneurial members who lost their seats in 1980 had devoted substantial amounts of resources to constituency service (Loomis 1988, 202–3). Although they had devoted substantial amounts of resources to the kinds of activities that should have kept them afloat in the changing electoral tides, they still had to answer for the positions they had staked out through their entrepreneurial activities.

bers devote to entrepreneurial activity, the fewer they have for providing pork and constituency service in their districts during a given Congress. The third argument is that there is a direct, negative relationship between legislative entrepreneurship and reelection because entrepreneurial activity on certain issues can alienate or upset constituents, prompting them to withdraw support from the incumbent in future elections.

These three arguments stand in contrast to the argument that there is a direct, positive relationship between legislative entrepreneurship and constituency response. In order to determine which of these arguments is correct, we need to conduct systematic empirical tests using appropriate measures of legislative entrepreneurship. In the sections that follow, I examine the relationship between Washington activities and the reelection goal by looking at constituents' responses to entrepreneurial activity. I do not measure the amount of resources devoted to entrepreneurial activity directly but use the measures of entrepreneurial activity I discuss in chapter 2. I merge the legislative entrepreneurship data from the 96th through 102d Congresses with survey data from the 1980 through 1992 American National Election Surveys (ANES) and with contextual data on members' characteristics (ANES and Miller et al., various years). The survey and contextual data enable us to look at several components of support and how legislative entrepreneurship relates to them.

Effects of Legislative Entrepreneurship on Visibility

One way in which members cultivate the personal vote is through activities that increase their visibility and promote a favorable image among their constituents. By engaging in legislative entrepreneurship, members may become more visible, for example, through media coverage of their entrepreneurial activities in Washington. However, as was discussed earlier, visibility can have a downside as well. One way to assess the relationship between legislative entrepreneurship and visibility would be to see how this activity correlates with measures of members' visibility in their districts such as the number of personal appearances made by members or the number of local news reports about them. Unfortunately, such data are not readily available. However, we can measure visibility indirectly by using survey data. Constituents' responses to survey questions about the visibility of their representatives are in some ways better than objective measures because what we care about is constituents' perceptions—what they actually get to see of their representatives.

Contact with the incumbent has a profound influence on how constituents come to know and evaluate House members (Abramowitz 1980), so we should examine how entrepreneurship affects visibility in terms of constituents' contact with their representatives. If members face the kinds of tradeoffs discussed earlier, then resources devoted to legislative entrepreneurship should decrease visibility through contact with constituents. The ANES asks respondents if they have come in contact with their representatives. We can use the responses to this question and the data on legislative entrepreneurship to test the following hypothesis:

> *Hypothesis 3.1: Contact with constituents decreases the more a member engages in legislative entrepreneurship.*

To test this hypothesis, I estimate a probit regression in which the dependent variable equals one if the respondent claims to have had contact with the member and zero if he or she does not. I include on the right-hand side of this regression the log of the scaled entrepreneurship score that was discussed in chapter 2. Positive coefficients on the entrepreneurship score would lead us to reject hypothesis 3.1 and provide support for the argument that legislative entrepreneurship is an important part of members' reelection strategies. A statistically insignificant coefficient on the entrepreneurship variable would support the argument that constituents do not pay much attention to entrepreneurial activity. A negative and significant coefficient is consistent with the argument that entrepreneurial activity saps resources from other activities that are more effective in enhancing incumbents' visibility.

In addition to the entrepreneurship score, I include other explanatory variables in the regression that might affect contact with constituents. These variables measure the characteristics of the incumbent, the respondent, and the challenger if there is one. In the set of variables that measure the incumbent's characteristics, I include a variable that is the number of terms that the incumbent has served in Congress.[6] I expect the coefficient on the terms variable to be positive because the more terms an incumbent serves the more likely it is constituents will come in contact with the incumbent. But the literature also suggests that there may be a negative relationship between the number of terms served and contact, as members who have served many terms tend to pay less attention to their districts (Hibbing 1991). To account for this possible effect, I include the square of the number of terms a member has served. I expect the coefficient on this variable to be negative.

I also include three dummy variables, which indicate a member's position in the House. Members in prestigious positions will have more resources that they can use to appeal to constituents. These members are also likely to get more media attention than rank and file members, and so we might expect

6. The terms data are from Inter-university Consortium for Political and Social Research (ICPSR) and Carol McKibbin 1993.

persons in these positions to be more visible to their constituents. Alternatively, the additional legislative responsibilities of members in these positions might leave them less time to devote to district-oriented activities. Including these variables also enables us to determine whether or not the entrepreneurship measures have effects that are independent of a member's position in the House. Given the additional resources for legislative activity that formal leaders in the House possess (Hall 1996), one might argue that the entrepreneurship measures are just proxy measures for the occupancy of a prestigious position in Congress.[7] The three dummy variables I include indicate whether the incumbent has a seat on a prestigious committee, is a member of the party leadership, or is a leader of a full committee or subcommittee.[8]

In the set of variables that measure the respondent's characteristics, I include a dummy variable that equals one if the respondent identifies with the same party as the incumbent and equals zero otherwise. Respondents who have the same party affiliation as the incumbent should be more likely to come in contact with him or her than respondents who do not have the same affiliation. I also include variables that measure the respondent's education and income levels.[9] Respondents with higher levels of education and income are more likely to follow and be better informed about politics than are those with lower incomes and less education. Thus, the coefficients on the education and income variables should be positive.

Finally, I include a variable that measures whether or not the incumbent faces a quality challenger. Jacobson and Kernell (1983) have argued that the quality of the challenger plays a significant role in congressional elections. Challengers with experience in elective office will be better known and better at running a campaign than inexperienced challengers would be. In response

7. As we will see in chapter 5, entrepreneurial activity increases the probability that a member of the majority party will obtain a prestigious position.

8. Prestigious committees include Appropriations, Rules, and Ways and Means. Party leadership positions for Democrats include Speaker, chair and secretary of the caucus, majority leader, whip, chief, deputy whip, assistant whip/zone whip, at-large whip, and chair and vice chair of the Democratic Congressional Campaign Committee. Party leadership positions for the Republicans include minority leader; chair, vice chair, and secretary of the Republican Conference; floor leader; whip; chief deputy whip; assistant minority (or regional) whip; assistant minority (or assistant to regional) whip; and chair of the National Republican Congressional Committee. Committee leadership positions include full committee and subcommittee chairs for Democrats and ranking minority member positions for Republicans. The committee assignment data for the 96th through the 100th Congresses were collected by Garrison Nelson. The assignment data for the 101st through the 102d Congresses and the data on committee and party leadership positions were compiled from *Congressional Quarterly (CQ)* special reports, *CQ*'s Washington Alert, Legi-Slate, and the *Congressional Directory*.

9. These measures are the respondent's self-reported income and education. Both of these variables are categorical.

to the more competitive campaigns that quality challengers mount, incumbents will step up their own reelection efforts, including efforts to increase contact with constituents. The efforts of a quality challenger might also increase incumbent visibility as the challenger attempts to inform voters about the incumbent's record, albeit in a way that is intended to convince voters to withdraw support from the incumbent. The measure of challenger quality that I use is a dichotomous variable, which equals one if the challenger has held elective office and zero if the incumbent runs unopposed or the challenger has not previously held elective office. I expect that the coefficient on this variable will be positive.[10]

I conduct the analysis separately for Republicans and Democrats. I expect that constituents will place different expectations on members of the majority and minority parties when it comes to legislative and other activities. Statistical tests confirm that analyzing Democrats and Republicans separately is appropriate.

Table 3.1 reports the effects of these variables on the probability that constituents will come in contact with the incumbent. Though the coefficients on the entrepreneurship score are negative for both Democrats and Republicans, the size of the standard errors prevent us from saying with much confidence that the effect differs from zero. These results do not provide support for hypothesis 3.1. The coefficients on the party identification, education, income, and quality challenger variables have positive and statistically significant effects for both Democrats and Republicans. None of the coefficients on the other variables are bounded away from zero.

We can explore this issue further by examining the ways in which constituents come in contact with their representatives. We might expect that entrepreneurship would affect the probability of constituents having *certain types* of contact with their representatives. Members who engage in higher levels of entrepreneurship might have less direct contact with their constituents because they spend more time in the Washington arena and less time in the district. Yet constituents of LEs might be more likely to see or hear stories about about their legislative efforts in the media. In order to determine the effects of entrepreneurship on contact, I test the following hypotheses:

Hypothesis 3.2: The more legislative entrepreneurship a member engages

10. Many other explanatory variables could be included in this statistical model and the models that follow. This specification, however, should do a reasonable job of accounting for the variation in the dependent variable so that we can obtain clean estimates of the effects of legislative entrepreneurship. For the sake of clarity and parsimony, I use the same set of explanatory variables for the analyses of the various aspects of constituent response to members' behavior.

TABLE 3.1. Effects of Legislative Entrepreneurship on Members' Contact with Constituents

Variable	Democrats	Republicans
Intercept	−.042	.115
	(.103)	(.128)
Entrepreneurship score	−.010	−.018
	(.011)	(.012)
Terms	.021	.061
	(.022)	(.034)
$Terms^2$	−.0003	−.003
	(.001)	(.003)
Exclusive committee	.019	−.002
	(.062)	(.102)
Party leader	.011	.003
	(.007)	(.012)
Committee leader	−.081	−.139
	(.069)	(.082)
Party	.215	.154
	(.046)	(.063)
Education	.131	.119
	(.020)	(.027)
Income	.016	.015
	(.004)	(.006)
Quality challenger	.285	.169
	(.080)	(.087)
N	3,901	2,293
−2 × log likelihood	3,966.668	2,152.336
Percentage correctly predicted	62.1	61.9

Note: Coefficients are probit MLEs. Standard errors are in parentheses.

in the less likely it is that he or she will have personal contact with constituents.

Hypothesis 3.3: The amount of contact a member has with constituents through the media increases with legislative entrepreneurship.

The ANES asks respondents what kind of contact they have had with the incumbent, if any. I estimated two probit regressions to determine the effect of entrepreneurship on contact. The dependent variable for the first regression is whether the constituent had personal contact with the member. Personal contact includes meeting the incumbent or attending a meeting where the incumbent was present. The dependent variable for the second regression is whether the constituent came in contact with the incumbent through print or electronic

TABLE 3.2. Effects of Legislative Entrepreneurship on Members' Personal Contact with Constituents

Variable	Democrats	Republicans
Intercept	−1.678	−2.155
	(.111)	(.151)
Entrepreneurship score	−.015	−.016
	(.010)	(.011)
Terms	.037	.100
	(.023)	(.035)
Terms^2	−.002	−.005
	(.001)	(.003)
Exclusive committee	−.149	−.021
	(.067)	(.102)
Party leader	.012	−.030
	(.007)	(.014)
Committee leader	−.185	−.087
	(.073)	(.089)
Party	.254	.200
	(.050)	(.067)
Education	.132	.139
	(.021)	(.030)
Income	.013	.021
	(.004)	(.007)
Quality challenger	.042	.056
	(.075)	(.089)
N	3,901	2,293
$-2 \times$ log likelihood	3,686.350	1,928.280
Percentage correctly predicted	61.8	65.5

Note: Coefficients are probit MLEs. Standard errors are in parentheses.

media. I estimated the effects of the explanatory variables I used earlier on the probability that a constituent has come in contact with his or her member in each of these ways. The results are reported in tables 3.2 and 3.3. While the signs of the coefficients on the entrepreneurship score are negative in the probits for personal contact, these coefficients are not bounded away from zero. Thus, we cannot infer that entrepreneurship decreases the amount of personal contact that members have with their constituents. For Democrats, entrepreneurship has a positive and statistically significant effect on the probability that constituents come in contact with their representatives through the media. This finding is consistent with the argument that the current electoral environment has led members to engage in entrepreneurship to appeal to constituents through the media. The negative and statistically significant coefficient on the entrepreneurship score for Republicans suggests that their legislative travails

TABLE 3.3. Effects of Legislative Entrepreneurship on Members' Contact with Constituents through the Media

Variable	Democrats	Republicans
Intercept	−.297	−.103
	(.095)	(.117)
Entrepreneurship score	.017	−.026
	(.009)	(.011)
Terms	−.010	.035
	(.020)	(.030)
Terms^2	.001	−.001
	(.001)	(.003)
Exclusive committee	−.041	−.018
	(.057)	(.090)
Party leader	.019	.008
	(.006)	(.011)
Committee leader	−.055	−.099
	(.064)	(.074)
Party	.182	.121
	(.043)	(.057)
Education	.129	.106
	(.018)	(.024)
Income	.008	.012
	(.004)	(.005)
Quality challenger	.217	.233
	(.070)	(.078)
N	3,901	2,293
$-2 \times$ log likelihood	4,994.242	2,821.625
Percentage correctly predicted	60.2	60.1

Note: Coefficients are probit MLEs. Standard errors are in parentheses.

consume resources that could be spent on activities that would increase visibility through the media.

Although the coefficients on the entrepreneurship score indicate that this variable has statistically significant effects on contact through the media, we should not make too much of these results because an analysis of the marginal effects indicates that these effects are not *substantively* significant. I simulated probabilities of contact with constituents through the media over the range of the values of the entrepreneurship score in the sample (the other variables in the specification are set to their median values). In order to realize a .03 increase in the probability that a constituent reports coming in contact with the Democratic incumbent through the media, the incumbent would have to increase his or her entrepreneurship score from the lowest to highest values in the sample. A Republican incumbent would have to change his or her score by the same amount in order to realize a .03 decrease in the probability of this kind of contact. Despite the statistical significance of the coefficient on the entrepreneurship variable, the small changes in the probability of contact in response to such large changes in the entrepreneurship score indicate that incumbents are neither helped nor hurt much by this activity.

Name Recall and Likes and Dislikes

The analysis in the previous section indicates that there is not much of a relationship between legislative entrepreneurship and visibility through either personal contact or media coverage. We can explore in more detail how legislative entrepreneurship relates to members' efforts to build winning coalitions in their districts by examining how this activity affects constituents' knowledge of and opinions about their representatives. Studies of voter behavior have found that voters who recall the name of the incumbent are more likely to cast their ballots for him or her (Stokes and Miller 1966; Cain, Ferejohn, and Fiorina 1987). Thus, reelection-seeking incumbents should undertake activities that will increase their name recall among constituents. One strategy that a member can adopt is to try to increase name recall by engaging in legislative entrepreneurship. Through legislative activity, members can try to attach their names to issues that are salient to the district. For example, a member from a district with a large number of farms may try to entrepreneur legislation on agricultural issues. Such activities might increase the probability that constituents will recall their member's name and find something that they like about the member.

But, as Fiorina argues (1974, 1989), this kind of strategy can be risky because legislative activity on any issue that is salient to constituents might provoke a negative reaction if they do not like the stand the member has taken on the issue. Fiorina's argument about saliency suggests that increased familiarity with the incumbent might lead constituents to discover things they do not like. So in addition to name recall, we should look at how entrepreneurship affects whether constituents like or dislike the candidate. These arguments lead to three testable hypotheses:

Hypothesis 3.4: Legislative entrepreneurship increases the probability that constituents will recall the incumbent's name.

Hypothesis 3.5: Legislative entrepreneurship increases the probability that constituents will like something about the incumbent.

Hypothesis 3.6: Legislative entrepreneurship increases the probability that constituents will dislike something about the incumbent.

To test hypothesis 3.4, I estimate a dichotomous probit regression in which the dependent variable is whether or not the respondent recalls the name of the incumbent. I include on the right-hand side of this regression the log of the scaled entrepreneurship score. Positive coefficients on the entrepreneurship score support hypothesis 3.4 and indicate that legislative entrepreneurship promotes reelection. The coefficient on the entrepreneurship variable should be statistically indistinguishable from zero if constituents ignore entrepreneurial activity but should be negative and significant if entrepreneurship forces tradeoffs with other activities that are better at placing a member's name before the public. The rest of the specification includes the set of explanatory variables used in the previous regressions.

Table 3.4 reports the effects of these variables on the probability that a respondent will recall the incumbent's name. The coefficient on the entrepreneurship score is statistically insignificant for Democrats but negative and statistically significant for Republicans, indicating that higher levels of entrepreneurship actually decrease the probability that constituents will recall their Republican member's name. The other variables that have significant coefficients have the effects that I expect, and these effects are similar for members of both parties. The longer a Democratic member has served the more likely it is that constituents will recall his or her name, although the negative coefficient on the squared terms variable indicates that Democrats with very high levels of seniority are less well known by their constituents. A Republican's seniority does not have an effect that is statistically distinguishable from zero. The institutional position variables do not have significant effects for either Democrats or Republicans. Constituents are more likely to recall the member's name the more education and income they have and if they belong to the same party as the incumbent. The quality of the challenger also has significant and positive effects.

Although the coefficient on the entrepreneurship score for Republicans is negative and statistically significant, this result still does not provide strong support for the argument that legislative entrepreneurship requires members to allocate fewer resources to activities that build name recall. The marginal effect of the entrepreneurship variable is quite small; the probability that a constituent will recall the incumbent's name is only about .08 less when the incumbent has the maximum entrepreneurship score in the sample than when he or she has the minimum score. Thus, Republicans are not hurt much in terms of name recall when they engage in high levels of legislative entrepreneurship.[11]

---

11. I also estimated the effect of the entrepreneurship score on the probability that constitu-

TABLE 3.4. Effects of Legislative Entrepreneurship on Name Recall of the Incumbent

Variable	Democrats	Republicans
Intercept	−1.791	−1.541
	(.094)	(.117)
Entrepreneurship score	.009	−.053
	(.010)	(.010)
Terms	.035	.040
	(.019)	(.029)
Terms^2	−.003	−.002
	(.001)	(.002)
Exclusive committee	−.038	.076
	(.055)	(.082)
Party leader	.007	−.004
	(.006)	(.010)
Committee leader	−.072	−.094
	(.060)	(.070)
Party	.261	.354
	(.040)	(.053)
Education	.209	.167
	(.017)	(.024)
Income	.016	.018
	(.004)	(.005)
Quality challenger	.222	.293
	(.059)	(.069)
N	4,809	2,711
−2 × log likelihood	5,368.859	3,040.022
Percentage correctly predicted	65.7	67.1

Note: Coefficients are probit MLEs. Standard errors are in parentheses.

To test hypotheses 3.5 and 3.6, I use the ANES items that ask respondents whether there is anything that they like or dislike about the incumbent. In the first probit, the dependent variable equals one if the respondent mentioned something he or she liked about the incumbent and zero otherwise. In the second probit, the dependent variable equals one if the respondent mentioned something he disliked about the incumbent and zero otherwise. The explanatory variables are the same as those employed earlier. Tables 3.5 and 3.6 report the results. The results are not consistent with hypothesis 3.5. The coefficient on the entrepreneurship score is not bounded away from zero for

ents will *recognize* the incumbent's name. The effect was statistically indistinguishable from zero for Democrats but positive for Republicans. However, the marginal effect for Republicans was quite small.

TABLE 3.5. Effects of Entrepreneurship on the Probability That Constituents Like Something about the Incumbent

Variable	Democrats	Republicans
Intercept	−.908	−1.086
	(.088)	(.112)
Entrepreneurship score	.0003	.009
	(.009)	(.010)
Terms	.002	.082
	(.017)	(.028)
Terms^2	.0004	−.003
	(.001)	(.002)
Exclusive committee	−.005	.086
	(.054)	(.081)
Party leader	.007	−.030
	(.006)	(.010)
Committee leader	−.037	−.157
	(.059)	(.068)
Party	.436	.426
	(.039)	(.052)
Education	.089	.092
	(.017)	(.023)
Income	.007	.009
	(.003)	(.005)
Quality challenger	.136	.098
	(.059)	(.070)
N	4,490	2,544
$-2 \times$ log likelihood	5,894.53	3,288.076
Percentage correctly predicted	60.8	64.7

Note: Coefficients are probit MLEs. Standard errors are in parentheses.

either Democrats or Republicans, so we cannot say with much confidence that entrepreneurship increases or decreases the probability that constituents like something about the incumbent. The only variables that have statistically significant effects that are in the same direction for members of both parties are the party identification and education variables. Both of these increase the probability that constituents will like something about their representative. More senior Republicans and Democrats who face quality challengers are also more likely to have constituents who like something about them. Unexpectedly, the party and committee leadership variables have negative effects for Republicans, suggesting that these positions might prevent members from attending to certain duties constituents favor more.

TABLE 3.6. Effects of Entrepreneurship on the Probability That Constituents Dislike Something about the Incumbent

Variable	Democrats	Republicans
Intercept	−2.149	−1.942
	(.128)	(.149)
Entrepreneurship score	.023	−.040
	(.015)	(.010)
Terms	−.002	.013
	(.025)	(.037)
$Terms^2$	−.001	−.002
	(.002)	(.003)
Exclusive committee	.114	.072
	(.070)	(.105)
Party leader	−.007	−.007
	(.008)	(.013)
Committee leader	.265	.019
	(.077)	(.088)
Party	−.305	−.534
	(.051)	(.070)
Education	.207	.161
	(.023)	(.030)
Income	.008	.030
	(.005)	(.007)
Quality challenger	.311	.529
	(.071)	(.080)
N	4,490	2,544
$-2 \times$ log likelihood	3,022.246	1,804.026
Percentage correctly predicted	69.9	71.4

Note: Coefficients are probit MLEs. Standard errors are in parentheses.

The results reported in table 3.6 do not support hypothesis 3.6 either because the entrepreneurship score does not have a statistically significant effect for Democrats and has a statistically significant and *negative* effect for Republicans. This means that entrepreneurship has essentially no effect on the probability that a constituent will dislike something about a Democratic incumbent and makes it less likely that constituents will dislike something about their Republican representative. Thus, entrepreneurship does not seem to hurt Democrats and it helps Republicans—albeit only slightly—in this regard. A Republican who has the highest values for the entrepreneurship score in the sample has a .16 probability that a constituent will dislike something about them, while this probability is equal to .21 for a member who has the lowest score in the sample. This difference indicates that Republicans are not helped much by legislative entrepreneurship when it comes to negative feelings toward incumbents.

As for the other variables in the model, having the same party identification as the incumbent decreases the probability of disliking something about the incumbent, while having more education increases the probability that a constituent will dislike something. Quality challengers also have a significant effect, suggesting that they have better success in pointing out incumbents' flaws than do those candidates who have not held elective office.[12]

Constituent-Initiated Contact with Representatives

So far we have looked at how entrepreneurial activity affects various aspects of representative-constituent relations. Another important aspect of cultivating the personal vote involves constituent-initiated contact. Constituents contact their representatives for a variety of reasons, from voicing opinions about various issues to seeking help with problems such as delays in receiving social security or veterans' benefit checks. Members believe that the latter kinds of contact are particularly important for building the personal vote because they involve requests that the member and his staff engage in casework on the behalf of constituents (Cain, Ferejohn, and Fiorina 1987). Yet, if those members who focus attention on legislative activity have fewer resources to devote to district-oriented activities like casework, then their constituents might be discouraged from requesting assistance. If this logic is correct, then the following hypothesis should be true:

> *Hypothesis 3.7: Constituents of members who engage in higher levels of legislative entrepreneurship will be less likely to contact their members.*

The ANES asks respondents whether they have initiated contact with their representative. I estimated probit regressions in which the dependent variable equals one if the respondent has contacted his or her member and zero otherwise. The independent variables are the same as in the previous specifications. Table 3.7 reports the results. The coefficient on the entrepreneurship variable for Democrats is negative and statistically significant, supporting hypothesis 3.7. Entrepreneurship does not appear, however, to affect the probability that a Republican's constituents will contact him or her. The marginal effects of

---

12. I also calculated the total number of likes and dislikes each respondent mentioned about the incumbent and challenger and regressed these variables on the independent variables in the previous equations. The results of these ordered probits were similar to the results of the dichotomous probits.

TABLE 3.7. Effects of Legislative Entrepreneurship on Constituent-Initiated Contact

Variable	Democrats	Republicans
Intercept	−1.969	−2.299
	(.113)	(.149)
Entrepreneurship score	−.020	−.002
	(.010)	(.013)
Terms	.068	.118
	(.023)	(.034)
Terms^2	−.003	−.005
	(.002)	(.003)
Exclusive committee	−.086	.028
	(.068)	(.095)
Party leader	−.004	−.023
	(.007)	(.013)
Committee leader	.018	−.094
	(.073)	(.090)
Party	.190	.140
	(.049)	(.064)
Education	.134	.159
	(.021)	(.029)
Income	.008	.016
	(.004)	(.006)
Quality challenger	.267	.039
	(.070)	(.090)
N	4,439	2,539
$-2 \times$ log likelihood	3,444.274	2,090.745
Percentage correctly predicted	62.7	66.8

Note: Coefficients are probit MLEs. Standard errors are in parentheses.

the entrepreneurship score on the probability of a constituent initiating contact indicate that, even though the coefficient is statistically significant for Democrats, the substantive significance of this effect is quite small. A Democratic incumbent would realize a drop of only about .02 in this probability if he or she went from having the lowest to the highest entrepreneurship score in the sample.

One explanation of why constituents might be less likely to initiate contact would be because they do not expect their representative to be very helpful. Consequently, we would expect that entrepreneurial activity would have a negative effect on constituents' perceptions of how helpful their member would be if they did seek help. Members who engage in high levels of entrepreneurship should be perceived as less helpful because they devote a substantial amount of their resources to the Washington arena. The ANES asks respondents how helpful they think their members would be if they sought help. Constituents' answers range from "not helpful" to "very helpful." To assess the claim about perceptions of helpfulness I estimated ordered probits in which the dependent variable ranges from zero to two depending on how helpful respondents perceive their member to be. A negative coefficient on the entrepreneurship variable would indicate that constituents perceive entrepreneurial members as less helpful with problems. Table 3.8 reports that, although the signs on the entrepreneurship variables for members of both parties are negative, the standard errors overwhelm the coefficients. Thus, it is not clear why constituents would be less likely to contact members who engage in higher levels of entrepreneurship.[13]

Entrepreneurship and Taking Care of the District

A key activity in members' reelection strategies is claiming credit for the delivery of particularized benefits to the district. Past studies have found that if constituents remember activities that the incumbent has performed for the district they are more likely to vote for him or her (Cain, Ferejohn, and Fiorina 1987). Cain et al. (175–76) argue that survey responses to questions like "Do you recall anything special that the incumbent has done for the district?" measure the amount of particularized benefits members have delivered and for which they have claimed credit.[14] But it is important for this analysis to determine specifically what sort of "special things" constituents remember. Are constituents more likely to remember special things that relate to legislative or nonlegislative activities? If constituents remember the former, then we should expect that higher levels of legislative entrepreneurship would increase the probability that constituents will remember special things the incumbents did. However, the statistical analysis discussed in this chapter so far indicates that general legislative activity (i.e., that which is not directly related to providing district-specific benefits) is not something that constituents tend to notice.

In all of the years that this study covers, the ANES included a question that asks whether respondents remember whether the incumbent has done anything special for the district. Ideally, we would like to know specifically whether

---

13. I also estimated the effects of legislative entrepreneurship on the probability that constituents had received constituency service from their representative. I found that entrepreneurial activity did not affect the probability that those who sought constituency service received a response from their representative.

14. Positive responses to this question do not necessarily indicate that constituents respond only to particularized or district-specific benefits. Incumbents can do things legislatively that benefit many districts besides their own.

TABLE 3.8. Effects of Legislative Entrepreneurship on Constituents' Perceptions of Helpfulness

Variable	Democrats	Republicans
Intercept 1	−.556	−.819
	(.089)	(.113)
Intercept 2	1.09	.827
	(.090)	(.113)
Entrepreneurship score	−.002	−.003
	(.009)	(.010)
Terms	.041	.039
	(.019)	(.028)
Terms^2	−.002	−.0001
	(.001)	(.002)
Exclusive committee	−.144	.022
	(.054)	(.082)
Party leader	.005	−.003
	(.006)	(.010)
Committee leader	−.244	−.082
	(.059)	(.067)
Party	.344	.287
	(.040)	(.052)
Education	−.022	.039
	(.017)	(.023)
Income	.001	.003
	(.003)	(.005)
Quality challenger	−.024	−.051
	(.059)	(.068)
N	3,563	2,005
$-2 \times$ log likelihood	6,638.747	3,769.548
Percentage correctly predicted	58.3	58.2

Note: Coefficients are probit MLEs. Standard errors are in parentheses.

or not constituents remember legislative activities that benefited the district. Unfortunately, ANES interviewers probed to find out what the respondent remembered in only one of the surveys that I use in this analysis, and even in that survey the ANES-specified categories of responses to the question do not tell us specifically what we would like to know.

The data from the one survey that does probe to find out what constituents remember give some indication that they are less likely to remember general legislative activity than activities that are "strictly local." Table 3.9 reports the percentages of respondents who claimed to have remembered various special things that the incumbent did for the district.[15] Very few individuals—

15. The categories are those defined by the ANES.

TABLE 3.9. Percentages of Constituents Who Recalled Their Incumbents Doing "Special Things" for Their Districts

What Kind of "Special Thing"?	Percentage of Constituents in Category
General competence in office	1.55
Congressman as means of access to government	.899
National legislation and policy	.93
Strictly local problems (where no particular group or self-interest is expressed)	3.63
Congressman as party member	.062
Congressman good for, knows problems of, or supports interests of various groups	2.14
Negative comments concerning congressman	.031
Miscellaneous	.465
Did not recall special thing	89.92
N	1,616

Source: 1980 ANES.

just over 10 percent—recalled the incumbent doing anything special for the district. About 3 percent recalled the incumbent doing something special regarding strictly local problems. Of those who recalled the incumbent doing something concerning strictly local problems, most mentioned that the incumbent "promotes local industry," has "helped bring/keep defense contracts for area," has "helped bring/keep jobs/projects for district," or has "secured federal grants/revenue sharing or aid for schools, roads, other municipal-local projects" (1980 ANES codebook). Less than 1 percent recalled the incumbent doing a special thing for the district through national legislation or policy. Legislative activity appears to be less visible than those activities that provide tangible benefits for the district. Still, it is questionable whether this survey question draws a fine enough distinction between activities to enable us to reach definitive conclusions about the impression that legislative activity has on constituents. For example, just over 2 percent of constituents remembered a special thing the incumbent did that indicated he or she was good for or sensitive to the interests of various groups. The incumbent could certainly have created this impression by acting as an entrepreneur for legislation that was of interest to these groups. An incumbent might even engage in legislative activities to address some of the strictly local problems that respondents mentioned. If this were the case, then we might see a positive relationship between legislative entrepreneurship and constituents remembering "special things" done for the district.

However, if members face tradeoffs between engaging in low-visibility legislative activity and high-visibility district service, then the following hypothesis should be true:

> *Hypothesis 3.8: Constituents of those incumbents who engage in higher levels of entrepreneurial activity are less likely to remember special things done by the incumbents.*

To test this hypothesis, I estimated probit regressions in which the dependent variable equals one if the respondent recalled a special thing that the incumbent had done for the district and equals zero otherwise. I use the same explanatory variables as in the previous regression. Table 3.10 reports the results. The entrepreneurship scores for Democrats and Republicans do not have statistically significant coefficients, and so they do not provide support for hypothesis 3.8. Seniority has a positive and significant effect on the probability that a constituent of a Democratic member will recall a special thing. Education, income, and having the same party identification as the incumbent all have positive and significant effects, as does the challenger quality variable.

Entrepreneurship and Job Approval

So far, we have found that entrepreneurial activity essentially has no substantive impact, positive or negative, on the types of interactions members have with constituents that are important for building the personal vote. Before we look at the effects that entrepreneurship has on constituents' vote choices, there is one more item—job approval—that is useful for understanding how entrepreneurship affects constituents' perceptions of their representatives. Cain, Ferejohn, and Fiorina (1987, 178) find that "job ratings constitute the single best measure of an incumbent's personal standing with constituents." Constituents ultimately might not care much about the level of interaction they have with the member in the district but instead might value the fact that their representative is an active legislator—a "mover and shaker" in Washington. Fenno (1978, 139) contends that "members believe that their supporters want their representative to be influential in Congress, and that they take a certain pride in having an effective congressman—the more so when he is effective on their behalf." Members might demonstrate such effectiveness through entrepreneurial activity. Even though we might find that entrepreneurship generally has null effects on the amount of interaction that members have with their constituents, members could cultivate the personal vote by developing positive records as active legislators. This leads to the following testable hypothesis:

> *Hypothesis 3.9: Legislative entrepreneurship increases the probability*

TABLE 3.10. Effects of Legislative Entrepreneurship on Respondent's Recall of a "Special Thing" the Incumbent Has Done for the District

Variable	Democrats	Republicans
Intercept	−1.635	−1.719
	(.103)	(.137)
Entrepreneurship score	−.003	.006
	(.010)	(.013)
Terms	.042	.021
	(.021)	(.033)
Terms^2	−.002	−.0003
	(.001)	(.003)
Exclusive committee	−.108	.107
	(.062)	(.094)
Party leader	−.007	−.00006
	(.007)	(.012)
Committee leader	.015	−.016
	(.067)	(.081)
Party	.340	.281
	(.045)	(.062)
Education	.103	.102
	(.019)	(.027)
Income	.007	.004
	(.004)	(.006)
Quality challenger	.298	.322
	(.065)	(.078)
N	4,432	2,532
$-2 \times$ log likelihood	4,320.437	2,176.384
Percentage correctly predicted	61.7	62.4

Note: Coefficients are probit MLEs. Standard errors are in parentheses.

that constituents will approve of the job their incumbent is doing.

The ANES enables us to determine how entrepreneurship affects constituents' perceptions of how well members are performing their jobs because it asks respondents whether they approve of the job their representative is doing. I estimated probits in which the dependent variable equals one if the respondent approves of the job the member is doing and equals zero if they do not. The explanatory variables are the same as those included in the previous regressions.

Table 3.11 reports the results. The coefficient on the entrepreneurship score is statistically significant for Republicans but not for Democrats, indicating that the constituents of Republican entrepreneurs are more likely to approve of the jobs their members are doing. The only variables that have

TABLE 3.11. Effects of Legislative Entrepreneurship on Incumbent's Job Approval

Variable	Democrats	Republicans
Intercept	1.201	1.106
	(.140)	(.182)
Entrepreneurship score	.001	.055
	(.015)	(.011)
Terms	.034	−.021
	(.029)	(.048)
Terms^2	−.003	.004
	(.002)	(.004)
Exclusive committee	−.083	−.042
	(.085)	(.138)
Party leader	−.003	−.022
	(.009)	(.015)
Committee leader	−.309	.010
	(.094)	(.110)
Party	.448	.870
	(.061)	(.090)
Education	−.029	−.072
	(.026)	(.036)
Income	−.001	−.006
	(.006)	(.008)
Quality challenger	−.209	−.325
	(.086)	(.101)
N	3,136	1,767
$-2 \times$ log likelihood	2,116.337	1,148.885
Percentage correctly predicted	64.4	73.9

Note: Coefficients are probit MLEs. Standard errors are in parentheses.

consistent and significant effects across parties are the party identification and quality challenger variables. Those constituents who identify with the same party as the incumbent are more likely to approve of the incumbent's record, while those who have the opportunity to vote for a quality challenger are less likely to approve. The coefficient on the education variable is negative and significant for Republicans, while the committee leadership variable is negative and significant for Democrats. None of the other variables has a coefficient that is bounded away from zero.

Even though the coefficient on the entrepreneurship variable is statistically significant for Republicans, simulated probabilities again indicate that the marginal effect of this variable is not substantively significant. A Republican incumbent would increase the probability that a typical constituent approves of the job he or she is doing only by about .07 if he or she increases the entrepreneurship score from the lowest to the highest value in the sample.

Legislative Entrepreneurship and the Vote

The previous sections have given us insight into the relationship between legislative entrepreneurship and members' efforts to build electoral support in their districts. The empirical analysis to this point supports the argument that legislative entrepreneurship does not have a direct, significantly positive impact on support. But ultimately we are interested in the effects that legislative entrepreneurship has on votes for the incumbent.

A methodological issue complicates the estimation of the effects of entrepreneurship on votes. Members' expectations about how their allocations of resources will affect their records will influence their allocation decisions. A member's level of legislative entrepreneurship is determined simultaneously with constituent responses (Fiorina 1981b). Unless we correct for this problem, we risk obtaining inconsistent estimates of the effects of entrepreneurial activity.[16]

To correct for this problem, I follow the two-stage method for models with mixed qualitative and continuous variables discussed by Maddala (1983, 244–45). This method involves setting up a two-equation system in which entrepreneurship and the vote are treated as endogenous variables. For this system of equations to be identified, we need to find some variables that affect a member's level of legislative entrepreneurship but not constituents' votes (or affect their votes only through entrepreneurship). The variables that I use in this procedure measure the workloads of committees. The larger the legislative workload of a committee the more opportunities its members should have to engage in entrepreneurial activity. A member of a more active committee should generally have more opportunities for entrepreneurship. However, committee activity might have a negative impact on certain aspects of legislative entrepreneurship. For example, if a committee addresses many bills in several different areas it may be difficult for its members to focus on a particular issue and acquire an adequate amount of policy knowledge. These committee-specific variables should be uncorrelated with how a particular member's constituents evaluate his or her performance. Many constituents do not even know their member's name let alone which committees he or she serves on and what these committees do (Miller and Stokes 1963).

I employ three committee workload variables to identify this system of

16. One could argue that the same problem exists in the analyses of constituent response to entrepreneurship discussed in the previous sections. While this is plausible, I expect that this problem is less serious for the items examined earlier than it is for the vote. Rather than trying to estimate a very complex system of equations that includes all of the different interactions between entrepreneurship and constituent response, I try to keep the analysis as simple and accessible as possible. But the results should be interpreted with appropriate caution.

TABLE 3.12. Descriptive Statistics of Members' Committee Workload Scores, 96th through the 102d Congresses

Variable	Mean	SD	Median	Minimum	Maximum
Avg. no. of bills referred	426.756	442.663	288	1	2,320
Avg. no. of bills reported	30.242	17.748	29	1	123
Avg. no. of hearings	112.704	50.322	106.5	1	242

Source: The data on bill referrals and bill reports are from the CRS's Legislative Data File. The data on committee hearings are from the Congressional Information Service's Congressional Masterfile.

equations. The first is the average number of bills that are referred to a member's committee(s).[17] This is a general measure of the demands that are placed on a committee that would affect its members and their opportunities for engaging in legislative entrepreneurship. The other two variables are measures of the actual work that a committee is doing. For each member in each Congress, I determine the average number of hearings that were held and the number of bills that were reported by their committee(s). Table 3.12 reports descriptive statistics for these data.

The right-hand variables in the first structural equation include the logs of the committee workload variables, the number of terms the member has served and its square, and the three institutional position dummies. Members who are better educated or have previous legislative experience might find it less costly to assume the entrepreneurial role. I include a dummy variable to crudely measure members' education in terms of whether they attended academically prestigious universities. I also include variables that indicate whether or not a member has previously held office in a state legislature or is a former congressional staffer. Experience as a state legislator or congressional staffer may help members with their entrepreneurial efforts after they become members of Congress.

The second-stage estimates from the structural equation when entrepreneurship is the dependent variable are reported in table 3.13. The vote choice instrument does not have statistically significant effects on legislative entrepreneurship for either Democrats or Republicans. The other variables do not have consistent effects across parties, and some have effects that are counterintuitive. For example, holding a leadership position in the Democratic Party increases entrepreneurship, while Democrats who have positions on exclusive committees engage in less entrepreneurship. This may be due to the fact that members of exclusive committees—particularly Rules and Appropriations—are limited in their entrepreneurial efforts by the nature of the work of their

17. I also computed the totals for the committee workload variables. The results were essentially the same for the averages and the totals.

TABLE 3.13. Effects of Constituent Response on Entrepreneurial Activity

Variable	Democrats	Republicans
Intercept	1.558	1.917
	(.650)	(.910)
Vote choice instrument[a]	−.112	.106
	(.084)	(.076)
ln of average number of bill referrals	.399	−.364
	(.089)	(.092)
ln of average number of bills reported	−.277	.930
	(.126)	(.122)
ln of average number of hearings	.117	−.098
	(.106)	(.183)
Terms	.217	.060
	(.060)	(.074)
Terms^2	−.006	−.002
	(.004)	(.006)
Exclusive committee	−.959	−.024
	(.182)	(.214)
Party leader	.050	.034
	(.018)	(.029)
Committee leader	−.234	.100
	(.193)	(.175)
Attended prestigious university	.091	.771
	(.134)	(.140)
State legislative experience	−.234	.475
	(.126)	(.154)
Former congressional staffer	.341	1.037
	(.301)	(.353)
N	1,573	880
R^2	.08	.12

Note: Coefficients are second-stage OLS estimates. Standard errors are computed from the covariance matrix given in Maddala 1983, 245.
[a]Average taken over individuals in the district.

committees. State legislative experience has a positive effect on entrepreneurship for Republicans but a surprisingly negative effect for Democrats. Attending a prestigious university and having served as a congressional staffer positively affect a Republican's entrepreneurial activity.

The exogenous variables in the second structural equation include the same variables that I included in the probits in earlier sections of this chapter. In addition to these variables, I include variables that measure the respondents' retrospective and prospective judgments about their personal financial situations and the performance of the national economy. Other studies of voting behavior have found these variables, especially ones concerning the national economy, to have significant effects upon the vote decision (Fiorina 1981a; Kiewiet 1983). The more favorably constituents evaluate the national economy and their personal financial situations, the more likely they are to vote for the incumbent.

Table 3.14 reports the estimates of the effects of these variables on the probability of voting for the incumbent. The key explanatory variable of interest is the entrepreneurship instrumental variable computed from the first-stage estimates. The coefficient on this variable is negative and statistically significant for Democrats but statistically insignificant for Republicans. This result for Democrats provides support for the argument that engaging in entrepreneurship makes it difficult for members to build supporting coalitions in their districts. For Republicans, we cannot say with much confidence that entrepreneurship has a positive or negative effect on the probability that constituents will vote for them.

The coefficients on the terms variable are not significant, while the coefficient on the squared terms variable is for Republicans, although its sign differs from what I expected. The coefficients on the party leadership variable are positive and bounded away from zero for both Democrats and Republicans. While the coefficient on the exclusive committee position variable attains statistical significance for Democrats, it has an unexpected negative sign. Constituents are more likely to vote for the incumbent if they share his or her party affiliation but less likely to do so if the incumbent faces a quality challenger. The only economic judgment variable that has a statistically significant coefficient is the prospective judgment of personal financial situation in the Republicans' equation, although this coefficient is unexpectedly negative.

Simulating the probability that a typical constituent will vote for the Democratic incumbent reveals that the marginal effects of the entrepreneurship score are substantial. A typical constituent will vote with probability .96 for a Democratic incumbent who engages in no legislative entrepreneurship. As a member's entrepreneurship increases, this probability drops precipitously. A Democrat with the median entrepreneurship score in the sample has a .65 probability that a constituent will vote for him or her. This probability drops below .5 for an incumbent who engages in the highest levels of entrepreneurship in the sample. This substantial drop in the probability of securing constituents' votes should strongly discourage members from engaging in this activity.

Discussion

The results of the empirical analysis of constituent response to legislative entrepreneurship indicate that legislative entrepreneurship does not contribute significantly to members' reelection goals. Using survey data, I examined the

TABLE 3.14. Effects of Legislative Entrepreneurship on the Probability of Voting for the Incumbent

Variable	Democrats	Republicans
Intercept	1.449	.084
	(.507)	(.345)
Entrepreneurship instrument	−.316	.021
	(.136)	(.089)
Terms	.031	−.088
	(.053)	(.076)
Terms^2	.001	.017
	(.003)	(.008)
Exclusive committee	−.696	−.014
	(.205)	(.195)
Party leader	.035	.070
	(.016)	(.029)
Committee leader	−.223	.184
	(.146)	(.134)
Party	1.287	1.649
	(.098)	(.125)
Education	−.034	−.008
	(.041)	(.049)
Income	.011	−.001
	(.009)	(.011)
Quality challenger	−.514	−.447
	(.122)	(.156)
National economy (prospective judgment)	−.094	−.026
	(.069)	(.086)
Personal financial situation (prospective judgment)	−.007	−.175
	(.078)	(.092)
National economy (retrospective judgment)	−.038	.017
	(.071)	(.076)
Personal financial situation (retrospective judgment)	.009	.088
	(.061)	(.072)
N	1,573	880
−2 × log likelihood	1,396.056	672.994

Note: Coefficients are second-stage probit MLEs. Standard errors are computed from the covariance matrix given in Maddala 1983, 245.

effects that entrepreneurial activity has on various factors that are important for building a winning coalition in the district. In most of the constituent response items examined, the coefficient on the entrepreneurship variable was not bounded away from zero, so we cannot say with much confidence that legislative entrepreneurship has any effect on the factors related to constituents' support for their incumbent representatives. In all but one of the cases in which the coefficient on the entrepreneurship score was statistically different from zero, the marginal effects of this variable were quite small. The only case in which the coefficient on the entrepreneurship score was statistically *and* substantively significant was the analysis of the vote decision. This analysis indicated that Democratic members who engage in high levels of entrepreneurship can seriously hurt their reelection chances.

The conservative conclusion to draw from the results reported in this chapter is that entrepreneurship does not directly help members achieve their reelection goals. Although the analysis of vote decisions indicated that entrepreneurship is detrimental for Democratic members' reelection bids, the lack of an effect of entrepreneurship on the other constituent response items that are important for building the personal vote indicates that there is not much support for the strong form of the argument that entrepreneurship forces members to make resource tradeoffs between the Washington and district arenas that put them in great electoral peril. But it is safe to say that there is little to no support for the argument that changes in the electoral environment have led members to engage in legislative entrepreneurship in order to appeal to their constituents and enhance their reelection prospects.

Reelection is one of the primary goals of members. The empirical analysis discussed in this chapter indicates that entrepreneurial activity does not directly help members in the attainment of this goal because it has essentially no impact on various items that are important for securing constituent support. At this point in the analysis, it would seem that the reelection imperative does not provide much motivation for engaging in legislative entrepreneurship. However, members do not seek reelection in a vacuum. They operate within a complex institutional environment that they themselves have created. In the next chapter, I consider how one feature of this institutional environment—campaign finance laws—might promote entrepreneurial activity.

CHAPTER 4

Legislative Entrepreneurship and Campaign Finance

The empirical results discussed in the last chapter indicate that direct constituent response to legislative entrepreneurship does not provide much motivation for members to engage in this activity. However, we should not conclude from these results that legislative entrepreneurship has no connection with members' reelection goals because this activity might be related indirectly to other factors that affect reelection. In particular, campaign contributions, which are an important resource for attracting the support of constituents, might be related to entrepreneurial activity. Even though ordinary constituents do not seem to pay much attention to entrepreneurial activity, politically attentive and active interest groups that can contribute to members' campaign coffers may consider this activity when making contribution decisions.

This chapter examines whether campaign contributions from PACs provide motivation for members of Congress to engage in legislative entrepreneurship. The analysis in this chapter is strongly motivated by rational choice models of service-induced campaign contributions and contributions as investments. The research on service-induced campaign contributions focuses on how members of Congress can use the authority and resources that their office confers on them to deliver services to different interest groups in exchange for campaign contributions (Baron 1989a, 1989b; Denzau and Munger 1986). These services range from intervening with government agencies on a group's behalf to voting for legislation that the group desires to more general legislative activities that benefit the group. The work on contributions as investments in members of Congress examines how PACs invest in members by giving them campaign contributions with the expectation of receiving some future return of services (Snyder 1990, 1992; Grier and Munger 1986, 1991).

This chapter extends the work on service and investment relationships by examining the role that legislative entrepreneurship plays in PACs' contribution decisions. I consider two opposing arguments. The first contends that PACs use campaign contributions to invest in members of Congress with the expectation that members will reciprocate by engaging in entrepreneurial behavior that benefits the PACs. Drawing on Hall and Wayman 1990, I contend that interest groups that want to influence policy should be concerned with the degree to which members are involved in the legislative process. Those members who engage in legislative entrepreneurship engage in the kinds of activities that are necessary to enact legislation and influence policy. A member who engages in entrepreneurial activity on a group's behalf can advance the group's policy goals more than a member who simply votes for legislation that the group favors. Thus, interest groups should invest in those individuals whom they think are capable LEs. An empirical implication of this argument is that we should observe that past entrepreneurial activity will affect the amount of contributions members receive.

The second argument contends that service and investment relationships are difficult to maintain because of constituency constraints and problems of enforcement. Taking care of constituents' needs and adhering to constituent preferences make it difficult for a member of Congress to provide services to groups affiliated with PACs. Tacit agreements involving the exchange of services for contributions are difficult to enforce because third parties such as courts are not available to ensure that the parties involved in the exchange fulfill their respective ends of the bargain (McCarty and Rothenberg 1996). Given these problems, PACs will be reluctant to contribute to a member on the basis of the services he or she can provide because of the high degree of uncertainty that they will see a return on their investments. If this argument is true, then empirically we will see little to no relationship between legislative entrepreneurship and PAC contributions.

It is important to note that if a relationship between legislative entrepreneurship and PAC contributions does exist this relationship is made possible by the campaign finance laws and legislative rules that members have established for themselves. If campaigns were publicly funded or individual members were severely restricted from initiating and pushing their own legislative proposals, then the exchange of entrepreneurial activity for campaign contributions would not be possible.[1] An assumption underlying the theoretical motivation of this chapter is that campaign finance laws are a feature of electoral institutions that members can design to promote individual and collective goals. If, as I argued in chapter 1, members value legislative entrepreneurship collectively, then it makes sense that they would enact campaign finance laws

1. Members of Congress, for example, have structured their electoral and legislative environments very differently in terms of campaign finance than their counterparts in the British Parliament have. Members of Parliament do not raise money individually and are severely restricted in the amount they can spend during their campaigns (Pinto-Duschinsky 1981). Members of Parliament have also gradually removed the power to initiate and advance legislation from those who are not part of a ministry (Cox 1987). The conditions that would make possible a relationship of contributions for legislative services between interest groups and backbenchers in Parliament do not appear to exist.

that would promote this activity. If campaign finance laws enable groups to reward a member who engages in the kinds of entrepreneurial activity that they favor, then there is an indirect connection between this activity and the reelection goal—a connection that is made possible by the fact that members in part determine the shape of electoral and legislative institutions.

The techniques that I use to estimate the effects of the entrepreneurship measures on PAC contributions take into consideration possible econometric problems raised by treating contributions as investments. If we think of contributions as investments, it follows then that entrepreneurship and contributions are simultaneously determined. To account for problems associated with simultaneity, I treat entrepreneurship as endogenous and employ two-stage least squares. This method gives us greater confidence in our estimates of the effects of legislative entrepreneurship. The results that I obtain indicate that legislative entrepreneurship does not play a significant part in PACs' contribution decisions. Thus, members' needs in terms of campaign finance do not appear to provide much motivation for legislative entrepreneurship.

Investment in Legislative Services

A substantial amount of research has attempted to determine which factors affect the decisions of PACs to make campaign contributions. Many important studies posit that PACs are goal-oriented, rational actors that seek to influence policy through contributions to candidates for Congress. PACs can be classified as one of two types based on the strategies they pursue in order to attain their goals. The first type, called "ideological PACs," attempts to influence policy by making contributions in ways that affect the composition of Congress (Wright 1985).[2] An ideological PAC tends to give money to candidates who are sympathetic to its views in the hope that the candidates will win office and then shape policy in ways the PAC favors. The contributions of an ideological PAC should be driven mainly by the degree to which candidates—both incumbents and challengers—are aligned with the PAC's interests.

PACs in the other category, which Snyder (1992) labels "investor PACs," are less concerned with shaping the composition of Congress than they are with influencing the behavior of individuals who are already members and are likely to remain so. Investor PACs are affiliated with corporations, labor unions, trade associations, or cooperatives. These PACs contribute money to incumbents who are not necessarily favorably disposed to the PACs' interests with the expectation that the contributions will encourage incumbents to be-

2. These PACs have been closely identified with what the Federal Election Commission (FEC) officially designates as *nonconnected PACs*—that is, they are not formally connected with a parent organization.

have in ways that further the PACs' goals. The contributions of investor PACs should mainly be driven by their beliefs about the degree to which an incumbent can promote the PACs' interests. At the very least, members must be in office if they are to provide services to groups, so the probability of winning the election should be a key determinant of contributions. Once in office, incumbents will vary in their ability to provide services. For example, a member's position in the institution will provide him or her with certain resources that can be used to a group's benefit. Some members may simply be better than others at browbeating recalcitrant bureaucracies or negotiating the legislative process to the benefit of groups.

One way in which members can serve the interests of PACs is by voting in favor of legislation that the PACs prefer. Numerous empirical studies have examined the relationship between PAC contributions and members' roll call behavior.[3] Many of these studies have failed to find a link between PAC money and votes. Hall and Wayman (1990) argue that these null findings are partly due to the fact that legislators face severe restrictions on the way they cast their votes on the floor. Because of the scrutiny that challengers can direct toward members' roll call voting records, constituency constraints prevent legislators from voting one way or another at the behest of an interest group. Consequently, campaign contributions aimed at influencing members' votes are relatively poor investments.

Hall and Wayman argue that members have more flexibility in how they can spend their time and allocate their legislative resources than they have when they cast floor votes. This is especially true at the committee stage of the legislative process, when members feel less constrained by their constituents than they do when they cast their votes on the floor (Hall 1996). The profound impact that committee deliberations can have on final legislative outcomes means that interest groups that give to members involved in these deliberations can receive large returns on their investments. Thus, we should observe a positive relationship between campaign contributions and members' involvement at early stages of the process. In their empirical analysis, Hall and Wayman find that contributions from concerned PACs in the previous election cycle had a positive impact on members' involvement during subsequent committee deliberations for three separate pieces of legislation.

However, the connection between contributions and legislative activity does not seem to extend beyond the committee room. Ragsdale and Cook (1987) examined the effect of bill sponsorship and cosponsorship on contributions to incumbents and did not find a statistically significant relationship between the two. But does the lack of a relationship between general legis-

3. See Snyder 1992, n. 1, for a detailed list of these studies.

lative activity (as measured by Ragsdale and Cook) imply that contributions related to this type of activity are poor investments, as is the case with roll calls and contributions?

For a PAC to invest in members with the expectation that they will engage in legislative entrepreneurship on the PAC's behalf, members must have some leeway in deciding how to allocate their resources, not just at the committee stage but during all stages of the legislative process. Morton and Cameron (1992) raise the possibility that members' accountability to their constituents imposes significant constraints that can prevent them from providing legislative services to groups. Morton and Cameron argue that providing services to interest groups can hurt members' reelection chances because their constituents might react negatively (cf. Denzau and Munger 1986). Since the provision of services to interest groups might decrease members' effectiveness in satisfying their constituents' demands, voters might punish members who "sell out" in exchange for campaign funds. If this is true, it would be unwise for groups to invest in members with the expectation that they will engage in activities like legislative entrepreneurship to the benefit of the groups.

But for such constituency constraints to be binding voters must have access to reliable information to determine whether or not their members have sold out. Essentially, there are two ways in which a constituent can assess whether a member has sold out: through personal experience and through information provided by a challenger or by groups aligned with a challenger. Constituents can personally determine whether members have sold out when they seek help from their members' offices. The logic is similar to that laid out in the last chapter: if members devote a substantial amount of their resources to providing services to interest groups, this can detract from their capacity to take care of their constituents' needs relating to casework and constituency service. A poor constituency service operation is something that constituents can directly observe and personally experience. However, the analysis in chapter 3 indicates that when members do provide services in the form of legislative entrepreneurship this does not have much of an impact on their direct relationships with constituents.

Constituents can also find out about an incumbent's fund-raising practices by looking at FEC reports to determine how much money he or she has raised. Constituents can infer that an incumbent who has raised substantial amounts of money has sold out and then punish him or her accordingly. The FEC's reporting requirements ensure the availability of a wealth of information about the amounts and sources of campaign contributions. However, it seems highly unlikely that the average constituent will expend the time and effort necessary to collect this information.

One might argue that constituents can infer whether their incumbent has sold out by observing campaign expenditures (cf. Morton and Cameron 1992, 84). For example, if constituents observe a large number of television or radio commercials in favor of the incumbent then they may conclude that the incumbent must have sold out in order to acquire the funds necessary to saturate the airwaves. But this can be a very poor indicator on which to base one's voting decision.

Recent Supreme Court decisions have made it possible for groups to spend unlimited amounts on *issue advocacy* ads, which provide information about candidates without explicitly telling voters to vote for or against a particular candidate. Expenditures on these types of ads are independent of incumbents' campaigns, and incumbents may have little control over the number and content of the issue ads aired by groups.[4]

Even if the ads are financed by incumbents, it may not be a good strategy for constituents to support a challenge to the incumbent if they observe a substantial number of ads favorable to the incumbent. Incumbents who spend a lot of money may be doing so in response to a strong challenger (Jacobson 1978). Unless a challenger has substantial personal wealth and spends his or her own money on the campaign, considerable amounts of money must be raised in order to mount a serious challenge.[5] Voters should be concerned that they could be removing one sellout from office in exchange for another. Constituents should be dubious about any signals from a challenger about the incumbent's shady fund-raising practices since the challenger may have engaged in similar practices in order to raise enough money to mount a serious challenge.

Generally, the size of an incumbent's war chest will be an unreliable indicator of whether he or she has sold out in the sense of providing services to interest groups and forsaking constituents. In terms of policy services, an incumbent can work in policy areas that concern constituents and in ways that benefit them as well as interest groups in order to amass campaign funds.

Interestingly, the amount of money an incumbent raises can determine whether he or she even faces a challenger who can inform constituents about the incumbent's behavior. Epstein and Zemsky (1995) show formally how war chests can discourage quality challengers from entering races. Box-Steffensmeier (1996) presents empirical evidence that war chests deter the timely entry of challengers into congressional races. The amount of money an incumbent has raised can affect election outcomes without the incumbent having to spend a dime to influence a constituent's vote. Although constituents might become upset if their member provides services to interest groups, the amount

4. For a journalistic account of the role that issue ads have played in recent elections, see Cassata 1998.

5. Jacobson (1997, 40) estimates that for recent elections challengers must raise and spend close to $600,000 in order to run a competitive campaign for the House.

of money the incumbent gets in return for such services can prevent a challenger from emerging to inform voters that they should be upset and to give them a viable alternative to vote for in the election.

Although incumbents are ill-advised to ignore the demands of their constituents when making decisions about how to spend their resources and allocate their time, the barriers that voters face in acquiring reliable information about their incumbents' relationships with interest groups seem to grant incumbents the leeway to provide services to groups. Furthermore, constituency constraints are less binding when groups share the same policy interests as members' constituents. If by looking after groups' policy interests a member is simultaneously looking after the policy interests of his or her constituents, it will be difficult to make the case that the member has sold out. Thus, a group that invests in a member whose constituents have policy interests similar to those of the group is more likely to realize a return on its investment (Denzau and Munger 1986).

McCarty and Rothenberg (1996) raise another objection to the contributions as investments argument. They find that the mechanisms necessary to enforce commitments between legislators and PACs concerning the exchange of services for contributions do not appear to exist. In order to have a viable *campaign contribution contract,* legislators and PACs must credibly commit to punishing each other when they deviate from the contract and deliver on promised rewards when they adhere to it. McCarty and Rothenberg do not find empirical evidence indicating that legislators and PACs can credibly commit to the necessary punishment strategies.

While the failure of previous studies to find a relationship between general legislative activity and contributions could be due to the problems of enforcing campaign contribution contracts, another possible explanation for the null findings is that these studies have poorly measured the kinds of activities about which groups should care. The number of bills sponsored or cosponsored is not a very accurate measure of the level of legislative services that members can provide to interest groups. An interest group will get little in return for campaign contributions if a member introduces a bill on a subject the group cares about but then does nothing with it. It seems reasonable that a group should want to see some sort of effort on the part of the members it supports so there is at least a credible possibility that something will happen on the issues the group cares about.

Box-Steffensmeier and Grant (1999) argue that PACs care about more than effort; they care about the effectiveness of a member of Congress in terms of the number of bills he or she sponsors that are enacted into law. Thus, PAC contributions should be correlated not simply with effort but with the legislative success of members' bills. Box-Steffensmeier and Grant find that the *hit rate* (measured as the percentage of bills a member sponsors that are enacted) has a positive and statistically significant effect on campaign contributions received in the previous Congress.

Although Box-Steffensmeier and Grant claim that this finding supports theories of contributions as investments, the size of the effect of the hit rate on contributions indicates only a very weak correlation with contributions. In the 103d Congress, an incumbent who was expected to increase his or her hit rate by 20 percent (approximately two standard deviations) would receive only about $15,000 in additional contributions.[6] In the 104th Congress, an incumbent who was expected to increase his or her hit rate by 24 percent (approximately two standard deviations) would receive only about $28,500 in additional contributions.

According to the FEC, the average incumbent in the 1992 and 1994 elections received $552,417 and $569,777 in campaign contributions, respectively. The increases in contributions that incumbents would receive from such large increases in legislative success would account for about 2 percent and 5 percent of the contributions they received in the 1992 and 1994 election cycles. This does not seem to be a very lucrative contract for incumbents.

Box-Steffensmeier and Grant argue that PAC contributions related to legislative effectiveness help members compensate for the neglect of home-style activities when they focus their resources on Washington work.[7] Yet the paltry sums of money that are related to legislative effectiveness would not seem to provide much incentive for individual members to devote resources to passing legislation.

Athough PACs are undoubtedly interested in end results, producing desired results through the enactment of legislation is not something that comes easily or often. Consistent with investment theory, PACs may contribute to an incumbent who exerts effort in the present, even though his or her efforts may

6. Since Box-Steffensmeier and Grant (1999) regress the total amount of PAC contributions from the previous Congress on the hit rate in the current Congress, causal inferences made from their analysis must be phrased in terms of expectations. For these inferences to be appropriate, PACs would have to perfectly anticipate members' hit rates. Considering how unpredictable the legislative process is and the low probability that any given bill will make it into law, it is unreasonable to assume that PACs would have this degree of foresight. This is especially problematic for Box-Steffensmeier and Grant's analysis of the 104th Congress, in which they assume that PACs anticipated the hit rate of members even though there was a change in the majority party, which was anticipated by few. Instead, I argue that we should allow for simultaneous causation between campaign contributions and legislative activity in a given Congress. I discuss the logic and the appropriate methodology for this approach in more detail later.

7. I must remind readers that the empirical analysis in the last chapter indicated that members who concentrate resources on legislative activity in Washington are not severly hurt in their efforts to build winning coalitions in their districts.

not immediately result in the passage of legislation, because these efforts may pay off in the future. Additionally, Congress does not necessarily need to pass legislation to change policy in a way that PACs would care about because a credible threat of passing legislation can change policy (Ferejohn and Shipan 1990).

Investor PACs should still be interested in the amount of effort that members are putting into their legislation and not necessarily whether the legislation is enacted into law. I contend that PACs should care about the effort members put into the activities that I define as legislative entrepreneurship. The measures of legislative entrepreneurship that I employ capture this effort and so avoid the problems of previous studies that have attempted to assess the relationship between campaign contributions and legislative activity. The measures of legislative entrepreneurship enable us to test the following hypothesis:

> *Hypothesis 4: The more legislative entrepreneurship a member engages in the more investor PAC contributions he or she will recieve.*

If the empirical analysis leads to a rejection of this hypothesis, then we should question the validity of theories of PAC contributions as investments for services, and we will have to keep looking for an explanation of legislative entrepreneurship. If we do not reject this hypothesis, then legislative entreprenuership is indirectly related to members' reelection goals and the standard electoral-connection rationale explains why members would engage in this activity.

Empirical Analysis

The recent theoretical work on which this analysis is based suggests that standard regression techniques are not appropriate for making inferences about the relationship between campaign contributions and entrepreneurial activity. This work suggests that campaign contributions and entrepreneurial activity might be simultaneously determined (cf. Hall and Wayman 1990). PACs should expect a return on their investments, and so past campaign contributions should affect a legislator's activities at some point. But members may also attempt to demonstrate their competency at entrepreneurial activities in order to attract campaign contributions. As members' needs for contributions increase, they should increase the activities that attract such contributions. It seems appropriate, then, to treat entrepreneurship and other activities as endogenous and employ methods that account for this problem.[8]

---

8. Another potential problem is that PACs might be interested in services that are not legislative in nature. It would be extremely costly to obtain data on all of the possible activities about

I use a two-stage procedure similar to that in the previous chapter to correct for these problems. A test for exogeneity developed by Spencer and Berk (1981) indicates that the same variables used in the previous chapters to purge the entrepreneurship score of its correlation with the disturbance term in the regression equation of interest are appropriate here.[9] The variables that I include in the specification to construct instruments are the committee workload variables as well as variables that account for a member's education and previous legislative experience.[10]

In addition to the legislative entrepreneurship score, I expect several other variables to have an effect on investor PAC contributions. As in the last chapter, I include three dummy variables that indicate whether the member has a seat on a prestigious committee, a committee leadership position, or a party leadership position. Members in these positions possess resources that enable them to exert more influence over bureaucrats as well as the legislative process. A PAC may want to give money to these individuals in an attempt to get them to use some of their influence on the PAC's behalf. These variables also enable us to determine whether entrepreneurial activity has an effect on contributions that is independent of the formal positions that members hold in the House.

Investor PACs might take into consideration the ideological extremity of members. PACs that seek to "buy" members' votes may find it less costly to

---

which PACs care. Yet not accounting for other activities will compromise the inferences we make about legislative entrepreneurship. Legislative entrepreneurship might be credited with affecting campaign contributions when that credit is due to other activities. Although panel data methods that account for individual-specific effects could help us get around this problem, the nature of the data available limits the usefulness of these methods. With the kind of congressional data used in this study, there will be attrition due to members leaving the institution. This causes serious sample selection problems. Preliminary work I have done using panel data methods indicates that these problems would be extremely difficult to overcome with the data available. While panel data methods hold some promise for analyzing campaign finance, we must wait until better data become available before we can employ these methods effectively.

9. Spencer and Berk's test is similar to that developed by Hausman (1978), but it has the advantage of not requiring specification of the full system of equations. The test involves checking to see whether particular variables are orthogonal to the disturbance in the purging regression. The χ^2 statistic from the Spencer and Berk test was 2.316, which has a p-value of .999 for 16 degrees of freedom. Thus, we cannot reject the null hypothesis of exogeneity.

10. Some may find it surprising that previous experience in a state legislature appears as an explanatory variable for legislative entreprenuership but not for campaign contributions given Jacobson's (1997) findings about the effect that holding prior elective office has on the electoral success of candidates. Experience in holding elective office is important for challengers who wish to mount successful campaigns against incumbents. In this analysis, we are focusing on incumbent members of Congress. It appears that the benefits of holding prior elective office do not extend to candidates after they become incumbent members of Congress, so it is valid to use this variable in the first-stage regression, where legislative entrepreneurship appears on the left-hand side of the equation.

influence the votes of moderate members than to influence the votes of members at the extreme ends of the ideological spectrum (Snyder 1991; Stratman 1992; Groseclose 1996). To measure this effect, I include the absolute value of the difference between a member's NOMINATE score and the median score in the chamber (Poole and Rosenthal 1997).[11]

The specification also includes the percentage of votes the incumbent received in the previous election.[12] Potential challengers might view an incumbent who barely squeaked by in the previous election as vulnerable, and PACs might want to help such an incumbent build a war chest with the expectation that he or she will face a quality challenger in the next election. Vulnerable incumbents might feel more indebted to their contributors than do those who are more secure. However, investor PACs might be reluctant to contribute to insecure incumbents because they may not remain in office to assist the PACs. Vulnerable incumbents might also decide to retire rather than face a difficult reelection campaign in the future. Following Snyder 1992, I include the square of previous vote share as well to account for possible nonlinear effects.

I also include variables that measure a member's age and seniority. Although more senior members will have accumulated human capital that they can use to further PACs' interests, older members may be less attractive investments because they might retire or die before the PACs can see a return on their investments. Thus, seniority should have a positive effect and age should have a negative effect on investor PAC contributions (Snyder 1992).

Finally, I include a variable that measures the number of districts in a state. Snyder (1992) argues that investor PACs should care about this variable because the fewer the number of districts in a state, the higher the probability that a House member will move to the Senate. Since a typical senator has more influence than a typical House member, senators are more valuable to PACs, so it is a good investment to contribute to House members who are likely to become senators. This variable is simply one divided by the number of districts in the state.

Tables 4.1 and 4.2 include descriptive statistics of the variables used in this analysis for Democrats and Republicans serving in the 98th through the

---

11. To be precise, I use the DW-NOMINATE first-dimension score. These scores range from -1 to $+1$, with increasing scores indicating the increasing conservatism of the member.

12. The analysis in the previous chapter suggests that the previous election margin is endogenous to legislative entrepreneurship. If entrepreneurial activity decreases the probability that constituents will vote for a Democratic incumbent, then incumbents who had a close call in the previous election might eschew entrepreneurial activity in the next Congress to minimize the chance of alienating voters. However, rather than estimating a more complex system of equations that would correct for this potential problem, I have sacrificed some empirical accuracy for simplicity and estimated a less complicated model.

102d Congresses.[13] Table 4.3 reports the results of the first-stage regressions in which the entrepreneurship score is the dependent variable.

Table 4.4 reports the results from the second-stage regressions in which the dependent variable is the log of investor PAC contributions. The coefficient on the entrepreneurship instrument is not statistically distinguishable from zero for either Democrats or Republicans. We cannot say with much confidence that entrepreneurship has any effect on investor PAC contributions. From these results, it does not appear that members will engage in legislative entrepreneurship in order to attract contributions from investor PACs.[14]

For Democrats, all but one of the other variables in the specification have statistically significant effects on contributions. Investor PACs contribute more to Democrats on exclusive committees and in party leadership positions but contribute less to those who hold committee leadership positions. Ideologically extreme Democrats also receive less money. The effects of the other variables—in terms of direction and magnitude of the effect—are similar to what Snyder (1992) found, except for the one over the number of districts variable, which does not have a statistically significant effect. Vote share has a nonlinear effect on contributions: contributions decrease as the incumbent's vote share increases but increase slightly for those incumbents who win with very high percentages of the vote. Older members get less in contributions, while more senior members get more.

For Republicans, all but one of the variables in the specification have statistically *in*significant effects on contributions. The only variable with a coefficient that is statistically distinguishable from zero is the Republican Party leadership dummy. Members holding party leadership positions collect approximately $36,000 more from investor PACs than those who do not hold such positions, all else being equal.[15]

Discussion

This chapter has attempted to assess whether a relationship exists between leg-

13. The campaign finance data are from the Federal Election Commission's Campaign Expenditures in the United States: Reports on Financial Activity Data, House Spread Data, from 1984 to 1992 (FEC, various years.)

14. I also performed this analysis using OLS and obtained results that differ from those reported here. The entrepreneurship score had a positive and statistically significant coefficient for Democrats and a statistically insignificant coefficient for Republicans. But even for Democrats the effect of entrepreneurship was not *substantively* significant. The different methods lead us to approximately the same inferences.

15. I also conducted the analysis separately on contributions from corporations, labor unions, trade associations, and cooperatives. In each case, the coefficients on the entrepreneurship score led to the same inferences as were drawn from the analysis reported in table 4.4.

TABLE 4.1. Descriptive Statistics of Variables for Democratic Members of Congress, 98th through the 102d Congresses

Variable	Mean	SD	Median	Minimum	Maximum
Investor PAC contributions	187,072	131,086	172,100	1	995,045
ln of entrepreneurship score[a]	4.072	1.879	4.277	0	6.204
ln of average number of bill referrals	5.690	.824	5.672	0	7.543
ln of average number of bills reported	3.149	.710	3.367	.693	4.595
ln of average number of hearings	4.626	.668	4.723	1.098	5.489
Attended prestigious university	.395	.489	0	0	1
State legislative experience	.453	.498	0	0	1
Former congressional staffer	.080	.272	0	0	1
Exclusive committee	.274	.446	0	0	1
Party leader	.353	.478	0	0	1
Committee/subcommittee leader	.515	.500	1	0	1
NOMINATE score (deviation from chamber median)	.270	.186	.246	0	.796
Vote share in previous election	.742	.160	.702	.471	1
(Vote share in previous election)^2	.577	.251	.493	.222	1
Age	1.805	10.893	50	30	87
Seniority	7.013	4.157	6	2	27
1/(number of districts)	.108	.132	.074	.019	1

$N = 996$.

[a]Entrepreneurship scale scores of zero were set equal to 1×10^{-10} so logs could be taken.

TABLE 4.2. Descriptive Statistics of Variables for Republican Members of Congress, 98th though the 102d Congresses

Variable	Mean	SD	Median	Minimum	Maximum
Investor PAC contributions	145,174	93,386	142,137	1	554,987
ln of entrepreneurship score[a]	3.590	2.583	3.922	0	5.569
ln of average number of bill referrals	5.692	.822	5.671	0	7.543
ln of average number of bills reported	3.163	.722	3.332	.916	4.812
ln of average number of hearings	4.654	.602	4.732	1.099	5.489
Attended prestigious university	.431	.496	0	0	1
State legislative experience	.503	.500	1	0	1
Former congressional staffer	.030	.170	0	0	1
Exclusive committee	.232	.423	0	0	1
Party leader	.148	.355	0	0	1
Committee/subcommittee leader	.605	.489	1	0	1
NOMINATE score (deviation from chamber median)	.558	.219	.559	.012	1.277
Vote share in previous election	.718	.155	.688	.412	1
(Vote share in previous election)^2	.539	.241	.474	.170	1
Age	51.357	9.591	52	28	80
Seniority	6.010	3.358	5	2	19
1/(number of districts)	.122	.149	.071	.019	1

$N = 673$.

[a]Entrepreneurship scale scores of zero were set equal to 1×10^{-10} so logs could be taken.

TABLE 4.3. First-Stage Regression of the Legislative Entrepreneurship Score on the Exogenous Variables

Variable	Democrats	Republicans
Intercept	−.107	−4.716
	(1.80)	(2.788)
ln of average number of bill referrals	.079	.110
	(.077)	(.133)
ln of average number of bills reported	.070	−.138
	(.104)	(.171)
ln of average number of hearings	.131	.258
	(.105)	(.192)
Attended prestigious university	−.128	.577
	(.125)	(.208)
State legislative experience	−.024	−.206
	(.122)	(.206)
Former congressional staffer	−.204	.550
	(.227)	(.598)
Exclusive committee	.151	.101
	(.155)	(.262)
Party leader	.255	.283
	(.131)	(.289)
Committee/subcommittee leader	.480	−.113
	(.158)	(.241)
NOMINATE score (deviation from chamber median)	.613	−.232
	(.346)	(.482)
Vote share in previous election	7.517	18.599
	(4.528)	(7.05)
(Vote share in previous election)^2	−5.358	−12.454
	(2.875)	(4.504)
Age	−.003	.004
	(.008)	(.0131)
Seniority	.006	−.004
	(.023)	(.044)
1/(number of districts)	.399	.667
	(.469)	(.687)
N	996	673
R^2	.05	.04

Note: Coefficients are OLS estimates. Standard errors are in parentheses.

TABLE 4.4. Effects of Legislative Entrepreneurship on Investor PAC Contributions, Second Stage Estimates

Variable	Democrats	Republicans
Intercept	907,683	451,608
	(116,388)	(99,762)
Entrepreneurship score	16,284	−10,932
	(23,902)	(10,184)
Exclusive committee	27,810	−138
	(10,053)	(9,279)
Party leader	46,334	35,772
	(10,488)	(10,660)
Committee/subcommittee leader	−25,853	−2,618
	(15,045)	(8,518)
NOMINATE score (deviation from chamber median)	−52,658	3,430
	(27,566)	(16,631)
Vote share in previous election	−1,691,861	−479,730
	(353,474)	(313,073)
(Vote share in previous election)^2	974,989	158,179
	(232,175)	(202,754)
Age	−2,229	−365
	(520)	(454)
Seniority	4,108	790
	(1,548)	(1,544)
1/(number of districts)	−23,193	187
	(32,317)	(24,609)
N	996	673
R^2	.16	.15

Note: Estimates and standard errors were obtained using two-stage least squares.

islative entrepreneurship and campaign finance. I have argued that the electoral and legislative instutions that members of Congress have established for themselves appear to make it possible for members of Congress to engage in legislative entrepreneurship in exchange for campaign contributions from PACs. However, empirical analysis did not reveal a relationship between entrepreneurial activity and PAC contributions. Thus, members' interest in acquiring campaign funds does not seem to provide them with much incentive to engage in legislative entrepreneurship.

These findings support the argument that commitment problems make it unattractive for PACs to invest in members with the expectation that they will engage in entrepreneurial activity to the benefit of the PACs. While the effects for the institutional position, age, and seniority variables are consistent with previous findings that support investment hypotheses, it does not appear that entrepreneurial activity is part of the implicit campaign contribution contracts between incumbents and PACs. It may simply be too difficult to enforce contract "clauses" concerning legislative entrepreneurship (cf. McCarty and Rothenberg 1996).

Another possible explanation for the null findings concerns the limitations of the legislative entrepreneurship measures. Even though the measures of legislative entrepreneurship used to produce these results improve upon the measures of legislative activity used in previous analyses, the improved measures are still somewhat problematic because they do not differentiate this activity according to policy type. Entrepreneurial activity on certain policy issues (e.g., banking policy) may be more lucrative in terms of campaign contributions than is entrepreneurial activity on other issues (e.g., childhood immunizations). The issue-neutral measures of legislative entrepreneurship used here would fail to pick up this variation. As with any empirical analysis, then, the results presented in this chapter should be interpreted with a degree of caution due to the limitations of the data employed.[16]

In this chapter, we began to consider in more detail how members might use their authority to structure their institutional environment in order to promote legislative entrepreneurship. In the next chapter, I continue this line of inquiry, considering how members of the House might use the committee and party hierarchies that they have created within their institution to promote legislative entrepreneurship.

---

16. The data limitations also extend to the variables used to construct the instrumental variable for the legislative entrepreneurship score. The low value for the R^2 statistic in the first-stage regression indicates that these variables are not capturing a good deal of the variation in the entrepreneurship score. A better model fit would decrease the standard errors in the second-stage equation and could lead to different inferences. Several other variables were included in the first-stage regression, but none of these substantially increased the model fit.

CHAPTER 5

Legislative Entrepreneurship and Intrainstitutional Mobility

The analyses in chapters 3 and 4 revealed no direct, substantively significant relationship among constituent response, campaign finance, and legislative entrepreneurship, and so they did not provide a satisfying answer to the question of why members of the House engage in entrepreneurial activity. In chapter 4, we began to think more explicitly about how members might use their authority to structure their institutional environment to promote legislative entrepreneurship. This chapter continues this institutional approach by moving the analysis inside the chamber. If members generally benefit when some of them assume the role of LEs, they should establish internal institutional features that provide incentives for each other to engage in this activity. In this chapter, I examine the incentives for entrepreneurship that exist within the committee and party hierarchies in the House.

As part of the "institutionalization" of the House, its members have established committee and party hierarchies and have divided the work of the chamber among subunits within these hierarchies (Polsby 1968). An important feature of this division of labor has been the creation of positions that grant their occupants more influence over matters of policy and process that affect the interests of other members. For example, the rules of the House divide its work among committees and subcommittees by granting them exclusive policy jurisdictions. Certain committees have jurisdiction over issues that are salient to all members, thus increasing the influence of those who sit on these committees (Fenno 1973; Smith and Deering 1990). House rules also assign much of the responsibility for the daily operation of the institution to leaders in the committee and party hierarchies, granting them special parliamentary rights and resources.

The creation and staffing of these prestigious positions are fundamental features of legislative organization. The analysis in this chapter builds on work on legislative organization, which considers how members design their institution to serve individual and collective interests. The resources and prerogatives that prestigious positions confer upon their occupants make them an important institutional determinant of how well the House functions as a policy-making body and how well it serves the collective interests of its members. Members who ascend to these positions acquire resources that help them achieve their individual goals of reelection, influence seeking, and formulating good public policy. In this chapter, I examine the possibility that prestigious positions are used by members to serve their individual and collective interests by promoting legislative entrepreneurship.

An important consideration is that members themselves have the authority to decide who will advance to prestigious positions in the House. In this chapter, I develop a theory of intrainstitutional mobility that considers what criteria members should apply when deciding who will advance to prestigious positions. A key consideration in the development of this theory is that members of the House can exploit each other's desires to advance to these positions in order to encourage them to engage in legislative entrepreneurship. Prestigious positions are a type of selective incentive that members can use to overcome the free-riding problem associated with legislative entrepreneurship. If members award these positions based on entrepreneurial activity, they will motivate each other to acquire policy knowledge, draft legislation, and build coalitions.

This argument has both supply-side and demand-side components. Members use the supply of prestigious positions to provide incentives by rewarding each other with "promotions" to these positions. But these positions increase the resources and the amount of influence that members have over how the House functions as a policy-making body in terms of the quality and quantity of the legislation it produces. Because they have a stake in how well the institution functions, members should demand "qualified" legislators to fill these positions—that is, individuals who are capable of handling the legislative duties and responsibilities of these positions. By basing decisions to promote on legislative entrepreneurship, members can ensure that more capable legislators occupy these influential positions.

Hall (1996) finds that a member's position in the House—specifically the "institutional endowments" associated with a position—in part determines the degree to which he or she will participate in the legislative process. The analysis in this chapter backs up Hall's analysis one step to determine whether participation in the form of legislative entrepreneurship affects a member's position in the institution in the first place. Members with superior entrepreneurial abilities are likely to use the endowments that accompany positions to make the House productive in terms of passing legislation, which ceteris paribus is something in which all members have an interest. One way to make it more likely that those who become institutionally endowed will engage in high levels of participation to the benefit of the collectivity is to promote those members who have participated at high levels in the past.

An important nuance is that it is difficult for those making promotion decisions to determine entrepreneurial ability because they only get to observe an individual's "legislative output," which is a noisy signal of ability. Drawing on the economics literature on *career concerns* (Fama 1980; Holmström 1982a), I argue that members consider entrepreneurial activity over their entire careers in order to ensure that qualified legislators will advance to prestigious positions.

The main purpose of this chapter is to determine whether an incentive system related to prestigious positions exists in the House. To achieve this purpose, I develop and test the following hypothesis:

> *Hypothesis 5 (the mobility hypothesis): The probability of advancing to a prestigious position within the House increases the more a member engages in legislative entrepreneurship.*

To test this hypothesis, I estimate the effects of entrepreneurial activity on the probability that a member will advance to a prestigious position. I develop a statistical model that addresses the problems of analyzing intrainstitutional mobility and the problems of assessing entrepreneurial ability. With this model, I perform a multivariate analysis to assess the effects of legislative entrepreneurship while accounting for other factors that previous studies have found to affect intrainstitutional mobility. The results indicate the existence of an incentive system based on prestigious positions for majority party members in the House, thus providing a solution to the puzzle of legislative entrepreneurship. These results have interesting implications for the literature on legislative participation and a possible reconciliation of the informational and partisan perspectives on legislative organization.

Career Concerns and the Mobility Hypothesis

One way in which members could promote entrepreneurial activity is by providing explicit incentives through written contracts, as is typically done in firms. But, as was discussed in chapter 1, the dubious ethical nature of such contracts renders them politically infeasible.

Alternatively, members could structure their institution in ways that encourage legislative entrepreneurship. An important part of the congressional literature has sought to explain how members have organized their institution to shape their behavior. Three competing theoretical perspectives on legislative organization—the distributive, informational, and partisan perspectives—have played a dominant role in congressional research in the past two decades.[1]

---

1. See Shepsle and Weingast 1994 for an excellent review of these theories.

While these theories of congressional institutions all offer some insight into why members would engage in activities that constitute legislative entrepreneurship, they do not provide satisfying solutions to the puzzle this book seeks to solve. These theories show how the different subunits in the committee and party hierarchies in Congress will behave under certain institutional arrangements. But they do not have much to say about how the behavior of *individuals* supports the behavior of the subunits. That is, they assume that individual members will engage in activities that are part of legislative entrepreneurship, such as building logrolling coalitions, acquiring policy knowledge, and pushing legislation, without making it clear why individual members would do so.

Distributive and informational theories focus their analysis on the committee level.[2] In a sense, these theories have lost sight of the trees for the forest (or, more precisely, subsets of the forest). Committees undoubtedly play an important role in the legislative process. But, by focusing on how parliamentary rules, procedures, and norms affect the behavior of committees as unitary actors, distributive and informational models have largely ignored the costs that individual members must bear if they contribute to the accomplishment of committee tasks. Members of a committee are members of a team involved in joint production, and so they face the oft-cited problem of free riding by team members (Alchian and Demsetz 1972; Holmström 1982b; Miller 1992). Freeriding by members can prevent the committee from getting its work done. Distributive theories focus on how the committee system keeps logrolling deals from unraveling, but it does not have much to say about why an individual member would incur the costs of putting such a deal together in the first place. Informational theories can help explain why individuals would acquire policy knowledge, but they do not have much to say about why individuals would engage in the other activities that constitute legislative entrepreneurship. Informational models assume that the only costs of legislating involve gathering policy-relevant information. These models assume that the legislative process is essentially frictionless beyond the information-gathering stage; proposals are always made, always make it to the floor, and always pass. Hence, there is no need for individual members to push their legislation and build coalitions after bills are reported from committee.

Cox and McCubbins's (1993) development of their partisan theory of legislative organization begins with the observation that members of Congress are engaged in team production. Indeed, their key claim is that members establish parties to solve problems associated with team production. While this partisan perspective has more to say about how institutional arrangements shape

2. An exception is Gilligan and Krehbiel 1997, which focuses on individual committee members' decisions to acquire and share policy-relevant information.

the behavior of individuals, their focus on party leaders does not give us much leverage for explaining the behavior of rank and file members of Congress. They contend that party leaders are elected to run the party as a cartel, policing the deals that members strike among themselves. But how do the deals originate? Cox and McCubbins argue that it is the job of party leaders to draft and push proposals. But clearly party leaders are not the sole source of legislative production. Why would those not in leadership positions engage in legislative entrepreneurship?

Although the distributive, informational, and partisan perspectives do not provide satisfying explanations for legislative entrepreneurship, their emphasis on the importance of the committee and party hierarchies in the House points us in the right direction. One way in which members could promote legislative entrepreneurship is through *implicit incentive* mechanisms related to the committee and party hierarchies. As developed in the literature on agency theory, "implicit incentives arise when a principal has some ex post discretion as to how to respond to an agent's performance and when the agent's current performance is informative about future performance" (Meyer 1995, 710). One type of positive implicit incentive is an agent's career concerns. Career concerns exist whenever the principal uses an agent's current performance to update beliefs about the agent's ability and adjusts the agent's compensation accordingly (Gibbons and Murphy 1992). Agents will exert effort in the present to enhance their reputations if they expect that they will receive rewards in the future.

Formal models have shown how career concerns can be a strong motivating force in firms (Fama 1980; Holmström 1982a). Career concerns relating to prestigious positions in the committee and party hierarchies can also be a strong motivating force in the House. While the intensity of the desire to move up will vary among members, it is reasonable to assume that the desire to advance to prestigious positions motivates members (Fenno 1973). Former Speaker Tom Foley (D–WA) has noted, "There may be some members who don't want to move up. . . . But most of the people around here are not like that."[3] In the next two sections, I describe the prestigious positions in the committee and party hierarchies in the House, explaining why members would find them attractive and why they would be concerned with the qualifications of those who occupy these positions.[4]

---

3. Foley is quoted in Loomis 1988, 236.

4. The descriptions of positions in the committee and party hierarchies that follow pertain to Congresses in the postreform era prior to the 104th Congress. The Republicans changed some of the characteristics of these positions when they assumed control in the 104th. Since my empirical analysis uses data gathered prior to the 104th, I describe the positions as they appeared under Democratic control.

Committee Hierarchy

Prestigious positions in the committee hierarchy include full committee and subcommittee chairs for majority party members and ranking minority member positions for those in the minority party. These positions within the committee hierarchy confer special resources such as additional staff and "the gavel," giving members more influence over committee deliberations.

Subcommittee chairs became especially attractive positions after the reforms of the 1970s increased the importance of subcommittees in the legislative process. These reforms devolved power from full committees to subcommittees, resulting in a shift from "committee government" to "subcommittee government" (Davidson 1981). The "Subcommittee Bill of Rights," which the Democratic Caucus put into effect in 1973, granted subcommittees procedural and jurisdictional rights that previously only full committees enjoyed: all legislation must be referred to the subcommittees with the appropriate jurisdictions, subcommittees can hold hearings and meetings to consider legislation, and subcommittees can hire their own staff (Rieselbach 1986, 50). As a consequence of the reforms, subcommittee chairs became more important players in the legislative process.

As a full committee or subcommittee chair, a member has significant influence over both the early and later stages of the legislative process. Chairs are typically "the chief 'agenda setters' " during the committee stages of the process and can enhance a bill's prospects for passage "by mobilizing staff resources, compressing the time for hearings and markups, and, in general, encouraging expeditious action by committee members" (Oleszek 1989, 94). Chairs have significant influence during floor deliberations as well. Full committee and subcommittee chairs are usually responsible for bill management on the floor.[5] Bill management is "an important final control," and how well bills are managed on the floor has a significant impact on the final outcome of the legislative process (Deering 1982).

The resources and authority of ranking minority members pale in comparison with those of committee and subcommittee chairs. Still, the agenda prerogatives and staff resources that are associated with these positions enable their occupants to be central players in committee activities (Hall 1996).

The prestige of positions in the committee hierarchy also varies with the jurisdictions of committees. The committees that consider taxing and spending measures—Ways and Means and Appropriations—have traditionally been the most sought after in the House (Smith and Deering 1990; Groseclose and Stewart 1998). The work of these committees and the issues they deal with

5. Since 1971, the rules of the Democratic Caucus have required bill managers to be subcommittee chairs whenever possible (Smith and Deering 1990, 129).

are salient to all members. Seats on these committees can help members obtain benefits for their districts as well as enhance their influence in the House. Fenno (1973, 276) notes that a member of Appropriations "can get funds for his constituency . . . while at the same time wielding a broader influence in the chamber." A third prestigious committee is Rules, which has jurisdiction over resolutions that set the conditions under which members consider legislation on the floor, making it extremely influential (Smith and Deering 1990, 88–90).

The central role that these committees play in matters of policy and process make them attractive, and a transfer to one of them should be considered a promotion for a member (cf. Munger 1988). Members of these committees can also exploit their positions to obtain certain benefits not directly related to the issues under their jurisdictions. For example, in order to get Rules to write a favorable rule for a bill, the drafters of the bill might include public works projects for Rules members' districts (Oleszek 1989, 124–25).

The rules of the party caucuses formally indicate the importance of these committees. The rules designate Appropriations, Rules, and Ways and Means as "exclusive" committees and preclude a member of one of these committees from serving on another without receiving a special exemption (U.S. House 1989).[6]

The Party Hierarchy

The top positions in the majority party hierarchy include the Speaker, the majority leader, and the majority whip. In the postreform era, the role of the Speaker in the policy-making process has been substantially enhanced. The Speaker plays a central role in directing the flow of the legislative process, from referring bills to committees to presiding over roll call votes. The Speaker also has special influence in the selection of members to Rules and the Steering and Policy Committee, which draws up committee slates. The majority leader is responsible for scheduling legislation for consideration on the floor and is the party's floor leader. The majority whip is responsible for "overseeing the whip system's extensive information-gathering and disseminating efforts" (Sinclair 1983, 52). These three positions work in tandem to ensure that the legisla-

---

6. House Republicans identify these as "red" committees, but they have the same restrictions on membership as the Democrats do (Smith 1995, 190–91.) Another prestigious panel is the Budget Committee. Although the rules designate Budget as a "major" committee, the role it plays in federal spending makes it as prestigious as the formally designated exclusive committees (Smith and Deering 1990, 86–87). A member serving on a major committee (or "blue" for Republicans) can serve on one other "nonmajor" committee (or "white" for Republicans). I do not include Budget in my empirical analysis because the process by which members are selected for it is very different from those of other committees.

tive process works as smoothly as possible to the benefit of the majority party (Sinclair 1995).[7]

Below the top leadership there are several prestigious positions in the whip system, including the chief deputy whip, deputy whips, assistant or zone whips, and at-large whips. Positions in the whip system increase their occupants' involvement in the legislative process. As whips, members become involved in deal making and legislation pushing in an official capacity. In addition to the traditional "nose-counting" job, whips in the House perform other important and more complex legislative functions. Whips assist the party leadership in developing legislative programs and strategies, transmit information about bills and leadership positions on bills to party members, and help build coalitions (Oleszek 1989, 33).

Other prestigious positions in the party hierarchy include the chair, vice chair, and secretary of the party caucuses. These leaders preside over the caucus meetings, where important decisions are made regarding institutional organization, rules, procedures, and the staffing of different positions in the committee and party hierarchies. The caucus leaders disseminate policy-relevant information to caucus members and use the caucus's resources to promote the party's policy objectives.

Positions in the minority party hierarchy mirror those in the majority. Although minority Republican positions carry much less influence than their Democratic counterparts, "for a Republican craving prestige, a party post supplies the best available substitute for the legislative power enjoyed by Democrats" in committee leadership positions (Connelly and Pitney 1994, 46).

As members advance to higher positions in the party hierarchies, they become more involved in the conduct of business in the House, from matters of policy to matters of institutional organization. The reinvigoration of the party caucuses during the past few decades has increased the influence of party leadership positions on the operation of the House, making these positions especially attractive (Rohde 1991; Sinclair 1995).

Prestigious Positions and Members' Goals

It is important to note that I use the term *hierarchies* loosely in that the prestige of positions is somewhat subjectively determined. Members will view some positions as more valuable and important than others, and this will affect their desire to advance to different positions. For example, some members will prefer to keep their current committee assignments rather than transfer in the

7. But see Krehbiel 1993, 1997, which question the degree of influence of parties and party leaders on legislative outcomes.

committee hierarchy and sacrifice "committee seniority, policy expertise, [and] contacts in the administrative bureaucracy" (Shepsle 1978, 45; Bullock 1973). Some members may consider it more advantageous to pursue positions in the party hierarchy than in the committee hierarchy.

Still it seems that members generally are interested in advancing to such positions because it helps them achieve their various goals. Clearly, advancing to these positions directly satisfies members' influence-seeking goals. A distinguishing feature of these positions is that the actions and decisions of their occupants have a substantial effect on the interests of other members. For example, the work of the Appropriations Committee affects the ability of those not on the committee to deliver pork barrel projects to their constituents. The role that full committee and subcommittee chairs play throughout the legislative process gives them increased influence over the fate of legislation that concerns other members. Although the nature of the hierarchical structure in the House is somewhat different from that in organizations such as bureaucracies or firms, the top positions in the committee and party hierarchies afford members a greater say in what goes on in the institution: "these positions count as distinctions with a legislative difference, in that they typically bestow certain procedural prerogatives, seats at important bargaining tables, special access to relevant political and policy networks, and other sources of legislative advantage" (Hall and Van Houweling 1995, 124).

Members can parlay these "sources of legislative advantage" to help them achieve their goals of reelection and enacting good public policy. As was mentioned earlier, members can use these positions to obtain federal benefits for their districts. The influence that members acquire with these positions makes them attractive investments for PACs (cf. Snyder 1990), so members can use their positions to obtain the funds necessary to mount successful reelection campaigns.[8] The occupants of influential positions generally have more resources "that subsidize the considerable opportunity costs that participation [in the legislative process] entails" (Hall 1987, 121). Members can devote these resources to enacting what they believe to be good public policy.

Members can exploit desires to advance to these positions by making appointment to them contingent on entrepreneurial activity. In terms of the definition of *career concerns,* some subset of members of the House (the principals) use the past entrepreneurial activity of a particular member (the agent) to determine whether they should reward the member with a promotion to a prestigious position within the institution. This kind of reward system will encourage members to engage in legislative entrepreneurship.

---

8. In chapter 4, I found that party leaders of both parties and Democrats on exclusive committees received a greater amount of PAC contributions than did those not in such positions (see also Box-Steffensmeier and Grant 1999).

For this reward system to work, it must be incentive compatible for the principals to promote LEs. Like other aspects of legislative organization, the selection of members for prestigious positions is essentially majoritarian (cf. Krehbiel 1991). That is, in some fashion majorities of members in the chamber—whether it be a majority of partisans on a committee or a majority of the party caucus—must agree to promote a member to a prestigious position.[9] What are the payoffs for the members who form these majorities to promote LEs?

As I argued in chapter 1, the production of legislation promotes the reelection chances of House members while the failure to produce legislation can hurt them. Thus, all members are better off when some members engage in legislative entrepreneurship because they have an interest in the legislative performance of the House. Promoting LEs will enhance legislative performance in two ways. First, it will provide incentives for members to become LEs. Second, it will ensure that more capable legislators assume positions that have an important effect on how well the House functions as a policy-making body, provided that members can determine entrepreneurial ability accurately.

This second point requires elaboration. Baker, Jensen, and Murphy (1988) argue that using promotions to motivate workers can be problematic because a worker who performs well at one level might not perform well in a position at a higher level. This is not a problem with regard to promoting LEs in the House. Congressional scholars have argued that members have created these various prestigious positions and endowed them with resources that their occupants are expected to devote to overcoming collective action problems associated with the passage of legislation (Cox and McCubbins 1993; Sinclair 1995).[10] When selecting individuals for these positions, members should consider whether those who are selected will effectively deploy the resources associated with the positions toward the passage of legislation. Members are confronted with a standard agency problem, which they can solve at least partly by carefully screening candidates for prestigious positions based on their characteristics or past behavior (Kiewiet and McCubbins 1991; Cox and McCubbins 1993).

Legislative entrepreneurship should be a key criterion that members use to screen candidates for prestigious positions. If advancement to these positions depends on possessing superior entrepreneurial ability and if those respon-

9. The agreement to promote can be considered "remote" in the case of appointive party leadership positions (cf. Krehbiel 1991). The individuals charged with appointing members to these positions are themselves elected and so should consider what effect their appointment decisions will have on their prospects for maintaining majority support for their own positions.

10. Cox and McCubbins and Sinclair are mainly concerned with party leadership positions, but their arguments easily extend to positions in the committee hierarchy (e.g., see Cox and McCubbins 1993, 91).

sible for determining whether a member will advance can infer such ability accurately, then more capable members will occupy positions that give them more control over the way the House conducts its business. Members should generally favor individuals with superior entrepreneurial ability because these individuals are best qualified to use the resources associated with prestigious positions to make the machinery of the legislative process work to enact legislation when there is adequate demand for it. Superior entrepreneurial ability implies that members have well-developed parliamentary skills, have a good grasp of how the legislative process works, know what it takes to build and maintain winning coalitions, and have a keen eye for spotting which proposals are worth the investment of resources. If members with superior entrepreneurial ability occupy the "management positions" in the House, this will improve the capacity of the House to produce legislation and satisfy the demands placed upon it as a collectivity.[11]

Thus, the use of promotions within the House's hierarchies has a dual effect on its performance as a legislative body. First, it will encourage members to contribute to legislative production through legislative entrepreneurship with the expectation of receiving promotions in the future. Second, if those making the promotion decisions infer entrepreneurial ability accurately, more capable members will end up in the influential positions in the House hierarchies.

However, the fact that ability is not directly observable complicates using a member's ability as a basis for promotion.[12] Others only get to observe a member's legislative output, which is a noisy signal of ability. This is problematic because members may try to inflate others' perceptions of their true ability by "overproducing" or try to conceal low entrepreneurial ability by blaming low output on forces beyond their control.

Holmström's (1982a) work on career concerns demonstrates how this problem can be solved in a dynamic setting. By observing an individual's output over time, the noise in the individual's production can be filtered out and more accurate inferences about his or her ability can be made. This model is fairly intuitive given how we typically think about reputation building—that is, reputations are built over time. Those involved in promotion decisions should

11. Rewarding LEs with promotions can also help the House maintain an adequate stock of entrepreneurial members. Ambitious LEs might decide to stay in the House rather than run for higher offices after they advance to prestigious positions in the institution (Hall and Van Houweling 1995).

12. Such a promotion scheme will be more effective if members base promotion decisions on ability rather than effort. While basing decisions on effort will encourage members to exert effort prior to receiving a promotion, there is no guarantee that they will continue to exert this level of effort once they receive the promotion. But, if ability is thought of as some "guaranteed" minimum level of effort, then this problem does not occur when promotion decisions are based on assessments of ability.

consider a member's "entrepreneurial output" over his or her entire career.

Anecdotal evidence suggests that members of the House do use observations over time to make inferences about entrepreneurial ability. MacNeil (1963, 14) notes how Speakers of the House have touted the institution's capacity for judging its members:

> "The House of Representatives," Sam Rayburn never tired of saying, "is the greatest jury in the world." The House, Rayburn meant, knew how to test and decide the qualifications of its own members and the recommendations they proposed as the House's judgments. Rayburn echoed a recurring theme throughout the House's history. Frederick Gillett of Massachusetts, Speaker in the 1920s, had expressed the same view that Rayburn reiterated. "This House," Gillett said, "becomes *in time* a pretty infallible judge of a member's merit." (emphasis added)

If we are to believe the claims of these former Speakers, members of the House apparently can determine their colleagues' abilities by observing them over time.

It is interesting to note that while the selection of members for prestigious positions is an important element of legislative organization, the selection of the method of selecting members for prestigious positions is itself an important aspect of legislative organization. It makes sense that members would choose elective methods as the primary selection mechanism for prestigious positions if they wanted LEs to occupy such positions. The skills that a member needs to win the support of others so that he or she can advance are similar to the skills needed for legislative entrepreneurship. Instead of pushing a legislative proposal and building a coalition of other members to support it, a member who seeks to advance strives to build a coalition in support of his or her promotion. The elective nature of prestigious positions gives the reward system something of a self-enforcing quality. Although members may be tempted not to vote for individuals with superior entrepreneurial abilities, those with superior abilities have the skills to convince them to vote in the "correct" way.

Some may argue that the fact that members have to vote others into prestigious positions is meaningless and that these "elections" are really just pro forma. I would argue that the elective nature of these positions is important. There is substantial evidence that the committee assignment process is not one of self-selection, especially for prestige committees (Cox and McCubbins 1993, chap. 1; Krehbiel 1991, chap. 4). Even those who claim that the process is one of self-selection note that the process of self-selecting involves extensive campaigning on one's behalf and building a supporting coalition of those who draw up committee slates (Shepsle 1978, 38–43). This type of campaigning and coalition building is also apparent in the selection of party leaders (Peabody 1976; Sinclair 1995, 64–65).[13]

Although assignment to subcommittees appears to be a process of self-selection (Hall 1996, 114–15), the selection of subcommittee leaders does not. Members can self-select themselves to subcommittees in such a way that their full committee seniority can give them an advantage (115), but seniority is not the only and perhaps not even most important factor in the selection of subcommittee chairs. It is not uncommon for junior members to wage campaigns to win the support of others for these positions.[14]

Anecdotal evidence gives hope that systematic analysis will indicate that members *are* rewarded for entrepreneurial activity in a way that is consistent with the mobility hypothesis. Several scholars have noted how Congress has evolved into a meritocracy in which the kinds of activities that constitute legislative entrepreneurship have become important determinants of a member's position in the institution (e.g., see Loomis 1988, 235). The reforms of the 1970s have weakened the role that seniority plays in the selection of members to prestigious positions and have made it possible for less senior members to lay claim to these positions on the basis of their entrepreneurial reputations. Oleszek (1989, 14) argues that members who abide by such norms as "legislative work (members should concentrate on congressional duties and not be publicity seekers)" and specialization "are rewarded with increased influence in the policy process, for example, by being appointed to prestigious committees." Mayhew (1974, 141, 146–47) contends that party leadership positions and seats on prestigious committees are part of a system of "selective incentives" that induces House members to work toward maintaining the institution, which involves "grueling and [electorally] unrewarding legislative work." Dodd (1977, 274) claims that "much pressure exists to establish norms by which members 'prove' themselves deserving of membership on an attractive committee" by demonstrating "specialization in limited areas of public policy, a willingness to work hard on legislation, [and] a commitment to the institution." Krehbiel (1991, chap. 4, n. 45) makes a similar argument, claiming that, since members' "ability to transfer [to a different committee] is likely to be a function of their having demonstrated at least a modicum of legislative competence . . . low-ranking members on undesirable committees have incentives to legislate their way to better committees." Although these observations support

13. For examples of competitive leadership elections and members waging campaigns for party leadership positions, see Hook 1989, Koszczuk 1997a, and Katz 1998.

14. Smith and Deering (1984, 197–98, n. 45) note 10 instances in which junior members vaulted over more senior members to become subcommittee chairs. For specific cases of seniority violations, see Cooper 1979.

the mobility hypothesis, it is necessary to test this hypothesis in a systematic fashion.

Analyzing Intrainstitutional Mobility

A systematic test of the mobility hypothesis requires a model that estimates the effects of individual characteristics on the probability that members will move from lower to higher ranking positions in the committee and party hierarchies. Sociologists and economists have developed and applied methods for analyzing mobility (Tuma, Hannan, and Groeneveld 1979; Lancaster 1990, chap. 5), though only a few studies examine mobility *within* hierarchies.[15] Analyzing mobility in hierarchies is problematic because in many hierarchies, including the House, individuals advance mainly through *vacancy competition*—that is, if a hierarchy contains a fixed number of positions, a member can advance to a higher position only if the current occupant vacates the position (Sorenson 1977).

Vacancy competition exists in the House because there are informal limits on the number of prestigious positions and members have informal property rights for the positions they occupy (Weingast and Marshall 1988). Since the Constitution grants members of the House the authority to organize their institution, they can determine the number of prestigious positions. Members may be tempted to expand the number of prestigious positions so that there are more rewards to go around. However, expanding the number of prestigious positions can reduce the value of these positions and defeat the purpose of having them in the first place. Although a member may want the number of positions to be increased so that it increases his or her chances of advancing to a position, that position may be worth less if the resources that are available with that position are fewer because they must be distributed more widely.

Shepsle (1978) argues that party leaders who have formal responsibilities for determining the size of committees face a tension between limiting the number of prestigious positions and expanding them to satisfy members' demands for them. Expanding the number of committee slots is a type of currency inflation that dissipates the worth of the slots. The value in having a particular committee seat stems from the fact that committee members have authority that nonmembers do not. Committee members can use their authority to benefit nonmembers who are concerned with the committee's business in

15. See Gibbons 1997 for a review of theoretical and empirical work on mobility within firms. Most of the empirical work in economics attempts to determine whether internal labor markets exist in firms and traces career paths within firms (e.g., see Baker, Gibbs, and Holmström 1994).

exchange for benefits that nonmembers can deliver. As the number of members on a committee increases, there are more individuals with whom nonmembers can exchange benefits, so the bargaining power of any single committee member decreases.

Both the distributive and informational models of legislatures contend that committee members can use their positions to obtain distributional benefits (Shepsle and Weingast 1987; Gilligan and Krehbiel 1987, 1989a). In distributive models, members exchange influence over different policy areas so that they can secure the benefits that are most valuable to them. In informational models, members obtain distributional benefits as rewards for information gathering. If the amount of distributional benefits that a committee controls is fixed, then as the number of committee members increases the share of each member decreases.

Munger (1988) finds empirical evidence to support the argument that the value of committee seats declines as the number of seats increases. Munger measures value by examining members' preferences for committee seats as indicated by committee transfers. As the number of slots on a committee increases, all else being equal, fewer members seek to transfer to the committee.

Similar arguments about limits hold for committee leadership and party leadership positions. The Subcommittee Bill of Rights gave subcommittee leaders authority that previously had been reserved for full committee leaders. While full committee chairs are still prestigious positions, they are not as important as they used to be because full committee chairs do not have the exclusive control over the legislative process that they once did. Further expansion of the number of subcommittee chairs would decrease the importance of these positions in a similar fashion. "The number of subcommittees can be changed but not willy-nilly and not infinitely" (Deering 1996, 20). The number of party leadership positions, particularly whip positions, increased substantially during the period under analysis (Rohde 1991, fig. 4.1). Even with these positions however, concerns about spreading resources too thinly and "too many cooks spoiling the soup" impose limits on the number of new positions that can be created and induce vacancy competition for these positions.

While House rules make it possible for challengers to oust those who hold prestigious positions, this rarely happens. Informal property rights that members have in these positions appear to discourage such challenges. The possibility of retribution after unsuccessful challenges also discourages efforts to unseat incumbents in prestigious positions. In almost all cases, those who seek to advance to prestigious positions wait until they become open through the retirement, death, or electoral defeat of those who hold the positions. Practically all of the vacancies in prestigious positions arise due to members exiting the House because, once members obtain prestigious positions, they rarely leave them until they leave the House.[16]

The limits on the number of prestigious positions and property rights induce vacancy competition, which complicates the analysis of intrainstitutional mobility. The probability that a member will make a transition to a different position is not only a function of his or her own characteristics but also of the availability of that position. When computing the transition probabilities, we need to condition the probability of moving on the number of positions that are available.

White (1970) has proposed *vacancy chain methods* to examine mobility in hierarchies with vacancy competition.[17] These methods explicitly account for the constraints that vacancies impose on mobility. The units of observation are not individual members of the hierarchy but individual vacancies. Instead of looking at how a particular individual moves up through the hierarchy, these methods examine how a vacancy "moves" through different levels in the hierarchy. A movement by the vacancy down through the hierarchy implies that individuals are moving up.

While vacancy chain methods recognize the interdependence of movement through a hierarchy, they are not well suited for analyzing the effects of individual-specific characteristics on the probability of moving. In order to use vacancy chain methods to determine the effects of legislative entrepreneurship, we would have to divide each position category into subcategories pertaining to individual characteristics. For example, to study the effects of entrepreneurship on mobility we would have to create different categories of levels of entrepreneurship from the continuous measures. We could then look at the probability that a vacancy on a prestigious committee "moves" to a position on a nonprestigious committee occupied by a person who has "high" entrepreneurship scores. The number of transition probabilities will be extremely large if we consider a number of different positions and also want to include variables that should affect advancement such as seniority and party loyalty. It

16. Members who do not leave the House may leave prestigious positions because of term limits for particular positions (such as assistant whip), because the positions are eliminated (as sometimes happens with subcommittees), or because they are challenged and defeated for the position by another member (which almost never happens). Members who vacate full committee leadership positions without leaving the House usually retire shortly thereafter. Members will give up subcommittee leadership positions without leaving the House if they transfer to a different committee. The challenges to incumbent Republican Party leaders for positions in the 106th Congress were extremely unusual, apparently sparked by another extremely unusual event: the failure of the party not controlling the presidency to pick up House seats in a midterm election. These internecine battles raise questions about the applicability of some of the assumptions of this analysis to the Republican-controlled House. I discuss these issues in more detail in the next chapter.

17. See also Stewman 1986.

is unlikely that we will have enough data on each type of movement to obtain reliable estimates of the probabilities (cf. White 1970, 257).

In appendix B, I derive a model that allows estimation of the effects of individual-specific characteristics on the probability of making a transition while accounting for vacancy constraints. This maximum likelihood method estimates the probability of making a transition conditional on the positions that members occupy initially and the opportunities for filling vacancies in other positions. The method also accounts for the fact that members can make a transition to an "exit state" (i.e., leave the institution), which prevents them from making a transition to a position within the institution. The interpretation of the coefficients estimated from this model is similar to that of coefficients from a logit regression, so readers not interested in the technical details of the model can still understand the results without fully grasping the appendix. The likelihood equation that I estimate is

$$L = \prod_i \{[(1-p_{i1w})(1-q_{i12})]^{d_{i11}} [(1-p_{i1w})q_{i12}]^{d_{i12}} (p_{i1w})^{d_{i1w}}\},$$

where

$(1-p_{i1w})(1-q_{i12})$ is the probability that member i stays in a nonprestigious position. Nonprestigious positions are denoted by a 1 subscript, prestigious positions are denoted by a 2 subscript, and the "exit position" is denoted by a w.

$(1-p_{i1w})q_{i12}$ is the probability that i will make a transition from a nonprestigious to a prestigious position.

p_{i1w} is the probability that i will exit the House from a nonprestigious position.

$$p_{i1w} = \frac{\exp(\beta'_{1w}\mathbf{x}_{i1w})}{1+\exp(\beta'_{1w}\mathbf{x}_{i1w})} \tag{5.1}$$

$$q_{i12} = 1 - \left[1 - \frac{\exp(\beta'_{12}\mathbf{x}_{i12})}{1+\exp(\beta'_{12}\mathbf{x}_{i12})}\right]^{N_{i12}} \tag{5.2}$$

$$d_{i11} = \begin{cases} 1 & \text{if } i \text{ stays in nonprestigious position} \\ 0 & \text{otherwise} \end{cases}$$

$$d_{i12} = \begin{cases} 1 & \text{if } i \text{ moves to a prestigious position} \\ 0 & \text{otherwise} \end{cases}$$

and

$$d_{i1w} = \begin{cases} 1 & \text{if } i \text{ leaves the institution from a nonprestigious position} \\ 0 & \text{otherwise} \end{cases}$$

The vectors $\mathbf{x}_{i1w}$ and $\mathbf{x}_{i12}$ contain variables measuring individual-specific attributes, and β_{1w} and β_{12} are vectors of parameters to be estimated. Since the model conditions on initially occupied positions and we are looking only at the advancement of those not in prestigious positions, we can be sure that any effects that legislative entrepreneurship has on advancement are not simply due to members expending resources associated with prestigious positions.

Explanatory Variables

Despite numerous studies that examine the importance of prestigious positions in the House, we know very little about what factors determine which members get to occupy them.[18] Except for a few important works that have looked at mobility in terms of what factors affect the probability that a member will transfer from one committee to another (Rohde and Shepsle 1973; Shepsle 1978; Smith and Ray 1983; Cox and McCubbins 1993), students of Congress have not paid much attention to members' mobility within the institution.[19] But these previous studies do give us some ideas about what explanatory variables we should include in the specification.

The first set of variables I include are measures of legislative entrepreneurship. In order to account for reputation building, I transform the entrepreneurship measures in the following way. For each Congress in which a member serves, I sum over the measures in the previous Congresses, take the log of this sum, and then divide by the number of terms the member has served.[20] This is a rough approximation of Holmström's (1982a) Bayesian learning model of reputation building. I refer to this transformation as the *entrepreneurship reputation score.*[21] The entrepreneurship reputation score essentially represents

18. Most studies of the advancement of House members have focused on *progressive ambition*—that is, ambition relating to decisions to seek higher office (Schlesinger 1966). Several studies have looked at the career paths of members in terms of decisions to remain in the House or run for a Senate seat or governorship (Rohde 1979; Brace 1984; Kiewiet and Zeng 1993).

19. Hall and Van Houweling (1995) examine how members' expectations about advancing to a better position within the House in the future affects their retirement decisions. Hall and Van Houweling focus on how prospects for advancement based on position in the seniority queue affect members' decisions to retire, but they do not consider what individual characteristics might affect advancement. Peabody (1976) looks at several case studies of contests for top leadership positions in the Democratic Caucus and Republican Conference. Deering (1996) and Nelson (1977) examine patterns of advancement within subcommittees and parties, respectively, but they do not focus on what individual-specific characteristics affect advancement.

20. Taking logs puts the entrepreneurship measures on the same scale as the other explanatory variables, making the model much more stable and easier to estimate.

21. A drawback of using these transformed measures is that we cannot use the data for members who entered Congress prior to the 94th Congress because we cannot observe their entrepreneurship scores between the time they began their congressional careers and the 94th. The

an interaction between inverse seniority and the log of the sum of the entrepreneurship scores over previous Congresses. Following standard econometric practice, I include the "uninteracted" variables as well. That is, I include a variable that is the log of the sum of the entrepreneurship scores over previous Congresses (the *cumulative entrepreneurship score*) and a variable that is one divided by the number of terms a member has served.

There are two advantages to including these other terms. First, it enables us to measure the cumulative effect of a member's entrepreneurial efforts. Instead of evaluating each other according to Holmström's model, members may consider the sum of their entrepreneurial activities without regard to seniority. Second, including inverse seniority allows us to account for the potential nonlinear effects of seniority that other studies have found.[22] Seniority on its own might affect advancement because it is a proxy for experience and the development of "organization-specific human capital" (Shepsle and Nalebuff 1990). Apart from their records of legislative entrepreneurship, more senior members are more likely to promote legislative production because they have a better grasp of how the legislative process works.

Partisan factors may also play an important role in advancement. At a minimum, partisanship is important in that members will be promoted only to positions controlled by their parties. That is, a member of the minority party will not be promoted to a full committee or subcommittee chair or to a majority party leadership position. The party caucuses make decisions regarding advancement of their members for most of the prestigious positions in the House. The party caucuses vote on committee slates drawn up by the parties' committees on committees. The party caucuses elect full committee chairs for all committees and subcommittee chairs for the Appropriations Committee. Members for the top leadership positions in each party are selected by the caucuses. Given the role that parties play in the selection of members to prestigious positions, it seems reasonable that loyalty to the party would be of central concern. Members who have demonstrated high levels of loyalty in the past might be considered good candidates because they will use the resources of their positions to advance party goals, which include passing legislation that creates a favorable image of the party with the electorate (Cox and McCubbins 1993).

Some would argue that party loyalty should play a more important role than legislative entrepreneurship in selection for prestigious positions because party leaders would not want to choose members who were activist LEs and

---

analysis of mobility includes cohorts of members from the 94th through the 103d Congress, although I analyze mobility only in the 96th through the 103d.

22. Including a quadratic term to allow for nonlinear effects for seniority did not change the results significantly.

might cause trouble for the leadership. Instead, party leaders should choose loyalists whom they can keep in their back pockets. There are two problems with this argument. First, though party leaders do have some say in who advances to certain prestigious positions, theirs is not the only say. Although for some positions party leaders have the power to propose slates of individuals, those slates must obtain the approval of majorities of others. The approval of majorities still matters in some sense for the few positions to which party leaders get to appoint members directly. As I argued earlier, party leaders themselves depend on the support of coalitions to obtain and maintain their positions, so they must consider how their choice of appointees will affect their support. Second, party leaders have an interest in promoting LEs because LEs can assist party leaders with one of the primary responsibilities of leaders: building coalitions (Sinclair 1983). Having a committee chair who is incompetent but loyal makes the job of party leaders difficult because they cannot rely on that individual to handle important day to day legislating and coalition-building tasks and so they must perform those tasks themselves. Nevertheless, the effect of party loyalty versus legislative entrepreneurship is something that the systematic data analysis reported in this chapter will determine. The measure of party loyalty that I include is the same as the measure Cox and McCubbins (1993) use to demonstrate that loyalty to the party leadership affects committee transfers.[23] If Cox and McCubbins's hypothesis about the role of parties in the House is correct, then this variable should matter in other types of advancement as well.

Another factor affecting mobility might be whether or not a member is a preference outlier. Members may not wish to promote an individual if his or her policy preferences are out of step with the rest of the chamber (Krehbiel 1991). Such a member is likely to use his or her position for causes to which many other members are opposed. To compute this measure, I take the absolute value of the difference between each member's NOMINATE score and the score of the median voter in the chamber.[24]

I also include a variable that measures whether a member of a legislator's

---

23. To compute this measure, they first identify *party leadership votes.* These are votes in which the majority leader and the majority whip vote the opposite of the way the minority leader and minority whip vote. They determine the number of times each member voted with the leaders of his or her party. They then standardize this measure in the usual fashion. The data used to compute the measure of party loyalty are from the United States Congressional Roll Call Voting Records (ICPSR and Congressional Quarterly, Inc. 1997). I do not transform the party loyalty variable in same way as the entrepreneurship variables so that I can compare my results with previous work.

24. I also tried including a variable that measures the absolute value of the difference between each member's NOMINATE score and the score of the median voter in the member's party. The results did not change significantly.

state delegation had vacated a position. For certain positions, maintaining a regional balance seems important to members (Shepsle 1978). For example, one criterion for advancing to an assistant whip position is that a member must be from a state that is in the geographic zone of the country represented by the position. When a member from a particular state vacates a position, the desire to maintain the state's representation should give those from that state a higher probability of advancing to the position. I expect a positive coefficient on this dummy variable, which equals one if someone from the member's state delegation leaves a prestigious position.

As for the part of the model that accounts for exiting the House, the specification includes several variables that studies of exits from the House have found to be important (Kiewiet and Zeng 1993; Groseclose and Krehbiel 1994; Hall and Van Houweling 1995). I include variables that measure the number of terms the member has served and his or her age. I include dummy variables that indicate whether there is an open seat in the Senate or an open governorship in the member's state. House members will be more tempted to leave the chamber to run for higher office if they do not have to face an incumbent. I also include a dummy variable that equals one if a member experiences an unfavorable redistricting and a variable that measures the vote share of the incumbent in the previous election.[25] An unfavorable redistricting or a close race in the previous election might mean that an incumbent will face a serious challenge in the next one, leading to preemptive retirement or electoral defeat in the next election. While clearly there are other variables that might affect the probability of exit, those I include should pick up enough variation in the data to estimate the probability of advancement, which is the theoretically more important part of the model.[26] Table 5.1 reports descriptive statistics for the explanatory variables included in this analysis.

Positive coefficients on the explanatory variables in q_{i12} mean that the probability of advancing to a prestigious position increases as the values of the variables increase. The mobility hypothesis predicts that the net effect of the cumulative entrepreneurship variable and the entrepreneurship reputation variable should be positive. A positive coefficient on the inverse terms variable indicates that length of service increases the probability of transferring, but this effect declines the longer a member serves. Previous work indicates that the loyalty to party leadership and the vacancy from state delegation variables should have positive effects on mobility. Informational theories of legislative organization suggest that the coefficient on the deviation from median voter

---

25. I used the same method as Hall and Van Houweling (1995, 127) to compute the redistricting variable.

26. Likelihood ratio tests indicate that these variables jointly improve the fit of the model over a model that assumes a constant rate for exits.

TABLE 5.1. Descriptive Statistics for Explanatory Variables

	Mean	SD	Median	Minimum	Maximum
	Democrats ($N = 1,242$)				
Entrepreneurship reputation score[a]	1.84	1.25	1.56	0	5.35
Cumulative entrepreneurship score[a]	5.08	1.38	5.15	0	7.22
1/(terms served)	.40	.28	.33	.111	1
Party loyalty	−.023	1.03	.37	−4.21	1.39
State vacancy in committee leadership	.12	.35	0	0	1
State vacancy in party leadership	.23	.42	0	0	1
Deviation from median voter	.30	.21	.27	0	.91
Terms served	3.63	2.02	3	1	9
Age	46.79	8.61	46	27	80
Open seat in Senate	.12	.32	0	0	1
Open seat in governorship	.19	.39	0	0	1
Previous vote share	.72	.16	.68	.50	1
Unfavorable redistricting	.04	.19	0	0	1
	Republicans ($N = 843$)				
Entrepreneurship reputation score[a]	1.97	1.37	1.69	0	5.85
Cumulative entrepreneurship score[a]	4.74	1.55	4.95	0	6.49
1/(terms served)	.47	.31	.33	.11	1
Party loyalty	.09	.93	.35	−3.65	1.46
State vacancy	.18	.39	0	0	1
Deviation from median voter	.55	.22	.552	0	1.28
Terms served	3.18	1.88	3	1	9
Age	47.36	9.10	47	27	80
Open seat in Senate	.13	.34	0	0	1
Open seat in governorship	.18	.39	0	0	1
Previous vote share	.67	.13	.65	.50	1
Unfavorable redistricting	.04	.20	0	0	1

[a] Entrepreneurship scale scores of zero were set equal to 1×10^{-10} so logs could be taken.

variable should be negative. I expect that the terms, age, unfavorable redistricting, and Senate and governorship open seat variables should have positive effects on the probability of exiting the House. The previous vote share variable should have a negative effect on the probability of exiting.

I analyzed mobility of Democrats and Republicans separately for theoretical and empirical reasons. Theoretically, I expect that the results should be stronger for Democrats since they were in the majority during the period analyzed and Republicans' opportunities for enacting legislation were severely limited. The positions that minority party members can fill are much less useful as rewards for entrepreneurial activity because the limits on the legislative authority of these positions detracts from their effectiveness in helping members achieve their goals (Connelly and Pitney 1994, 46). Minority party members have an interest in promoting LEs, though to a much lesser extent since the positions that minority party members occupy have much less influence than positions filled by majority party members. Empirically, likelihood ratio tests indicate that pooling members of the two parties is inappropriate. When Republicans are analyzed separately, neither the entrepreneurship reputation score nor the cumulative entrepreneurship score has statistically significant effects on mobility in the committee or party hierarchies for Republicans. I report the results for Republicans in Tables 5.2 through 5.4 but focus on the details of the results for Democrats in the text.[27]

Analysis of Mobility in the Committee Hierarchy

I pooled the data for the 96th through the 103d Congresses and estimated the effects of the explanatory variables on advancement to committee leadership positions. Committee leadership positions are full committee and subcommittee chairs for Democrats and ranking minority member positions for Republicans.[28]

---

27. One justification for pooling across the parties is that the distributive and informational models that in part motivate this analysis and help define the model specification are blind to party affiliation. I conducted the analysis by pooling observations for Democrats and Republicans, and the results on the entrepreneurship variables were qualitatively the same as the results reported for Democrats. The results for Democrats appear to be strong enough to overwhelm the null effects for Republicans.

28. In this analysis, N_{i12} is equal to the number of full committee or subcommittee chairs that left *i*'s *full* committee. In approximately 40 percent of transitions to committee leadership positions, those making the transitions did not assume the leadership position of a subcommittee that they served on in the previous Congress. Apparently, any member of a full committee is eligible for any open leadership position on its subcommittees. In only 2 percent of the transitions made between the 96th and 103d Congresses did a member assume a subcommittee leadership position upon securing a transfer to an exclusive committee.

TABLE 5.2. Effects of Legislative Entrepreneurship on Mobility in the Committee Hierarchy, Full Committee and Subcommittee Chairs

Variable	Democrats	Republicans
	Probability of Advancing	
Intercept	−7.187	−3.043
	(1.865)	(2.273)
Entrepreneurship reputation score	−1.133	−.147
	(.348)	(.470)
Cumulative entrepreneurship score	1.101	.187
	(.331)	(.423)
1/(terms served)	4.913	.986
	(1.975)	(2.369)
Party loyalty	−.086	−.500
	(.138)	(.291)
State vacancy	.573	.323
	(.438)	(.583)
Deviation from median voter	−.650	.255
	(.761)	(1.188)
	Probability of Exiting	
Intercept	−3.756	−2.456
	(.625)	(.684)
Terms served	.392	.153
	(.063)	(.078)
Age	−.002	.005
	(.013)	(.012)
Open seat in Senate	−.164	.044
	(.294)	(.293)
Open seat in governorship	.052	.463
	(.260)	(.245)
Previous vote share	.578	.265
	(.599)	(.818)
Unfavorable redistricting	−.296	−.528
	(.574)	(.499)
N	802	439
−2 × log likelihood	1,032.58	713.80

Note: Entries are the coefficients in the vectors β_{12} and β_{1w} from equations 5.2 and 5.1. Standard errors are in parentheses.

N denotes the number of individuals not in committee leadership positions.

Table 5.2 reports the effects of the explanatory variables on the probability of advancing to a committee leadership position. The results reveal an interesting effect with the cumulative entrepreneurship score and the reputation score. The coefficients on these variables are both statistically significant and approximately equal but have opposite signs. This means that for freshmen members the effect of these two variables cancel each other out, suggesting that the norm of apprenticeship might not be quite as dead as some recent studies contend. Although freshman members may no longer be pressured to be "seen and not heard," those who make themselves heard through legislative entrepreneurship are not rewarded in the same way as LEs who are not freshmen. Beyond the first term however, the value of the cumulative score is greater than the reputation score, so the net effect of the entrepreneurship variables is positive. The only other variable that has a significant effect on the probability of making a transition to a committee leadership position is the inverse terms of service variable, which has a positive coefficient. As for exiting the House, the number of terms served has a positive and significant effect on the probability of exiting the House.[29]

To determine the marginal effects of the variables of interest, I simulate the probability of advancing. Given the specification of the model, we are interested in how a member's entrepreneurial activity affects the probability of advancing to a committee leadership position throughout his or her career. Figure 5.1 contains simulated transition probabilities for Democrats, which are computed for the different percentiles of the entrepreneurship score in the sample and for the number of terms served. The other variables are held constant at their median values. The figure shows that members who have entrepreneurship scores in the lowest percentiles have almost no chance of advancing to a committee leadership position regardless of seniority. Those members in the highest percentiles have a substantially greater probability of advancing to committee leadership positions, and this effect appears to peak at the fifth term.

Neither of the legislative entrepreneurship variables has a statistically significant effect on the probability of Republican members making a transition to a ranking minority position.[30] In fact, as table 5.2 reports, the only explanatory variable that has even a marginally significant effect on the probability of a nonranking Republican making any transition is the party loyalty variable. However, this variable has a negative coefficient, indicating that a Republican member's probability of becoming a ranking member decreases the more loyal he or she is to the party's top leaders. This counterintuitive result may be due to the split that developed in the 1980s between the old guard Republicans led by then minority leader Robert Michel (R–IL) and the more conservative and confrontational Republicans led by Newt Gingrich (R–GA), who were much less willing to compromise with Democrats (Connelly and Pitney 1994). The

29. I should note that using the mobility model to take into account the number of vacancies gives results that differ from simple logit regression. The effect of the entrepreneurship variables was smaller and the party loyalty variables had a positive sign.

30. I did not simulate probabilities for Republicans since neither of the entrepreneurship variables was statistically distinguishable from zero.

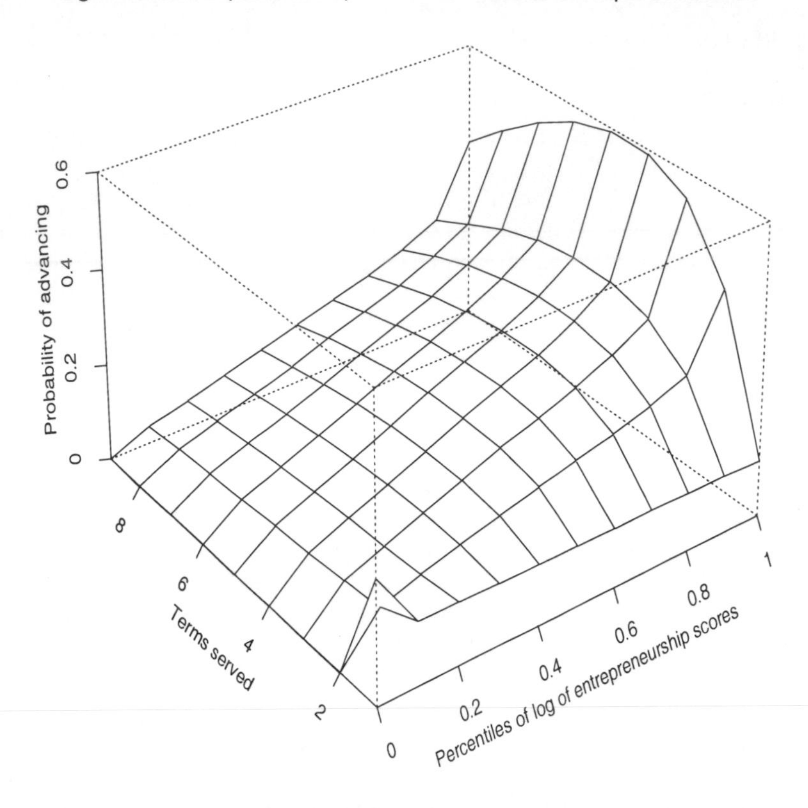

Fig. 5.1. Effect of legislative entrepreneurship and terms served on the probability of advancing to a full committee or subcommittee chairmanship, Democrats

open governor's seat variable is the only one that has a significant effect on the probability of exit.

I also estimated the effects of the explanatory variables on mobility with respect to seats on prestigious committees.[31] Table 5.3 reports the results of this analysis. The coefficients on the entrepreneurship variables follow the same pattern as in the analysis of advancement to committee leadership positions: the coefficient on the cumulative entrepreneurial activity variable is positive while the coefficient on the entrepreneurship reputation measure is

31. The committee transfers data for the 96th through the 100th Congresses were created using the committee assignments collected by Garrison Nelson. The transfers data for the 101st through the 102d Congresses were compiled from *CQ* special reports, CQ's Washington Alert, Legi-Slate, and the *Congressional Directory.*

TABLE 5.3. Effects of Legislative Entrepreneurship on Mobility in the Committee Hierarchy, Exclusive Committees

Variable	Democrats	Republicans
	Probability of Advancing	
Intercept	−3.471	−2.068
	(1.370)	(1.092)
Entrepreneurship reputation score	−.378	.114
	(.265)	(.308)
Cumulative entrepreneurship score	.347	−.077
	(.234)	(.200)
1/(terms served)	.747	−.694
	(1.547)	(1.444)
Party loyalty	−.128	−.581
	(0.096)	(.179)
State delegation vacancy	.606	−.074
	(.216)	(.309)
Deviation from median voter	−.173	1.272
	(.546)	(.787)
	Probability of Exiting	
Intercept	−4.354	−4.648
	(.903)	(.983)
Terms served	−.569	−.248
	(.123)	(.110)
Age	.001	−.007
	(.018	(.018)
Open seat in Senate	.717	.093
	(.335)	(.421)
Open seat in governorship	−.665	.165
	(.529)	(.396)
Previous vote share	1.300	1.663
	(.835)	(1.090)
Unfavorable redistricting	−.045	.637
	(1.019)	(.621)
N	954	714
−2 × log likelihood	1,022.22	854.10

Note: Entries are the coefficients in the vectors β_{12} and β_{1w} from equations 5.2 and 5.1. Standard errors are in parentheses.

N denotes the number of individuals not in prestigious positions.

negative. However, given the size of standard errors for these coefficients, I cannot say with much confidence that they have an effect that differs from zero. These results may be due to the fact that legislative entrepreneurship may be jurisdiction specific, making it less attractive for members to transfer to committees with different jurisdictions.

As predicted, the coefficient on the state vacancy variable is positive and statistically significant, indicating that the probability of a member advancing to a prestigious committee increases if another member from his or her state on that committee leaves the House. The coefficients on the inverse terms variable, the party loyalty variable, the southern Democrat dummy, and the deviation from the median voter variable do not have coefficients that are bounded away from zero.

The number of terms served has a statistically significant effect on the probability that a member not on a prestigious committee will leave the House. However, this coefficient is negative, indicating that the probability of a member leaving the House decreases the longer he or she serves. I expect that this result stems from the fact that when I compute the entrepreneurship reputation scores I lose members with high seniority because the legislative data only go back to the 94th Congress. Open seats in the Senate have a positive effect on leaving, as predicted, but the coefficient is only marginally statistically significant. The coefficient on the age variable is much smaller than its standard error.

The model does not do very well in explaining Republican mobility with respect to exclusive committees. None of the variables in the model save party loyalty has a statistically significant impact on the probability of advancing to an exclusive committee, but age has a significant and unexpectedly negative impact on the probability of leaving the institution.

Analysis of Mobility in the Party Hierarchy

An analysis of all of the possible transitions a member could make into the party hierarchy and to different positions in that hierarchy would require an entire chapter by itself. Instead of analyzing all of these transitions, I simply look at whether a member made a transition from not having a party leadership position to having one. Although treating all party positions the same is a substantial simplification, it makes the analysis much more tractable.[32]

Table 5.4 reports the analysis of mobility in the party hierarchy. For Democrats, the coefficients on the entrepreneurship variables follow the same

32. Party leadership positions for the Democrats include the positions of Speaker, majority leader, majority whip, chief deputy whip, deputy whip, assistant whips/zone whips, and at-large whips. I also count the chair and vice chair of the Democratic Congressional Campaign Committee and the chair and secretary of the Democratic Caucus as party leadership positions. Republican Party leadership positions include minority leader; minority whip; chief deputy and deputy whips; assistant minority whips (regional and assistant to regional whips); the chair, vice chair, and secretary of the Republican Conference, and the chair of the National Republican Congressional Committee. In this part of the analysis, N_{i12} equals the number of party leadership positions that became vacant plus the number of new positions created in a Congress.

TABLE 5.4. Effects of Legislative Entrepreneurship on Mobility in the Party Hierarchy

Variable	Democrats	Republicans
	Probability of Advancing	
Intercept	−5.085	−2.679
	(1.514)	(1.160)
Entrepreneurship reputation score	−.631	−.005
	(.298)	(.270)
Cumulative entrepreneurship score	.623	−.0001
	(.262)	(.207)
1/(terms served)	2.421	−.263
	(1.682)	(1.365)
Party loyalty	−.160	−.631
	(.099)	(.176)
State delegation vacancy	.986	.565
	(.215)	(.257)
Deviation from median voter	−.350	1.604
	(.546)	(.771)
	Probability of Exiting	
Intercept	−5.085	−2.550
	(1.514)	(.949)
Terms served	−.631	.195
	(.298)	(.098)
Age	.623	−.048
	(.262)	(.017)
Open seat in Senate	2.421	.626
	(1.682)	(.351)
Open seat in governorship	−.160	.585
	(.099)	(1.168)
Previous vote share	.986	−.624
	(.215)	(.392)
Unfavorable redistricting	−.350	−.339
	(.546)	(1.034)
N	867	723
−2 × log likelihood	1,263.13	933.86

Note: Entries are the coefficients in the vectors β_{12} and β_{1w} from equations 5.2 and 5.1. Standard errors are in parentheses.

N denotes the number of individuals not in prestigious positions.

pattern as that seen in the analysis of mobility in the committee hierarchy. The coefficient on the entrepreneurship reputation score is negative and slightly larger in size than the coefficient on the cumulative entrepreneurship score. Because both coefficients are statistically significant, we can infer that the net effect of legislative entrepreneurship is slightly negative for freshman members

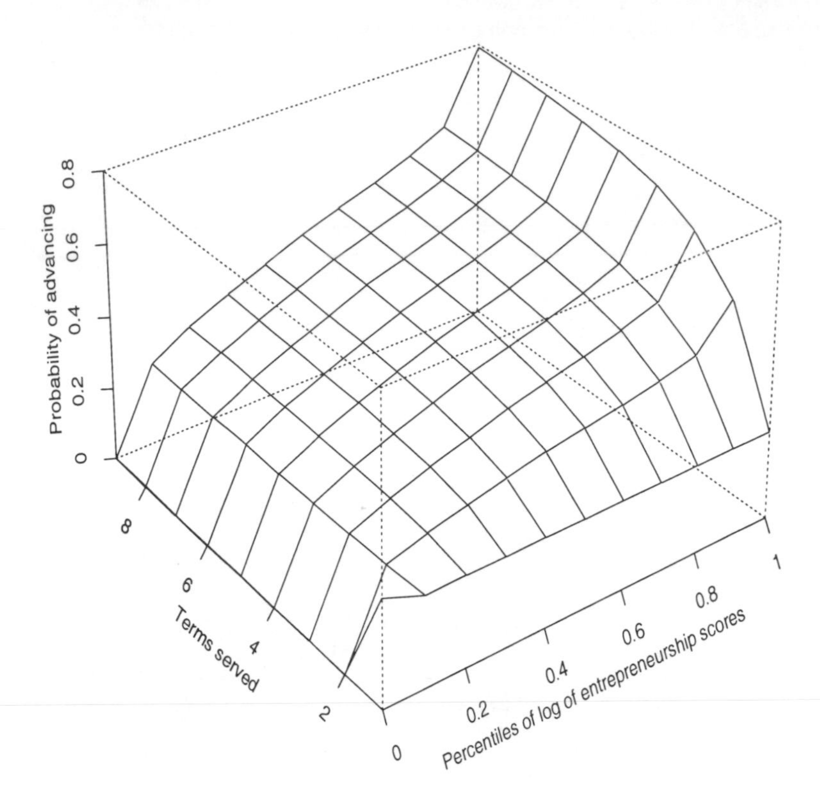

Fig. 5.2. Effect of legislative entrepreneurship and terms served on the probability of advancing to a party leadership position, Democrats

but positive for nonfreshmen. The coefficient on the state vacancy variable is positive and statistically significant, as expected. None of the other variables has a coefficient that is bounded away from zero.

As far as exits go, the previous vote share variable has a positive and statistically significant impact on exiting, as expected. The age variable also has a statistically significant coefficient, but it is unexpectedly negative.

Figure 5.2 shows simulated transition probabilities for members across the range of entrepreneurship scores and terms served in the sample. The marginal effects of legislative entrepreneurship are quite large. After the first term, the probability of a member with an entrepreneurship score in the top percentiles advancing to a party leadership position is three to four times higher than that of a member with a score in the bottom percentiles.

For Republicans, neither of the entrepreneurship variables has a coefficient that is bounded away from zero. Three variables have a statistically significant impact on the probability that a Republican will advance to a party leadership position. A Republican member's probability of advancing increases the farther his or her NOMINATE score is from that of the median voter and whether a position is vacated by someone from his or her state. The more loyal the member is to the leadership the lower is the probability of advancing. The results on the deviation from median voter and party loyalty variables seem to be driven by the ascension in the leadership ranks of more extreme and confrontational Republicans (cf. Connelly and Pitney 1994). As with the analysis for Democrats, age has a negative effect on the probability of exiting.

Discussion

In this chapter, I have argued that members engage in legislative entrepreneurship because institutional features of the House provide incentives for them to do so. I considered how members could use the prospect of promotion to prestigious positions in the committee and party hierarchies in the House to encourage legislative entrepreneurship. The analysis of mobility within these hierarchies provides support for this argument. Democrats who engage in higher levels of legislative entrepreneurship increase their chances of advancing to full committee, subcommittee, and party leadership positions. Promotions appear to be rewards for entrepreneurial activity. The analysis of Republican mobility does not provide support for this argument, as legislative entrepreneurship did not have significant effects on any type of advancement in committee or party hierarchies.

The analysis in this chapter has important implications for the recent work on participation in the legislative process. Hall (1996) draws a distinction between his behavioral focus and institutional focuses. He claims (239–40) that the

> "division of labor" in Congress is no structural feature, no matter of organizational design, rational or otherwise, that is somehow imposed and maintained. Rather, it bubbles up from the day-to-day decisions of individual members as they decide how to best allocate the time, energy, and other resources of their enterprise on the numerous issues that arise both within and beyond the panels to which they are assigned.

Hall finds that one way institutions enter into the participation equation is that a member's institutional position—specifically whether or not he or she is a full committee or subcommittee leader—has consistently positive effects on participation.

While this analysis strongly concurs with Hall's behavioral focus on individuals and their quotidian decisions to engage in legislative activity, it also reemphasizes the importance of institutions in shaping those decisions. While the parliamentary rights and resources that accrue to members when they obtain a prestigious position enhance their capacity to participate, members who advance to these positions generally have displayed a propensity for participating at high levels as LEs *prior* to advancing. It is not clear how much of their participation after they obtain prestigious positions is due to the institutional resources they obtain when they advance to these positions.

Furthermore, institutional arrangements can have a profound effect on participation by providing incentives for members who are not in prestigious positions to engage in legislative entrepreneurship. Since LEs have a higher probability of advancing to prestigious positions, members should be motivated to participate at high levels. Although Hall contends that participation is not matter of organizational design, my analysis suggests that organizational factors—in terms of who gets to serve in prestigious positions—can play an important role in influencing participation. While institutional features cannot guarantee that members will participate as LEs, they serve to encourage individuals to choose to participate to that degree.

The analysis in this chapter also has important implications for the recent literature on information and parties in Congress. Although the informational and partisan perspectives appear to be competing explanations of legislative organization, prominent congressional scholars have argued that future research on Congress should focus on the possible connections between these perspectives (Shepsle and Weingast 1994; Rohde 1994). The analysis in this chapter is a step in that direction.

Informational theories are primarily concerned with how legislators organize their institution to promote the gathering and sharing of information. Partisan theories are concerned with how party organizations solve collective decision-making problems so that their members can pass legislation that enhances party reputations. Although proponents of informational theories have discounted the importance of parties in Congress (e.g., Krehbiel 1993, 1997), my analysis indicates that party organizations play a role in ensuring that members who are competent at informational activities occupy important positions in the institution. I have presented empirical evidence that indicates that legislative entrepreneurship is a determinant of advancement to party leadership positions for members of the majority party.[33] I have also argued that an im-

33. These results are not driven solely by the informational component of legislative entre-

portant part of legislative entrepreneurship is gathering and communicating policy-relevant information. Individuals with superior entrepreneurial ability are predisposed to use the resources associated with party leadership positions to engage in informational activities that benefit members individually and collectively (Gilligan and Krehbiel 1990). Promoting those who have demonstrated superior entrepreneurial ability to institutional leadership positions is one way in which party organizations promote the passage of collective benefits legislation (cf. Cox and McCubbins 1993). In order to understand intrainstitutional mobility in the House and explain legislative entrepreneurship, it is necessary to consider how the informational and partisan theories interact and to integrate elements from these different theoretical perspectives.

Although my analysis is not a coherent synthesis of the different theories of congressional institutions, it illustrates how the different behaviors and institutional features that these theories are concerned with can interact. By pushing the analysis down to the individual level and looking at how individuals move within committee and party structures, I have found that both of these structures are important for understanding why members would acquire policy information, build logrolling coalitions, and push legislation through the House.

A remaining question has to do with the generalizability of the results of this analysis to the House under Republican control. The analysis presented in this chapter found that neither the entrepreneurship reputation score nor the cumulative entrepreneurship score has statistically significant effects on mobility in the committee or party hierarchies for Republicans. My interpretation of these results is that minority party members have a much smaller interest in promoting LEs since the positions that minority party members occupy are much less important legislatively than positions controlled by the majority party. During the period under analysis, Republicans saw themselves as cut out of the legislative process (Rohde 1991, 120–38), and the severe limits on opportunities for enacting legislation are reflected in the rejection of the mobility hypothesis for the minority party. In the next chapter, I consider how matters have changed with regard to legislative entrepreneurship since the Republicans assumed the majority in the 104th Congress.

---

preneurship. I reestimated the models discussed earlier, treating the policy knowledge measure as separate from the other legislative entrepreneurship measures. The measure of policy knowledge by itself did not have statistically significant effects on advancement.

CHAPTER 6

Legislative Entrepreneurship and the Republican Takeover

The most compelling explanation for why members of the House would engage in legislative entrepreneurship is that this activity enhances their prospects for advancement to prestigious positions in the committee and party hierarchies. This explanation, however, seems valid only for members of the majority party—that is, Democrats for the period analyzed in the previous chapter. In this chapter, I consider how this explanation extends to Republicans after they assumed the majority in the 104th House.

Any extensions of the arguments I have made in this book to the Republican-controlled House must be speculative at this time. In some sense, congressional scholars were fortunate to have the variable of majority status held constant for the past four decades. The "structural break" of the Republican takeover in the 104th Congress will no doubt cause many headaches for congressional scholars who undertake longitudinal analysis, and the analysis presented in this book is no exception. The Republicans changed the structure of the institution in important ways, some of which call into question whether the incentive mechanisms that I claim the Democrats employed to promote legislative entrepreneurship will have the same effect for the new majority party. These institutional changes were every bit as sweeping as the reforms of the 1970s, and they make it unlikely that we can apply to the Republican-controlled Congress the same models we used when the Democrats were in the majority. The change in majority status and the subsequent institutional upheaval and general tumult that has characterized the Republican-controlled House unfortunately place limits on the kind of analysis we can perform for recent Congresses. Systematic analysis similar to what I presented in previous chapters is of dubious reliability until we can reasonably assume that the institution has settled into a "steady state."

Although one of the key innovations of this book is the systematic analysis of legislative entrepreneurship, the change of the majority in the House requires a shift in the mode of analysis. In this chapter, I present more qualitatively oriented analysis to demonstrate how my arguments about legislative entrepreneurship and career concerns extend to the Republican House. I concede that this analysis amounts to at best storytelling and at worst selection on the dependent variable. I remind the reader that what follows is not meant to provide definitive answers. I hope only to allay the initial concerns of those who object to the generalizability of my arguments until a more systematic analysis is feasible. The evidence that I present in this chapter gives hope that such a systematic analysis will reveal that the mobility hypothesis will hold for the Republican majority.

The Republican Takeover, Institutional Reform, and the Contract with America

The Republicans took control of the House after the 1994 elections with an extremely ambitious legislative agenda. As part of their electoral strategy to end their minority status in the House, more than 300 Republican candidates endorsed a platform known as the Contract with America. The "contract" was a list of 10 legislative items that Republican incumbents and challengers promised to bring to a floor vote within the first 100 days of the 104th Congress (Kaplan 1994). The items included legislation to balance the federal budget, grant the president a line item veto, crack down on crime, cut taxes for the middle class, reduce the capital gains tax, reform welfare and product liability law, and impose term limits on members of Congress ("Republicans' " 1994; "House GOP" 1994).

It would have been quite a feat to have floor votes on this kind of legislation over an entire session of Congress. Yet, after the electorate gave them the opportunity to deliver on their promises, the Republicans accomplished the Herculean task of drafting, introducing, amending, debating, and holding floor votes on legislation addressing all of the contract's 10 items in the first 100 days (Cassata 1995a).[1] It is astonishing that the Republicans were able to make the transition from a minority, allegedly cut out of the legislative process by the Democrats, to a majority party and crank out sweeping legislation at a rate that equaled the push for the agendas of the New Deal in 1933 and the Great Society in 1965 (Cassata 1995b). Although most of the contract legislation died in the Senate or fell victim to the president's veto pen, threatening to make the 104th Congress one of the most *un*productive in modern times (Babson 1995b; Doherty 1996), the relative ease and speed with which Republicans pushed this legislation through the House have important implications for the arguments about legislative entrepreneurship that I make in this book.

The Republicans' goal of getting the contract legislation to the floor in the first 100 days required a substantial amount of entrepreneurial activity. I have

1. Some Democrats would argue that not much debate and deliberation took place, however (Hook 1995).

argued that whether or not members engage in legislative entrepreneurship depends crucially on the institutional features of prestigious positions. The new Republican majority changed the structure of the institution in ways that call into question whether the incentive mechanisms that I claim the Democrats employed to promote legislative entrepreneurship will have the same effect for the new majority party.

Some of the changes that are most relevant for whether the mobility hypothesis will hold for the Republican House have to do with subcommittees. The number of subcommittees was reduced, and the power of subcommittees and their chairs was weakened as more authority was placed in the hands of full committee chairs (Aldrich and Rohde 1997). Full committee chairs not only were given control over all committee staff, including staff associated with subcommittees, but they were also given the power to appoint subcommittee chairs. Thus, subcommittee chairs lost two sources of power that granted them independence from full committee chairs (Smith and Lawrence 1997). These changes have rendered subcommittee leadership positions less attractive and have reduced their capacity to motivate members to engage in legislative entrepreneurship.

Although full committee chairs were strengthened at the expense of subcommittees, reforms also limited the power of full committee chairs. Chairs were limited to serving six-year terms and were prohibited from using proxy votes in committees. Under Democratic control, chairs used proxy votes "to create quorums and to control the outcomes of votes when no other members of their party were physically present at committee meetings" (Aldrich and Rohde 1997, 551). Some committees and their chairs were bypassed altogether as the Republicans resorted to ad hoc task forces to perform functions typically performed by committees (Kalb 1995). The power of full committees was generally weakened as more authority was concentrated in the central party leadership (Aldrich and Rohde 1997).

These reforms should lead to a decrease in the ability of committee leadership positions to provide incentives for members to engage in legislative entrepreneurship. Yet these reforms also appear to have increased the attractiveness of party leadership positions. The lasting impact of these changes cannot be known at this time.[2] However, anecdotal evidence indicates that Republicans

---

2. Some evidence suggests that the impact of these changes may not extend beyond the 104th Congress. The 105th Congress seemed much more like the textbook Congress under Democratic control in the postreform era (Koszczuk 1997b). For example, one of the goals of the central party leadership at the beginning of the 105th was to shift power back to committee chairs and allow committees to play their traditional roles in the legislative process (Freedman 1996). Thus, it may be that the institution in subsequent Congresses will operate more as it did when Democrats were in the majority.

are using these prestigious positions in a way that is consistent with the mobility hypothesis.

Party Leadership in the 104th: Dick Armey Revisited

Despite the unity fostered by the Republicans' sweeping electoral victory in 1994, they still needed individuals to assume the role of LEs if the contract legislation was going to make it to the floor as they had promised. They needed individuals to push this legislation and build and maintain supporting coalitions, which involved soothing tensions within the nascent majority. A unified block of conservative freshman Republicans clashed with moderates, making it difficult for some bills to progress through the legislative process (Koszczuk 1995a). Given the length of time that the Republicans had languished in the minority, there was considerable doubt that their party had an adequate stock of entrepreneurial members who could rise to the task (cf. Fenno 1997).

A key institutional reform of the 104th that would affect the ability of Republicans to deliver on their contract promises was the strengthening of party leaders, especially Speaker Newt Gingrich (Koszczuk 1995b). While the strengthening of the Speakership substantially enhanced his potential influence over the legislative process and the fortunes of contract proposals, Gingrich lacked the experience necessary to accomplish much legislatively. Prior to assuming the Speakership, Gingrich did not have much of a legislative record, having never authored or pushed a major piece of legislation (Gettinger 1994). In half of the eight Congresses in which Gingrich served prior to the Republican takeover, his legislative entrepreneurship scores fall at or below the bottom 10 percent of Republican scores. Gingrich's approach to leadership in the Republican Party had more to do with "throwing bombs" (i.e., exposing scandals) that would hurt the Democratic Party and its leaders than it did with passing a legislative program (Connelly and Pitney 1994; Barry 1989). Although he clearly had considerable support from the Republican conference due to his devotion to and eventual success in wresting the Republicans from their seemingly permanent minority status, Gingrich did not seem to have the practical legislative skills necessary to put together coalitions and push the contract legislation through the House.

That task fell to the new majority leader, Dick Armey. With Gingrich's blessing, Armey assumed responsibility for the quotidian duties of pushing and passing contract legislation: "The flashy Gingrich [was] usually out front, articulating the Republican vision. Armey hammer[ed] together the policy" (Koszczuk 1996, 524). While Gingrich carried with him a laminated copy of the contract, often displaying it proudly it at press conferences as the Republicans passed contract items, Armey symbolically carried a copy of the House's weekly legislative schedule. Armey accomplished the often difficult job of holding together the coalitions of conservative and moderate Republicans that were necessary to pass the contract legislation (Babson 1995a).

The case of Dick Armey provides support for my arguments concerning legislative entrepreneurship. I began this book by recounting one of Armey's entrepreneurial efforts involving the closing of military bases. The success that Armey realized on the difficult issue of base closings sent a strong signal about his entrepreneurial ability. Armey's entrepreneurship concerning the base-closing bill contributed to his rapid rise in the Republican Party leadership. Armey ascended to the top rungs of the party leadership after he successfully campaigned for the chairmanship of the Republican Conference in the 103d Congress. He won the number three spot in the Republican leadership by means of the same methodical vote gathering that led to the passage of his base-closing bill (Kuntz 1992). In the 104th Congress, Armey was elected to the position of majority leader even though he had served only five terms in Congress. His past entrepreneurial efforts and subsequent rise in the House Republican Party hierarchy are consistent with the argument that members motivate each other to engage in entrepreneurial activity by promoting LEs. I have also argued that by using entrepreneurship as a criterion for promotion members can ensure that more competent legislators will assume influential positions in the House and that this will enhance the House's capacity for producing legislation. As majority leader, Armey's entrepreneurial ability enabled him to orchestrate the passage in the House of many of the key bills in the GOP's contract.

Although Newt Gingrich's ascendancy in the Republican Party is not consistent with the mobility hypothesis, his difficulty in holding onto the Speakership is. Gingrich's tenure as Speaker was very short and extremely tumultuous. After his narrow reelection as Speaker in the 105th Congress, his Speakership was threatened by a coup attempt orchestrated by Republican insurgents. After the Republicans lost House seats in the 1998 elections, Gingrich vacated the Speakership.

Gingrich's *lack* of legislative entrepreneurship helps to explain the disaffection that many in the Republican Conference—including Dick Armey—felt toward Gingrich. While his ethics problems were clearly a factor, Gingrich's troubles as Speaker also stemmed from his lack of legislative savvy: "Gingrich conceives of himself not as a legislative sausage-maker but as a social visionary whose talents are best suited to such pursuits as designing the future of America and inspiring democracies worldwide" (Koszczuk 1997a, 2031). Gingrich demonstrated his lack of "sausage-making" skills by taking actions that were detrimental to holding coalitions together. For example, he promised Transportation Committee chair Bud Shuster (R–PA) that he could offer an amendment to the 1997 budget agreement that would increase funds for transportation projects. Shuster's amendment threatened to sink the historic budget deal, forcing members to make the politically difficult decision between sending more federal money back to their districts and providing the collective good of a balanced budget. Gingrich's lieutenants scrambled to hold together a coalition that narrowly defeated Shuster's amendment, but "once again, they felt they had been left to clean up the Speaker's mess" (Koszczuk 1997c, 1415).

Gingrich's behavior strained his relationship with fellow Republicans, leading to an abortive coup attempt in July of 1997 by GOP insurgents, which included some of Gingrich's top lieutenants. Interestingly, the coup attempt helped to reemphasize Gingrich's dependence on Armey. Armey had participated in the meetings where Gingrich's ouster was discussed, and later he informed the Speaker of the coup attempt. Despite Armey's participation in the plot to oust him, Gingrich reaffirmed Armey's importance to his Speakership and his central role in getting things done in the House. In an interview shortly after the coup attempt, Gingrich claimed, "I said to Dick in the middle of all of this nonsense that the morning I had to put armor on to stand with him I will leave, that I am always vulnerable to Dick Armey. And I would not stay here if I were not capable of doing all that" (Eilperin and Vande Hei 1997). It is telling that in the aftermath of the coup attempt Gingrich grew closer to Armey but not to the other leaders, including Bill Paxon (R–NY), Majority Whip Tom Delay (R–TX), and then Conference chair John Boehner (R–OH), who participated in the plot.[3]

Gingrich's troubles did not end with the coup attempt. Instead of gaining seats, as the party that does not control the presidency typically does in a midterm election, Republicans lost a net of five seats in the 1998 election, leaving them with the thinnest majority in the House since 1955. Gingrich received much of the blame for the Republicans' disappointing show at the polls. Republican House members in part blamed the loss of seats on Gingrich's failed strategy of focusing on the impeachment of President Clinton instead of on legislative accomplishments (Katz 1998b). Members expressed interest in replacing Gingrich out of the fear that his continuing leadership missteps would land the Republicans back in the minority.

Gingrich resigned the Speakership after Robert Livingston (R–LA) announced that he would challenge Gingrich for the post. At the beginning of the 104th Congress, Gingrich had picked Livingston for the chair of the Appropriations Committee over four more senior members. I discuss in detail in the next section how Livingston's ascension to the chair of Appropriations might be consistent with the mobility hypothesis, and so I will not go into much

3. Gingrich denied that the reason he remained close with Armey was because Armey alerted him to the coup attempt (Eilperin and Vande Hei 1997).

detail here about how Livingston's record of legislative entrepreneurship made him an appealing alternative to Gingrich. In his campaign for the Speakership, Livingston called attention to Gingrich's lack of attention to legislative matters and how his own experience would enable him to perform better. As Speaker, Livingston would "concentrate more on the nuts and bolts of advancing a legislative agenda than Gingrich" (Katz 1998b, 2990).

Though Livingston won the Republicans' nomination for Speaker, he withdrew his name from consideration and announced that he would quit the House (43 days after Gingrich announced his resignation) after his marital infidelities came to light. Republicans quickly turned to Dennis Hastert (R–IL) to fill the Speakership. Like Livingston, Hastert was viewed as more pragmatic than Gingrich and well equipped to handle the difficult task of managing a thin majority.

This perception of Hastert in part stemmed from his strong record of legislative entrepreneurship. Hastert's "ability to forge consensus made him a go-to guy for Gingrich" on key pieces of legislation and won him the reputation of "an effective legislative tactician" (Katz 1999, 58). In the Congress preceding Hastert's ascension to Speaker, the *Congressional Quarterly Weekly Report* identified him as one of the 12 members who made a critical difference because he "was a guiding force in practically everything [the Republicans] accomplished" ("Scandal" 1998). Hastert forged legislation to give more authority to managed care patients, diffusing criticism that Republicans were ignoring the issue and removing a possible campaign issue for Democrats ("Scandal" 1998). He also won a major legislative success as chair of an antidrug task force when he managed to tack $690 million for antidrug efforts onto the fiscal 1999 omnibus appropriations bill. However, "his biggest contribution was not in pushing any particular legislative intitiative but in advancing all of them as chief deputy majority whip" ("Scandal" 1998).

Hastert's skills with respect to coalition building and pushing legislation made him an attractive choice for Speaker. In a gesture meant to symbolize that his leadership would be more concerned with the day to day legislative activities of the House, Haster broke with precedent and delivered his acceptance speech from the well of the House, claiming, "My legislative home is here on the floor with you, and so is my heart" (Katz 1999, 59). Hastert's advancement to the top position in the Republican Party hierarchy in the House appears to support the mobility hypothesis.

The Speakership was not the only position to experience turmoil in the aftermath of the 1998 elections. Dick Armey drew challenges for the majority leader position from Steve Largent (R–OK) and Jennifer Dunn (R–WA).[4]

---

4. Dennis Hastert was nominated for the majority leader slot, though he did not actively

Armey came under fire for a variety of reasons, including concerns about his political judgment, his poor media skills, and his trustworthiness after the aborted coup against Gingrich. Armey retained his slot, and his record of legislative entrepreneurship seemed to play a key role in his victory. In promoting their candidacies, Largent and Dunn argued "that the party need[ed] a more telegenic leader who is capable of forging coalitions across the ideologically divided party" ("Majority" 1998). Yet, "neither Largent nor Dunn [was] considered a master of the legislative process—a serious concern when running for a position responsible for managing the House floor" (Katz 1998c). In contrast to Largent's and Dunn's campaigns, Armey "emphasized his record of shepherding bills through the legislative process and building momentum behind proposed policy reforms on issues such as taxes and education" ("Majority" 1998). Armey's campaign was successful, though it became clear that his role in the new leadership team would draw less on his weak communications skills and more on the strengths he has demonstrated on the floor (Doherty 1998a). Even though Armey does not enjoy the stature he did when Gingrich was Speaker, Hastert has been "relying heavily" on him to help with the difficult task of running the House with such a thin majority (Koszczuk 1999; Martinez 1999).

Although the selection process for Republican Party leaders for the 106th Congress was one of the most raucous on record, as the dust has settled we find support for the mobility hypothesis. Members' records on activities that constitute legislative entrepreneurship were a key consideration in the selection of individuals for the top slots in the Republican Party hierarchy. House Republicans have opted for individuals who have demonstrated their ability to tackle the difficult tasks that are necessary to advance a legislative agenda.

Seniority Violations in the Republican Congress

Seniority violations in the selection of committee chairs in the 104th Congress also provide support for the mobility hypothesis. At the beginning of the 104th Congress, Carlos J. Moorhead (R–CA) was in position to take over the chair of either the Commerce Committee (formerly known as Energy and Commerce) or the Judiciary Committee. Moorhead had served as the ranking minority member on Energy and Commerce in the 103d Congress and was the most senior Republican member on the Judiciary Committee to return to the 104th. However, Newt Gingrich, who handpicked the committee chairs for the 104th Congress, passed over Moorhead for *both* of these slots.[5] Instead he selected

campaign for the position. Hastert pledged support to Dick Armey in the race, and honored this pledge after Armey refused to release him from it (Eilperin 1998).

5. Even though Gingrich's choices had to be approved by the Republican Committee on

Henry Hyde (R–IL) for the chair of Judiciary and Thomas Bliley (R–VA) for the chair of Commerce.

Why did Gingrich violate the seniority norm twice to deny Moorhead a committee chair? A possible answer lies in the entrepreneurial records of the three members involved. Moorhead was not a very dynamic legislator. He was "a soft-spoken, little-noticed member who depend[ed] on cue cards for his public comments" (Hosansky 1994). Prior to the 103d Congress, Moorhead's unassertive style was seen as limiting his ability to advance the Republican's agenda on Energy and Commerce. The longstanding dissatisfaction with Moorhead led House Republicans to discuss overstepping him for the ranking minority member slot in the 103d Congress (Duncan 1993, 182). Although he had won some legislative victories with his "nonthreatening" approach in previous Congresses, this approach seemed ill suited for tackling the issues on the Republican agenda in the 104th.

"The widely respected" Hyde and "the more aggressive" Bliley, however, have been much more assertive in their legislative efforts (Foerstel 1994). Hyde is best known for his entrepreneurial activity on the issue of abortion. As a freshman, he sponsored an amendment that prohibited federal funding for abortions. The first time he introduced the measure he did so at the request of better known Republican legislators who thought that Hyde, a less visible freshman, would draw less fire than they would. Since that time, Hyde has made the issue his own, displaying a mastery of legislative strategy in keeping the issue on the agenda and winning passage of his legislation concerning abortion. Hyde "has pursued the issue with great ingenuity and persistence" (Barone, Ujifusa, and Matthews 1979, 248) and "has been ingenious in finding programs to which he can attach his amendments and in devising procedures that require them to be considered" (Barone and Ujifusa 1983, 340). His proposals have consistently won passage in the House, and although the Senate has generally been less willing to accept bans on abortion funding, he has usually prevailed in conference committee deliberations. In the 1980s, Hyde expanded his legislative agenda to include other issues. He has become "indispensable to Republicans as a point man on defense and foreign policy issues" (Duncan 1991, 432). His efforts on these issues and abortion have helped him establish a reputation as the best debater in the House and one of the Republican Party's "most competent legislators" (Barone and Ujifusa 1983, 340).

Bliley has also established a favorable reputation as an LE. As a minority member of Energy and Commerce, he demonstrated an ability to work with the often contentious chair, John Dingell (D–MI), and became one of the most activist Republicans on a committee dominated by Democrats (Duncan 1993,

---

Committees and then submitted as nominations for a vote by the entire Republican Conference, there was little doubt that he would get his way (Foerstel 1994).

1589). Bliley "has taken the Republican lead on health issues on the committee, resolving several legal disputes relating to drug companies" (Hosansky 1994). He has earned a reputation as "an expert on pharmaceutical issues" and both Republicans and Democrats have given him "high marks" for "for fairness and hard work" (Hosansky 1995). Bliley "steered legislation through the 101st Congress to resolve legal conflicts over the production of so-called orphan drugs, which treat diseases so rare that there may not be a great enough market to support their development" (Hosansky 1995). He has also negotiated compromises that resulted in the passage of bills concerning generic drugs and drug discounts for purchases made by the Department of Veterans' Affairs.

The anecdotal evidence about the relative legislative activity of Moorhead, Hyde, and Bliley is supported by the data on legislative entrepreneurship. Figure 6.1 is a time-series plot of the entrepreneurship scale scores for Moorhead, Hyde, and Bliley in each of the Congresses in which they served together.[6] Hyde's scores exceed Moorhead's in eight of the 10 Congresses in which they served together. Despite being several terms junior to Moorhead, Bliley's scores are greater than Moorhead's in five of the seven Congresses in which they served together.

The patterns of legislative entrepreneurship for these three members help explain the seniority violations on the Commerce and Judiciary Committees. These committees had jurisdiction over key items on the Republican agenda—about half of the items in the Contract with America fell under the jurisdiction of these committees (Jacoby and Kahn 1994). These items included the reform of product liability law, crime control, congressional term limits, health care for illegal immigrants, telecommunications law, food safety regulations, and the reauthorization of hazardous waste and safe drinking water laws. I contend that one of the main reasons why Gingrich selected Bliley and Hyde over Moorhead is because they had greater potential for building coalitions and pushing the legislation addressing these items. The Republicans had promised major legislative action if they attained a majority in the House. Gingrich saw Bliley and Hyde as two individuals qualified to deliver on those promises. Thus, by rewarding Bliley and Hyde for demonstrating their entrepreneurial abilities with chairs to important committees, Gingrich sent a strong signal to Republicans about the rewards of entrepreneurial activity as well as ensuring that he had entrepreneurial legislators in positions where they could get things done in the House.

The other major seniority violation that occurred in the 104th Congress

6. Although the empirical analysis indicated that the cumulative entrepreneurship score and the entrepreneurship reputation score are what matters for advancement for Democrats, I could not compute these scores for Moorhead because he entered Congress before the legislative data I use became available.

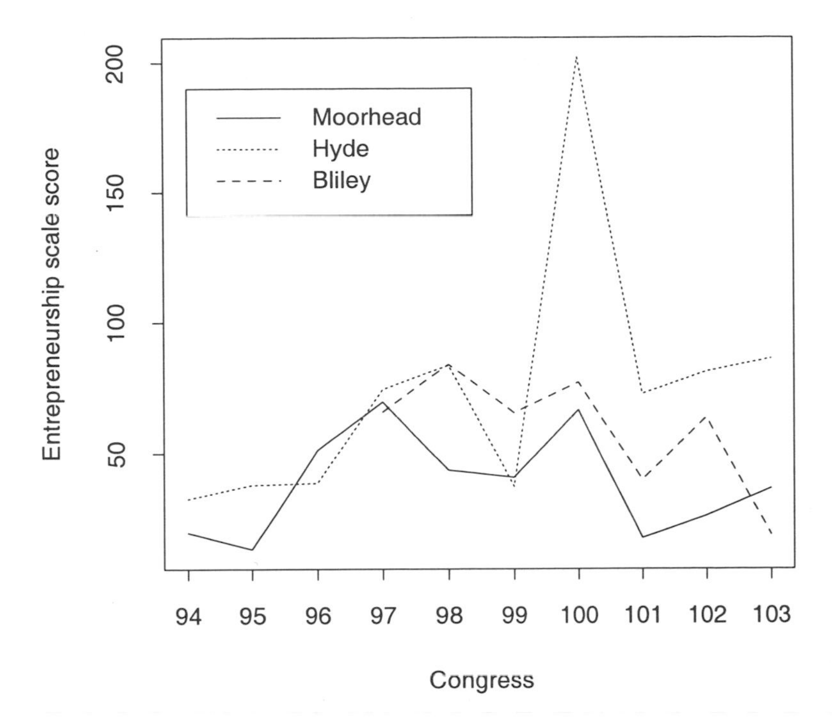

Fig. 6.1. Entrepreneurship scale scores for representatives Moorhead, Hyde, and Bliley

does not unambiguously support the mobility hypothesis. The most senior Republican member on Appropriations, Joe McDade (R–PA), was prevented from assuming the chairmanship because he was under indictment at the time. The leadership passed over the next most senior member, John Myers (R–IN) because it did not consider him to be "the right person to initiate the huge budget cuts favored by Republicans" (Kahn and Burger 1994). It is not clear whether this means that the leadership thought Myers did not have the legislative skills to push the cuts through the House or whether he was simply too pro-spending. As the ranking member of the Energy and Water Development Subcommittee of Appropriations, Myers was a staunch defender of spending for public works projects that more fiscally conservative Republicans sought to cut. "Myers had particularly irked Gingrich and his loyalists in 1993 when he actively lobbied against the Penny-Kasich proposal to cut $90 billion in federal spending over five years" (Duncan and Lawrence 1995, 471). Myers appeared to be more

TABLE 6.1. Party Leadership Loyalty Scores for the Top Five Republicans on Appropriations, 94th through the 103d Congresses

Congress	McDade	Myers	Young	Regula	Livingston
94th	.456	.844	.745	.739	—
95th	.527	.888	.720	.797	.720
96th	.616	.904	.766	.846	.877
97th	.457	.825	.578	.722	.831
98th	.512	.769	.658	.688	.893
99th	.457	.648	.638	.601	.815
100th	.506	.678	.632	.629	.728
101st	.600	.729	.715	.711	.819
102d	.686	.763	.807	.736	.866
103d	.753	.779	.825	.813	.892
Mean (95th through the 103d)	.568	.776	.704	.727	.827

loyal to the Appropriations Committee than to the Republican leadership. Bill Young (R–FL) and Ralph Regula (R–OH) were also passed over for the chairmanship of the full committee, although they each obtained Appropriations subcommittee chairs.

The full committee chairmanship went to Robert Livingston, who ranked fifth in seniority among Republicans on the committee. One possible reason for these seniority violations is that Livingston's ethos on spending appeared to be much more in tune with the Republican leadership than that of the more senior members of the panel (Kahn and Burger 1994). Prior to the 104th, Livingston's party leadership loyalty scores were substantially higher than those of Myers, Young, Regula, and especially McDade (see table 6.1), but there is some evidence that Livingston's legislative skills also played a part in his selection. Prior to becoming chair, Livingston had developed a reputation for sensitivity to the central role that bipartisanship plays in coalition building on Appropriations. Livingston had "developed a respect for the bipartisanship that keeps work on the committee's must-pass bills humming without the acrimony that tends to paralyze other legislation" (Koszczuk 1994, 3350). Despite his fervently conservative voting record, Livingston "has cut deals with moderates and liberals alike," demonstrating that he knows what it takes to build a coalition (3350). These skills proved crucial for pushing through the spending cuts that were central to the Republican agenda. They also seemed crucial in Livingston's abortive quest to succeed Gingrich as Speaker (Katz 1998a, 1998b).

The data on legislative entrepreneurship provide a modicum of support for this argument. Table 6.2 contains the entrepreneurship scale scores for the five most senior Republican members of Appropriations. Livingston's mean entre-

TABLE 6.2. Legislative Entrepreneurship Scale Scores for the Top Five Republicans on Appropriations, 94th through the 103d Congresses

Congress	McDade	Myers	Young	Regula	Livingston
94th	38.288	21.417	32.819	50.775	—
95th	22.546	21.544	45.151	40.670	12.048
96th	49.877	11.822	48.193	36.723	37.113
97th	53.166	56.806	36.007	52.056	51.723
98th	42.861	28.863	59.525	65.760	101.462
99th	42.638	4.941	39.997	54.244	23.080
100th	57.520	34.189	34.529	84.023	27.227
101st	79.213	27.084	39.371	72.161	13.291
102d	29.151	14.109	38.732	70.676	33.698
103d	18.549	45.367	16.761	64.393	113.096
Mean (95th through the 103d)	43.947	27.191	39.807	60.078	45.860

preneurship scale score for the 95th through the 103d Congresses exceeds the mean scores for all but one of his more senior colleagues, though not by much. It is interesting that Livingston's entrepreneurship score for the Congress prior to the one in which he was promoted to chair was much higher than the scores of the others.

It is also interesting that a seniority violation did not occur on the Rules Committee. Gerald Solomon (R–NY), the senior Republican member on the committee, was selected as chair despite his questionable loyalty to Gingrich. Many knowledgeable observers expected Gingrich to bypass Solomon as a payback for Solomon's brief but vocal challenge to Gingrich to replace the retiring minority leader, Bob Michel (Kahn 1994). Yet Solomon assumed the chairmanship despite expectations that it would go to David Dreier (R–CA), the third-ranking Republican on Rules, or Robert Walker (R–PA), a parliamentary expert and close friend of Gingrich (Kahn and Burger 1994).

Loyalty to party leaders and entrepreneurship help explain why Solomon won out over the second-ranking Republican, James Quillen (R–TN), but not necessarily over Dreier. Both Solomon's entrepreneurship and loyalty scores are noticeably higher than Quillen's in every Congress in which they served together (see Tables 6.3 and 6.4). Solomon and Dreier's entrepreneurship and loyalty scores are comparable, but Dreier has somewhat higher scores in four out of the seven the Congresses in which they served together. So support for the mobility hypothesis in this case is mixed at best.

Discussion

The analysis in chapter 5 did not provide empirical support for the mobility

TABLE 6.3. Loyalty to Party Leadership Scores for Republicans on Rules, 95th through the 103d Congresses

Congress	Quillen	Solomon	Dreier	Goss
94th	.860	—	—	—
95th	.760	—	—	—
96th	.807	.934	—	—
97th	.807	.861	.964	—
98th	.860	.944	.910	—
99th	.773	.958	.916	—
100th	.778	.912	.976	—
101st	.759	.916	.928	.861
102d	.782	.932	.966	.919
103d	.661	.895	.947	.952

hypothesis for Republicans when they were the minority party in the House. I have presented evidence in this chapter suggesting that the mobility hypothesis may hold for Republicans now that they are in the majority. For example, the case of Dick Armey suggests that providing incentives for entrepreneurial activity through promotion to prestigious positions in the House paid off for the GOP in the 104th Congress. With entrepreneurial individuals like Armey in key positions, House Republicans were able to make the transition from minority to majority status with relative ease and accomplish the impressive feat of passing all but one of the items in the Contract with America in the House.

Except for a few pieces of legislation, these legislative successes did not extend beyond the House and result in the enactment of new laws. The failures

TABLE 6.4. Legislative Entrepreneurship Scale Scores for Republicans on Rules, 94th through the 103d Congresses

Congress	Quillen	Solomon	Dreier	Goss
94th	25.017	—	—	—
95th	18.434	—	—	—
96th	20.288	25.427	—	—
97th	20.960	50.718	40.506	—
98th	16.609	37.397	31.470	—
99th	15.954	17.493	64.417	—
100th	22.605	65.614	55.560	—
101st	7.636	50.546	82.482	24.805
102d	15.562	27.484	60.889	75.930
103d	3.674	39.150	65.302	102.952

of the 104th Congress accentuate the importance of taking into consideration the Senate and the president when building coalitions (Fenno 1997). The LEs who pushed the contract items through the House were somewhat shortsighted in this regard. Nevertheless, the Republicans were successful in delivering on their promise to bring up the contract items in the first 100 days, a major legislative feat that should not be discounted.

The Republicans' legislative accomplishments were more modest in the 105th and were largely overshadowed by the impeachment of the president. Splits within the Republican Conference and between the House and the Senate made the task of building coalitions especially difficult, and this was reflected in the legislative productivity of the House. The low point came when the House and Senate failed to pass a budget plan for fiscal year 1999—the first time that has happened since the existing budgeting procedures were established in 1974 (Doherty 1998b). Although several important pieces of legislation made significant progress or became law in the 105th, this Congress seems to be marked more for what it did not accomplish legislatively than for what it did. It is not clear whether the legislative shortcomings of the Republican House in the 105th are related to the amount of entrepreneurial activity undertaken by individual members. The anecdotal evidence discussed in this chapter indicates that as the majority party Republicans are using the structure of the institution to provide incentives for entrepreneurial activity, so we should expect to see no shortage of legislative entrepreneurship. We have yet to see what long-term effects this incentive system will have on the Republicans' ability to maintain control of the House and be effective as the majority party.

CHAPTER 7

Conclusion

Summary of Findings

The purpose of this book has been to explain why members of the House engage in legislative entrepreneurship. Understanding how and why members engage in this behavior is important to understanding how the House functions as a policy-making body. LEs drive much of the legislative production of the House, whether it be legislation involving major innovations in federal policy or more mundane "housekeeping" measures. If individual members of the House did not become LEs, the House as an institution would not be able to perform its fundamental duty of legislating.

The first potential explanation that I explored involved how legislative entrepreneurship directly affects members' efforts to win the support of their constituents. In chapter 3, I evaluated competing arguments about constituency response to legislative entrepreneurship. Some congressional scholars have argued that constituents respond positively to legislative activity, and in an electoral environment dominated by electronic media engaging in this activity is an important component of members' reelection strategies. Others have argued that constituents respond more to district service than legislative activities and that devoting resources to legislative activities at best does not help and at worst actually hurts members' reelection chances.

In the empirical analysis in chapter 3, I sought to evaluate these competing claims using data that are more appropriate for studying legislative entrepreneurship than those that have been employed previously. I examined several different dimensions of direct constituent response to legislative entrepreneurship and found little evidence that constituents respond to this activity in a way that would enhance members' reelection prospects. I did not find much support for the argument that members face severe tradeoffs between legislative activity in the Washington arena and constituency service activities in the district arena. However, I did find that entrepreneurial activity has a substantial negative effect on the probability that constituents will vote for a Democratic incumbent. The conservative conclusion that I drew from these results is that legislative entrepreneurship does not promote members' reelection chances through direct constituent response, so constituents' responses to this activity do not motivate members to become LEs.

I then considered another potential link between the reelection motive and legislative entrepreneurship by examining the relationship between campaign finance and this activity. Drawing on the recent literature on service-induced campaign contributions and contributions as investments, I considered the possibility that members provide entrepreneurial services to interest groups in exchange for campaign contributions. An underlying assumption of this analysis was that members of Congress have structured their electoral environment by enacting campaign finance laws that would enable them to provide legislative services to PACs in exchange for contributions. PACs seeking to influence the policies enacted by Congress would get more bang for their political buck if, instead of giving campaign money to those who simply cast a vote for or against a piece of legislation, they contributed to those who helped shape the legislation on which members voted. I also considered the argument that these kinds of investment relationships were not viable because of commitment and enforcement problems. The empirical analysis presented in chapter 4 failed to find a positive correlation between entrepreneurial activity and PAC contributions, indicating that legislative entrepreneurship is not an important factor in PACs' contribution decisions. Thus, members' needs in terms of campaign finance will not motivate them to engage in legislative entrepreneurship because PACs do not appear to respond to this activity by investing in entrepreneurial members.

After looking at how members structure their interactions with those outside of the House with respect to legislative entrepreneurship in chapter 4, I then looked inside the institution for further explanations of this behavior. In chapter 5, I argued that incentives for entrepreneurship are embedded within the committee and party structures that members have established in the House. These structures contain positions that members value because the positions confer on their occupants additional resources that they can use to accomplish their various goals. I posited that members use promotions to prestigious positions to encourage legislative entrepreneurship. If such an incentive system exists, then members who engage in higher levels of entrepreneurial activity should have a higher probability of advancing in the committee and party hierarchies.

I analyzed patterns of advancement to full and subcommittee chairmanships, exclusive committees, and party leadership positions. The results of this analysis are consistent with the argument that members use advancement to reward each other for their entrepreneurial efforts. The more entrepreneurial activity that members of the majority party undertake, the more likely it is that they will advance to committee and party leadership positions. Members of the majority party (in this case Democrats) appear to use prestigious positions to provide incentives for each other to engage in entrepreneurial activity. Thus, intrainstitutional mobility seems to be the crucial piece in solving the puzzle of legislative entrepreneurship.

In chapter 6, I considered how Republicans as the majority party might be using prestigious positions to provide incentives for legislative entrepreneurship. I presented qualitative evidence indicating that legislative entrepreneurship has played an important role in Republicans' selection of key party and committee leaders. While more systematic analysis is necessary to confirm this preliminary analysis, the evidence presented in chapter 6 provides confidence that the mobility hypothesis will hold for the Republican majority.

Members' Goals, Institutional Design, and Legislative Performance

The findings of this study have implications for our understanding of the interaction between members' goals, institutional design, and legislative behavior and productivity. In the traditional "electoral connection" view of legislative behavior, members are single-minded seekers of reelection. Yet recent studies argue that a narrow focus on the reelection motive can inhibit our understanding of legislative behavior. For example, Hall (1996) argues that members' interest in enacting good public policy strongly motivates them to participate in the legislative process. This interest no doubt contributes to members' entrepreneurial efforts as well. However, this goal can conflict with the reelection goal. Fiorina and Noll (1979, 1101) posit that reelection-seeking members will not focus on activities that are necessary to enact legislation and "consequently, societies may experience a shortfall in public policy accomplishments which could contribute to increasing cynicism about the potential of democratic government." Mayhew (1974, 141) contends that if "all members did nothing but pursue their electoral goals, Congress would decay or collapse."

It appears as if members of the House have prevented this dire situation from occurring. Although Congress as an institution perennially receives low approval ratings, the institution certainly has not collapsed, nor has cynicism about its capacity to enact policy become so great that the citizenry has sought to replace it with some other governing institution. Members have tempered the detrimental effects of reelection-seeking behavior in part by recognizing that they have goals in addition to reelection and that these are intertwined with the reelection goal. Members have used institutional features to exploit the links between the goals of enacting good public policy, reelection, and obtaining influence within the House to help ensure that the House does not realize a shortfall in policy accomplishments or become legislatively enervated due to members' primary interest in securing reelection. Members who work hard to advance legislation that they believe to be good public policy increase their chances of acquiring influence within the House because they are more likely to be promoted to leadership positions in the committee or party hierarchies, which in turn increases the amount of resources at their disposal to advance their reelection goals. Members who pursue their policy goals in the near term through legislative entrepreneurship advances their other goals in the long term. We would miss these connections between goals, and possibly miss the most compelling explanation for entrepreneurial behavior, if we narrowly focused on members as single-minded seekers of reelection, as the long-standing "electoral connection" view of Congress would have us do. One implication of this study is that a broader focus on members' goals is necessary if we are to gain a thorough understanding of legislative entrepreneurship and possibly other types of legislative behavior.

Although this study has argued that ambition and legislative entrepreneurship are linked, we have not explicitly examined how legislative entrepreneurship varies with a member's ambition, mainly because of the difficulties with measuring ambition. One variable that appears in the analysis in chapter 4 crudely taps members' intrainstitutional ambitions. The number of House seats in a member's state affects members' ambitions for the Senate as opposed to their ambitions for staying in the House and advancing to a leadership position. The more House seats there are in a state, the more difficult it is to advance to the Senate because there is more potential competition from other House incumbents who seek to advance to the Senate. We would expect that more House seats in a state would lead to more legislative entrepreneurship by members in that state as they pursue ambition within the House instead of progressive ambition to the Senate. The variable one divided by the number of House seats in a state does not have an effect on entrepreneurial activity that is statistically distinguishable from zero, however. This variable may simply be too crude a way to examine intrainstitutional ambition, and so one way to extend this analysis is to collect and analyze better data on this type of ambition.

Focusing on members' goals related to their ambitions is also important for understanding larger issues of legislative organization. Hall and Van Houweling (1995) lament the dearth of studies of members' institutional positions that connect theories of legislative organization with theories of ambition, especially intrainstitutional ambition. Hall and Van Houweling attempt to connect ambition theory and theories of legislative organization by considering how members' current positions and expectations about advancing to committee or party leadership positions affect their decisions to retire from the House. My work explicitly connects ambition theory with theories of legislative organization. A main thrust of the literature on legislative organization focuses on how members organize their institution to shape their own behavior. My work indicates that members have taken into consideration their intrainstitutional ambitions when organizing the House. Members have organized their institution to harness the internal ambition of members to maintain the House as a viable partner in the separation of powers system. By providing incentives for legislative entrepreneurship through institutional design, members help to ensure that the House can function as a legislative body and accomplish its fundamental duty of legislating.

Thus, another implication of this study concerns how goals, legislative institutions, and legislative productivity are intimately related. Researchers have recently become more interested in what factors determine the legislative productivity of the federal government. The main focus, however, has been on partisan control of institutions and the preferences of key players within them. Mayhew (1991) examines how divided party control of the chambers of Congress and the executive affects lawmaking and finds that legislative productivity in terms of "significant legislation" does not vary much with unified versus divided government.[1] Krehbiel (1998) develops a "basic" theory of U.S. lawmaking, which holds that the enactment of legislation is driven by the relationship among the policy preferences of key political actors whose approval is necessary for enactment. These actors include the president, the members of the House and Senate whose votes are necessary to achieve the two thirds majority required to override a presidential veto, and the member of the Senate whose vote is necessary to form a three-fifths majority to stop a filibuster. According to Krehbiel's theory, the distribution of the ideal points of these individuals on a given policy issue determines whether or not a new law will be passed.

The research presented in this book indicates that these studies have missed an important factor in legislative productivity by focusing primarily on ideological preferences of individuals for policy and ignoring individuals' preferences for doing the day to day work of producing legislation. Legislative productivity depends on individuals investing time and resources in entrepreneurial activity. Whether or not individuals make these investments surely depends on their beliefs about how the preferences of important political actors affects the probability of enacting new legislation. But, as my research shows, members' investments in entrepreneurial activity depend crucially on incentives embedded within the institutional structure of the House. Explaining lawmaking requires us to think not just about relationships between the preferences of members of the different branches of government but also about the activities of individuals within the branches and how these activities af-

1. But see Binder 1999, which finds that divided government does matter when legislative output is measured in proportion to the policy agenda.

fect legislative productivity. Policy making depends not just on the ideological preferences of key legislators, as these works suggest, but also on the skills and effort that legislators invest in passing legislation.[2]

A crude look at legislative productivity and legislative entrepreneurship reveals a relationship between them. The mean of the entrepreneurship scale score and the number of bills passed (accounting for the number of bills introduced) have a correlation coefficient of .785 ($p = .007$). Of course, we should be cautious about making too much of this result. From figure 7.1 we can see that the ratio of bills passed to bills introduced and the mean of the entrepreneurship scale score both trend upward, which accounts for the correlation.[3] One way to check whether this correlation is real and not spurious would be to examine more closely how measures of changes in institutional structure correlate with these series. Changes over time in institutional structure and patterns of entrepreneurial activity and legislative productivity should be inextricably linked.

An interesting extension of the work presented here would involve conducting historical research on the development of institutions that support legislative entrepreneurship by members of Congress. This research would involve examining basic rules and procedures, such as those governing bill introduction, as well as more complicated institutional features such as the procedures governing the selection of committee and party leadership positions. One of the shortcomings of this study is that it conducts systematic analysis of only the postreform Congress under Democratic control—a period of relative institutional stability. Although in chapter 6 I argued that my theories of legislative entrepreneurship extend to the House under Republican control, it is questionable whether the key findings presented here will hold up for other periods.

Consider the "textbook Congress" between the Legislative Reorganization Act of 1946 and the reforms of the 1970s (Shepsle 1989). The 1946 reorganization reduced the number of full committees, and consequently the number of full committee leadership positions, from 48 to 19. Although the act increased the amount of resources available to committees, these resources were concentrated in the hands of an elite group of committee chairs who used them

2. A valid criticism of my analysis is that it does not pay enough attention to the ideological preferences of LEs. The measures of legislative entrepreneurship that this analysis employs are ideologically neutral. The measures cannot tell us how the entrepreneurial activity of members of various ideological stripes might bias policy outcomes in particular directions. Yet, as Hall (1996) cogently argues, important questions about the representativeness of Congress depend on the ideological preferences of those who participate heavily in the legislative process.

3. The data used to compute the ratio of bills passed to bills introduced are from Ornstein, Mann, and Malbin 1996.

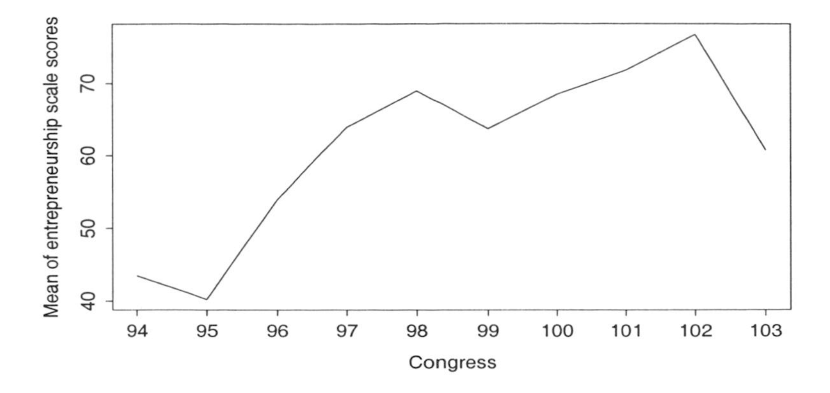

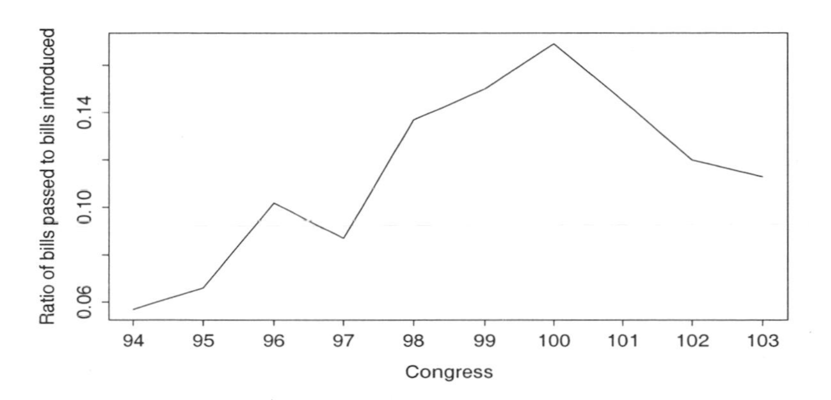

Fig. 7.1. Ratio of bills passed to bills introduced and the mean of the entrepreneurship scale score, 94th through the 103d Congresses

to dominate the legislative process in the House. The stylized view of the power structure during this period is that the authority of party leaders paled in comparison with that of the chairs and rank and file members had little hope of getting anything done legislatively that did not have the imprimatur of the relevant committee chair. In fact, the norm of apprenticeship discouraged junior members from having active legislative agendas (Asher 1973).[4] Non-chairs could do little more than wait their turns to assume positions of power in the House, as advancement to a full committee chairmanship seems to have

4. Hall (1996) claims that there never was such a norm, although informal barriers to participation led to a type of apprenticeship.

depended only on one's seniority in the institution.[5]

The general effect of these reforms would be to dampen legislative entrepreneurship. Although the resources and authority of committee chairs were substantially increased and would make these positions more attractive, there were many fewer positions to which members could aspire. Members' expectations about advancing to a committee chair position were greatly reduced, limiting the usefulness of these positions for promoting legislative entrepreneurship by nonchairs. The concentration of resources in chairs would also have reduced the motivating power of subcommittee and party leadership positions. Although Mayhew (1974, 146–47) seems to argue that during this period an incentive system existed that involved using prestigious positions to promote legislative activity, the relatively small number of positions suggests that we would see less legislative entrepreneurship during this period.

Interestingly, this period is considered to be one of decline for the Congress vis-à-vis the president, especially with respect to legislative initiative. Beginning with the presidency of Franklin Delano Roosevelt and continuing during the postwar period, the president assumed the role of "chief legislator," becoming more and more involved in all stages of the legislative process (Sundquist 1981, 127–54). During this period, "the initiative in formulating legislation, in assigning legislative priorities, in arousing support for legislation, and in determining the final content of the legislation enacted [had] clearly shifted to the executive branch" (Huntington 1973, 28).

How much of this decline is explained by the lack of incentives for individuals to engage in legislative entrepreneurship? Before we could answer this question, we would have to determine how much legislative entrepreneurship occurred and how this activity correlates with advancement within the House during this period. Unfortunately, there are substantial barriers to performing the kind of systematic analysis that is necessary to answer these questions. The detailed legislative data that I use in this analysis exist only as far back as the 93d Congress (1973–74). It would be incredibly costly and perhaps impossible to assemble a data set on legislative activity prior to the 93d comparable to what is available for later Congresses. Although readily available data on bill sponsorship exist prior to the 93d, I have argued that we need to look at more than just sponsorship when examining entrepreneurial activity. But collecting data as detailed as those found in the Congressional Research Services legislative files would result in costs that very few researchers (including myself) would be willing to bear. Hall's work (1996) on participation provides some encouragement, though. In addition to providing a model for how to collect

5. But see Cox and McCubbins 1993, which claims that seniority was not inviolable during this period.

detailed data on legislative activity in earlier eras, he finds that his results on participation in the postreform era extend to the 87th Congress (1961–62). His results suggest that this earlier period may not be very different from the period covered by my analysis when it comes to legislative activity, though it is unclear whether this applies to legislative entrepreneurship.[6]

Legislative Entrepreneurship and the Reforms of the 1970s

For the most part, I have constrained my analysis to the the textbook Congress that existed after the sweeping reforms of the early 1970s. The changes that occurred in the 1970s are important because they shaped several of the features of the institutional environment that promote legislative entrepreneurship.

One important change concerns the norms of the institution. In the 1970s, the norm of apprenticeship allegedly disappeared as junior members assumed active roles in proposing and pushing legislation (Asher 1973). Seniority norms that affected members' positions in the institution eroded in the 1970s, making it easier for junior members to vault over more senior colleagues into prestigious positions in the House.

The structure of the institution with respect to prestigious positions also changed dramatically in the 1970s. One consequence of these reforms was the creation of "many new points of access for policy ideas in the congressional process" (Dodd and Oppenheimer 1977, 50). Two of the institutional features that provided access and that I found to promote entrepreneurial behavior—subcommittee and party leadership positions—probably did not have much motivating force prior to the 1970s. Subcommittee leadership positions did not have much value prior to the Subcommittee Bill of Rights. The rejuvenation of congressional party organizations during the 1970s substantially enhanced the value of party leadership positions, and positions below the top tier of the leadership became much more influential and attractive (Rohde 1991; Sinclair 1995).

The changes that took place within the House should have affected how it functioned as a legislative body. The reforms helped create an atmosphere that was much more conducive to legislative entrepreneurship than that which existed in the prereform era. It is not surprising, then, that entrepreneurial activity

---

6. Prospects seem to be much better for studying entrepreneurship in the present and future. The Internet and advances in computer technology have made it easy to access a vast amount of information about legislative activity. In addition to official government sites on the World Wide Web, numerous privately maintained sites contain information about legislative activity in Congress. Some examples of free sites include the House of Representatives home page (http://www.house.gov/), THOMAS (http://thomas.loc.gov/), and Congress.Org (http://congress.org/).

by members increased during this period. The fact that the 1970s is regarded as a period of the resurgence of Congress in the separation of powers system lends credence to my arguments about the connections between legislative entrepreneurship and the performance of the House as a legislative body.

The institutional changes of the 1970s were part of a general attempt by members of Congress to reassert the role of their institution in the federal government. The reforms were partly a congressional response to expansions of presidential power during the Nixon administration. Although Congress had acceded to the steady expansion of presidential power throughout the twentieth century, many members of Congress saw Nixon's actions as an unacceptable usurpation of legislative authority. A major motivating force behind the reform movement was the desire to reverse the trend in the expansion of executive power at the expense of congressional power (Sundquist 1981). The reforms that increased the number and authority of prestigious positions in the House were part of this attempt, serving to provide more incentives for members to undertake the tasks that are necessary if the House is to be a viable legislative body.

The relationship between legislative entrepreneurship and intrainstitutional mobility helps explain a paradox of the 1970s reforms. The decentralization of power that occurred would appear to have made it more difficult for the House as an institution to take legislative action because it would have made it more difficult to coordinate and integrate legislative efforts and would have created additional hurdles in the legislative process. Such fragmentation would seem to have hindered Congress's comeback against the executive in the legislative arena. Yet the decentralization of power served to provide incentives for members to undertake legislative activity in the first place. The desire to advance to the augmented positions of subcommittee and party leaders should have led individual members to take back legislative initiative from the president, proposing their own legislation instead of just disposing of the president's legislative agenda.

Legislative Entrepreneurship and Recent Institutional Reforms

In closing, I consider what implications the findings in this book have for evaluating the institutional reforms recently implemented or considered by the Republican majority. As was discussed in chapter 6, when the Republicans assumed the majority they changed certain institutional features that should have implications for the incentive system that drives legislative entrepreneurship. Although I contend that the selection of particular members for prestigious positions indicates that the Republicans are using these positions in a way that will promote legislative entrepreneurship, some of the reforms that they instituted will dampen incentives for it.

One institutional change that limits the committee hierarchy's motivational capacity is the use of task forces instead of standing committees for action on important pieces of legislation. Though Democrats employed task forces when they were in the majority, Republicans have relied on these panels to a much greater degree. While selecting entrepreneurial members to serve on task forces would promote entrepreneurial activity, the ephemeral nature of these panels detracts from their capacity to motivate LEs. Members should be interested in building seniority on a committee, which, along with legislative entrepreneurship, is a determinant of advancement to committee leadership positions. But it is not possible to build seniority on a task force, nor do members have any property rights in seats on them, because they do not survive beyond a given Congress.

While positions on task forces do not provide as much incentive for legislative entrepreneurship as standing committee positions, the use of task forces can decrease the motivational value of committee leadership positions if party leaders can arbitrarily bypass committees and appoint task forces. The jurisdictions of committees, which are set in the House rules, are supposed to ensure members of committees that they have exclusive claims to particular bills. Members work to obtain seats on certain committees and advance to leadership positions on those panels with the expectation that they have special rights to consider proposals under their committees' jurisdictions. They have less incentive to work as LEs if they are not guaranteed special rights over legislation they care about. Circumventing the committee system with task forces makes positions in the committee hierarchy less attractive.

In chapter 6, I discussed the strengthening of full committee chairs at the expense of subcommittee chairs. This reform also dampens incentives for legislative entrepreneurship because it decreases the capacity of subcommittee chairs to satisfy members' goals. Although concentrating power in the hands of full committee chairs seemed necessary for delivering on the promises made in the Contract with America, Republicans should consider whether or not a more decentralized system would serve their interests better in the long term.

Term limits for committee leadership positions will also decrease incentives for legislative entrepreneurship. In the 104th Congress, Republicans adopted a rule that limits full committee and subcommittee chairs to three consecutive terms. One could argue that term limits ensure periodic turnover in these positions and increase the likelihood of vacancies that ambitious, entrepreneurial members can fill. Yet limiting members' tenure in these positions decreases their attractiveness and dampens incentives for legislative entrepreneurship, both for those not in these positions and for those who hold them and want to retain them. Members may spend more time waiting to advance to a chair position than they would actually serve in it. Speaker Dennis Hastert recently claimed that the term limit rule does not prevent chairs from assuming the chairmanship of a different full committee or from taking over a subcommittee chair on the full committee on which they currently serve. This move would help preserve some of the capacity of these positions to motivate members to engage in entrepreneurial activity and suggests that Republicans recognize the disincentives term limits impose (Foerstel and Koszczuk 1999).

Limits on the number of terms that members can serve in Congress are also detrimental to legislative entrepreneurship. A proposal for these kinds of term limits was part of the Contract with America, but it was the only item in the contract that did not pass the House. Term limits place constraints on the upward mobility of members. Members need time to demonstrate their entrepreneurial ability, cultivate reputations as LEs, and move up to prestigious positions. They also need time to enjoy the fruits of their labors after advancing to prestigious positions. By constraining the amount of time members serve in Congress, term limits inhibit the usefulness of prestigious positions in motivating members to engage in legislative entrepreneurship. Term limits would decrease legislative entrepreneurship in the House, which would have detrimental effects on its performance as a legislative body.

In their attempt to restore themselves to majority status, Democrats have tried to make the legislative performance of the House an issue, arguing that Republicans have been running a "do nothing" Congress. While the Republicans have achieved some important legislative accomplishments, Democrats appear to have been successful in making this charge stick. Republicans have responded by advancing an agenda in the 106th Congress that is far less ambitious than what they sought in the 104th, concentrating on a few key proposals and the passage of appropriations bills in a timely and orderly fashion. Republicans hope this strategy will demonstrate their competence at governing and help them maintain their majority status.

The arguments in this book suggest that if Republicans are concerned about the legislative performance of the House they should rethink some of the institutional reforms they have adopted. The motivation behind many of the institutional changes Republicans instituted after assuming the majority was to eliminate features that they saw as undemocratic and employed by Democrats to oppress Republicans when they were in the minority. Yet these institutional changes may be hurting the legislative performance of the House. Legislative performance and institutional organization are connected by the incentives that individual members have to engage in entrepreneurial activity. Any debate about institutional reform should consider this connection and how the reforms will affect the incentives of members to engage in legislative entrepreneurship.

Appendixes

APPENDIX A

Data for a Reality Check of Entrepreneurship Scores

This appendix lists the names, legislative entrepreneurship scale scores, and profile scores for a random sample of members from the 96th, 98th, 100th, and 102d Congresses.

TABLE A.1. Scaled Entrepreneurship and Profile Scores for Selected Members

Name	Party	Scaled Entrepreneurship Score	Profile Score
		96th Congress	
Evans, Billy Lee	Dem.	30.649	1
Florio, James	Dem.	94.181	3
Gephardt, Richard	Dem.	82.620	3
Glickman, Dan	Dem.	84.236	3
Hall, Sam	Dem.	63.642	2
Hightower, Jack	Dem.	77.298	3
Montgomery, G. V.	Dem.	41.141	1
Pease, Donald	Dem.	69.906	1
Synar, Michael	Dem.	14.449	1
Whitten, Jamie	Dem.	88.543	3
Williams, Pat	Dem.	46.953	1
Findley, Paul	Rep.	64.936	1
Heckler, Margaret	Rep.	40.280	1
Kindness, Thomas	Rep.	52.660	2
Marks, Marc	Rep.	3.233	1
Martin, James	Rep.	61.250	2
Moorhead, Carlos	Rep.	51.282	2
Robinson, J. K.	Rep.	24.053	1
Shumway, Norman	Rep.	31.535	1
Spence, Floyd	Rep.	44.451	1

(continued)

TABLE A.1. —Continued

Name	Party	Scaled Entrepreneurship Score	Profile Score
		98th Congress	
Barnard, Doug	Dem.	33.467	2
Bonker, Don	Dem.	94.847	3
Chappell, William	Dem.	61.765	1
Dorgan, Byron	Dem.	77.602	1
Hayes, Charles	Dem.	59.797	1
Kleczka, Gerald	Dem.	0	1
Miller, George	Dem.	128.251	3
Mitchell, Parren	Dem.	59.337	1
Panetta, Leon	Dem.	109.242	3
Torres, Esteban	Dem.	17.881	1
Wyden, Ron	Dem.	150.915	3
Archer, William	Rep.	73.638	2
Coats, Daniel	Rep.	49.133	2
Coleman, E. Thomas	Rep.	48.697	2
Emerson, Bill	Rep.	49.181	2
Fish, Hamilton, Jr.	Rep.	129.323	3
Green, S. William	Rep.	93.193	3
Lagomarsino, Robert	Rep.	39.102	1
Lewis, Thomas	Rep.	88.765	1
Vucanovich, Barbara	Rep.	42.969	1
		100th Congress	
Bilbray, James	Dem.	61.422	1
Byron, Beverly	Dem.	41.125	2
Downey, Thomas	Dem.	81.301	3
Hertel, Dennis	Dem.	50.510	2
Hoyer, Steny	Dem.	59.282	1
Jones, Walter	Dem.	90.709	1
Kennelly, Barbara	Dem.	56.659	2
Murphy, Austin	Dem.	58.017	1
Ortiz, Solomon	Dem.	45.577	1
Rostenkowski, Daniel	Dem.	162.524	3
Swift, Allen	Dem.	78.745	3
Synar, Michael	Dem.	77.777	2
Vento, Bruce	Dem.	124.780	3

(continued)

TABLE A.1. —Continued

Name	Party	Scaled Entrepreneurship Score	Profile Score
Yates, Sidney	Dem.	135.530	3
Coble, Howard	Rep.	25.033	1
Hastert, Dennis	Rep.	33.368	1
McEwen, Bob	Rep.	37.489	1
Quillen, James	Rep.	22.605	1
Walker, Robert	Rep.	54.074	2
Young, C. W.	Rep.	95.091	3
102nd Congress			
Andrews, Michael	Dem.	86.915	1
Bilbray, James	Dem.	76.969	1
Durbin, Richard	Dem.	94.688	2
Lloyd, Marilyn	Dem.	71.815	1
McCurdy, Dave	Dem.	101.720	3
Mineta, Norman	Dem.	166.220	3
Penny, Timothy	Dem.	94.875	2
Price, David	Dem.	191.510	3
Sarpalius, Bill	Dem.	32.546	1
Slaughter, Louise	Dem.	86.781	2
Tanner, John	Dem.	20.041	1
Waters, Maxine	Dem.	61.809	2
Waxman, Henry	Dem.	187.170	3
Barrett, Bill	Rep.	21.114	2
Gekas, George	Rep.	33.533	2
Grandy, Fred	Rep.	90.463	2
Hansen, James	Rep.	45.641	1
Myers, John	Rep.	14.109	1
Roukema, Marge	Rep.	67.039	3
Skeen, Joseph	Rep.	51.112	1

APPENDIX B

Derivation of the Mobility Model

To test the mobility hypothesis, it is necessary to assess the effect of legislative entrepreneurship on the probability that a member makes a transition from a nonprestigious to a prestigious position in the House.[1] The probability that a member will advance to a prestigious position is constrained by the number of vacancies in such positions, so the maximum likelihood method that I propose estimates the probability of making a transition conditional on the positions that members occupy initially and the opportunities for filling vacancies.

In order to see how I build in constraints imposed by vacancy competition, consider the following thought experiment. Suppose that in a Congress each member is presented with a set of urns, each of which contains a number of white and black balls. The number of urns represents the number of vacancies that open up in a class of prestigious positions (e.g., the number of vacant subcommittee chairs). If a member draws a white ball from an urn, he or she is awarded the position represented by that urn and does not draw any more balls. If the member draws a black ball, then he or she is not awarded that position and moves on to the next urn. The member continues these independent Bernoulli trials until he or she either draws a white ball (i.e., advances) or runs out of urns (i.e., does not advance).

Let N_{ikl} be the number of trials (i.e., the number of urns) member i gets to make a transition from his or her current position k to a prestigious position l in a given Congress, where N_{ikl} is equal to the number of vacancies that open up in l. Let p_{ikl} denote the probability of success on a given trial. A member can make a transition only if he or she realizes a success on one of the N_{ikl} trials. If the random variable R_{ikl} denotes the trial at which the first success occurs in a sequence of independent Bernoulli trials, then R_{ikl} follows a geometric distribution:

$$\Pr(R_{ikl} = r | p_{ikl}) = p_{ikl}(1 - p_{ikl})^{r-1}.$$

1. I assume that members can make transitions only at the beginning of a Congress. If a member makes a transition during a Congress, then I treat that member as if he or she had made the transition at the beginning.

We only get to observe whether the member was successful for the entire sequence of trials—that is, we do not get to observe on which trial in the sequence he or she was successful. All we know is that $R_{ikl} \leq N_{ikl}$. Since R_{ikl} follows a geometric distribution,

$$\Pr(R_{ikl} \leq N_{ikl}) = \sum_{r=1}^{N_{ikl}} p_{ikl}(1 - p_{ikl})^{r-1},$$

which can be rewritten as

$$q_{ikl} = 1 - (1 - p_{ikl})^{N_{ikl}}. \tag{B.1}$$

We can see from equation B.1 how this model accounts for vacancies. If $N_{ikl} = 0$, it is not possible to make a transition, and so $q_{ikl} = 0$. As N_{ikl} becomes larger, q_{ikl} approaches 1, indicating a "demand-side effect"—that is, all positions must be filled. Since I get to observe N_{ikl}, I can plug this value into equation B.1 and estimate parameters in p_{ikl}.[2]

To estimate the transition probabilities, the model must account for all of the possible moves that members in nonprestigious positions can make. First, members can leave the institution by dying, retiring, running for higher office, or losing their reelection bids. The probability that a member leaves is p_{ikw}, where w denotes the exit state. If the member returns to the next Congress, then he or she can either move to a new position in Congress or stay in the current position. If the ith individual returns to the next Congress and advances to a prestigious position, then his or her contribution to the likelihood function is $(1 - p_{ikw})q_{ikl}$. The probability that an individual in a nonprestigious position

---

2. To be precise, we need to consider all of the possible sequences of vacancies that a member faces. For N_{ikl} vacancies, there are $N_{ikl}!$ sequences that a member can follow to try to fill a vacancy. That is, we can order the trials for the N_{ikl} vacancies in $N_{ikl}!$ different ways. Since there is no observable information on the likelihood of each sequence of vacancies, I assume that all sequences are equally likely, so the probability of a particular sequence is $1/N_{ikl}!$. Let s denote a sequence. Then the expectation of the probability of a transition is given by

$$\sum_{s=1}^{N_{ikl}!} \frac{1}{N_{ikl}!} \sum_{r=1}^{N_{ikl}} (1 - p_{ikl})^{r-1} p_{ikl},$$

which simplifies to q_{ikl}. We could also try to model the fact that once a member makes a transition other members have one less opportunity to do so. In terms of the thought experiment, all members should not have the same number of urns from which to draw. However, it would be extremely difficult to model all possible permutations of positions and trials, and it is not clear that we would gain much by doing so.

remains in that position is $(1 - p_{ikw})(1 - q_{ikl})$.[3]

The likelihood function for transitions that members can make is

$$L = \prod_i \left\{ \prod_{k \ni i} [(1 - p_{ikw})(1 - q_{ikl})]^{d_{ikk}} [(1 - p_{ikw}) q_{ikl}]^{1 - d_{ikl}} (p_{ikw})^{d_{ikw}} \right\},$$

where

$$d_{ikk} = \begin{cases} 1 & \text{if } i \text{ remains in a nonprestigious position} \\ 0 & \text{otherwise} \end{cases}$$

$$d_{ikl} = \begin{cases} 1 & \text{if } i \text{ moves to a prestigious position} \\ 0 & \text{otherwise} \end{cases}$$

and

$$d_{ikw} = \begin{cases} 1 & \text{if } i \text{ leaves the institution from a nonprestigious position} \\ 0 & \text{otherwise} \end{cases}$$

To test the mobility hypothesis, I use this method to estimate the effects of explanatory variables on the probability of moving from a nonprestigious position ($k = 1$) to a prestigious position ($l = 2$) in the committee and party hierarchies.

---

3. In these derivations I assume that the probability of leaving the institution is independent of the probability of advancing to a prestigious position. The work of Hall and Van Houweling (1995) suggests this assumption may be inappropriate. A member's decision to retire or run for higher office (thereby leaving the institution) may depend on their expectations about advancing to a higher position within the House in the future. However, relaxing this independence assumption makes the model much more difficult to derive and estimate, so I leave this for future work.

References

Abramowitz, Alan. 1980. "A Comparison of Voting for U.S. Senator and Representative in 1978." *American Political Science Review* 74:633–40.

Achen, Christopher H. 1985. "Proxy Variables and Incorrect Signs on Regression Coefficients." *Political Methodology* 11:299–316.

Alchian, Arman A., and Harold Demsetz. 1972. "Production, Information Costs, and Economic Organization." *American Economic Review* 62:777–95.

Aldrich, John H., and David W. Rohde. 1997. "The Transition to Republican Rule in the House: Implications for Theories of Congressional Politics." *Political Science Quarterly* 112:541–67.

Arnold, Douglas. 1990. *The Logic of Congressional Action.* New Haven: Yale University Press.

Asher, Herbert B. 1973. "The Learning of Legislative Norms." *American Political Science Review* 67:499–513.

Babson, Jennifer. 1995a. "Armey Stood Guard over Contract." *Congressional Quarterly Weekly Report,* 8 April, 987.

Babson, Jennifer. 1995b. "Senate Slows GOP's Progress to 'Contract's' Dotted Line." *Congressional Quarterly Weekly Report,* 8 July, p. 1983.

Bach, Stanley, and Steven S. Smith. 1988. *Managing Uncertainty in the House of Representatives.* Washington, DC: Brookings Institution.

Baker, George B., Michael Gibbs, and Bengt Holmström. 1994. "The Internal Economics of the Firm: Evidence from Personnel Data." *Quarterly Journal of Economics* 109:881–919.

Baker, George B., Michael C. Jensen, and Kevin J. Murphy. 1988. "Compensation and Incentives: Practice vs. Theory." *Journal of Finance* 43:593–616.

Baron, David P. 1989a. "Service-Related Campaign Contributions and the Political Equilibrium." *Quarterly Journal of Economics* 104:45–72.

Baron, David P. 1989b. "Service-Induced Campaign Contributions, Incumbent

Shirking, and Reelection Opportunities." In *Models of Strategic Choice in Politics,* ed. Peter C. Ordeshook. Ann Arbor: University of Michigan Press.

Barone, Michael, and Grant Ujifusa. 1983. *Almanac of American Politics, 1984.* Washington, DC: National Journal.

Barone, Michael, Grant Ujifusa, and Douglas Matthews. 1979. *Almanac of American Politics, 1980.* Washington, DC: National Journal.

Barry, John M. 1989. *The Ambition and the Power.* New York: Viking.

Binder, Sarah A. 1999. "The Dynamics of Legislative Gridlock, 1947–1996." *American Political Science Review* 93:519–34.

Box-Steffensmeier, Janet. 1996. "A Dynamic Analysis of the Role of War Chests in Campaign Strategy." *American Journal of Political Science* 40:352–71.

Box-Steffensmeier, Janet, and J. Tobin Grant. 1999. "All in a Day's Work: The Financial Rewards of Legislative Effectiveness." *Legislative Studies Quarterly* 24:511–23.

Brace, Paul. 1984. "Progressive Ambition in the House: A Probabilistic Approach." *Journal of Politics* 46:556–71.

Bullock, Charles S. 1973. "Committee Transfers in the United States House of Representatives" *Journal of Politics* 35:85–120.

Cain, Bruce E., John Ferejohn, and Morris Fiorina. 1987. *The Personal Vote: Constituency Service and Electoral Independence.* Cambridge: Harvard University Press.

Campbell, James E. 1982. "Cosponsoring Legislation in the U.S. Congress." *Legislative Studies Quarterly* 7:415–22.

Cassata, Donna. 1995a. "Republicans Bask in Success of Rousing Performance." *Congressional Quarterly Weekly Report,* 8 April, 986–90.

Cassata, Donna. 1995b. "Swift Progress of 'Contract' Inspires Awe and Concern." *Congressional Quarterly Weekly Report,* 1 April, 909–12.

Cassata, Donna. 1998. "Independent Groups' Ads Increasingly Steer Campaigns." *Congressional Quarterly Weekly Report,* 2 May, 1108–14.

Cavanaugh, Thomas. 1981. "The Two Arenas of Congress." In *The House at Work,* ed. Joseph Cooper and G. Calvin Mackenzie. Austin: University of Texas Press.

Clapp, Charles L. 1963. *The Congressman: His Work as He Sees It.* Washington, DC: Brookings Institution.

Connelly, William F., and John J. Pitney, Jr. 1994. *Congress' Permanent Minority? Republicans in the U.S. House.* Lanham, MD: Rowman & Littlefield.

Cooper, Ann. 1979. "New Setbacks for the House Seniority System." *Congressional Quarterly Weekly Report,* 3 February, 183–87.

Cooper, Joseph. 1977. "Congress in Organizational Perspective." In *Congress Reconsidered,* ed. Lawrence C. Dodd and Bruce I. Oppenheimer. 2d ed. New York: Praeger.

Cox, Gary W. 1987. *The Efficient Secret: The Cabinet and the Development of Political Parties in Victorian England.* Cambridge: Cambridge University Press.

Cox, Gary, and Mathew D. McCubbins. 1993. *Legislative Leviathan.* Berkeley: University of California Press.

Davidson, Roger H. 1981. "Subcommittee Government: New Channels for Policy Making." In *The New Congress,* ed. Thomas E. Mann and Norman J. Ornstein. Washington, DC: American Enterprise Institute.

Davidson, Roger H., and Walter J. Oleszek. 1985. *Congress and Its Members.* 2d ed. Washington, DC: CQ Press.

Davis, Joseph A. 1986. "Garrison Irrigation Plan Revived Once Again." *Congressional Quarterly Weekly Report,* 26 April, 908.

Deering, Christopher J. 1982. "Subcommittee Government in the U.S. House: An Analysis of Bill Management." *Legislative Studies Quarterly* 7:533–46.

Deering, Christopher J. 1996. "Career Advancement and Subcommittee Chairs in the U.S. House of Representatives." *American Politics Quarterly* 24:3–23.

Denzau, Arthur T., and Robert J. Mackay. 1983. "Gatekeeping and Monopoly Power of Committees: An Analysis of Sincere and Sophisticated Behavior." *American Journal of Political Science* 27:740–61.

Denzau, Arthur, and Michael C. Munger. 1986. "Legislators and Interest Groups: How Unorganized Interests Get Represented." *American Political Science Review* 80:98–106.

Dodd, Lawrence C. 1977. "Congress and the Quest for Power." In *Congress Reconsidered,* ed. Lawrence C. Dodd and Bruce I. Oppenheimer. New York: Praeger.

Dodd, Lawrence C., and Bruce I. Oppenheimer. 1977. "The House in Transition." In *Congress Reconsidered,* ed. Lawrence C. Dodd and Bruce I. Oppenheimer. New York: Praeger.

Doherty, Carroll J. 1996. "GOP's First Half is Marked Mostly by Sound and Fury." *Congressional Quarterly Weekly Report,* 20 January, 119–98.

Doherty, Carroll J. 1998a. "Armey, an Architect of the Revolution, Nearly Becomes One of Its Casualties." *Congressional Quarterly Weekly Report,* 21 November, 3163.

Doherty, Carroll J. 1998b. "Congress Compiles a Modest Record in a Session Sidetracked by Scandal." *Congressional Quarterly Weekly Report,* 14 November, 3079–80.

Duncan, Phil, ed. 1991. *Politics in America, 1992.* Washington, DC: CQ Press.

Duncan, Phil, ed. 1993. *Politics in America, 1994.* Washington, DC: CQ Press.

Duncan, Phil, and Christine D. Lawrence, eds. 1995. *Politics in America, 1996.* Washington, DC: CQ Press.

Durr, Robert H., John B. Gilmour, and Christina Wolbrecht. 1997. "Explaining Congressional Approval." *American Journal of Political Science* 41:175–207.

Ehrenhalt, Alan, ed. 1983. *Politics in America, 1984.* Washington, DC: CQ Press.

Ehrenhalt, Alan, ed. 1987. *Politics in America, 1988.* Washington, DC: CQ Press.

Eilperin, Juliet. 1998. "Hastert May Be Drafted for House GOP Contest." *Washington Post,* 15 November, A21.

Eilperin, Juliet, and Jim Vande Hei. 1997. "House GOP Leadership's Fractured Present Pits Gingrich-Armey Alliance Against DeLay-Paxon." *Roll Call,* 9 October, 1.

Enelow, James M., and Melvin J. Hinich. 1984. *The Spatial Theory of Voting: An Introduction.* Cambridge: Cambridge University Press.

Epstein, David, and Peter Zemsky. 1995. "Money Talks: Deterring Quality Challengers in Congressional Elections." *American Political Science Review* 89:295–308.

Fama, Eugene F. 1980. "Agency Problems and the Theory of the Firm." *Journal of Political Economy* 88:288–307.

Federal Election Commission. 1985. Campaign Expenditures in the United States, 1983-1984 [Computer file]. Washington, DC: Federal Election Commission [producer]. Ann Arbor, MI: Inter-university Consortium for Political and Social Research [distributor].

Federal Election Commission. 1988. Campaign Expenditures in the United States, 1985-1986: Reports on Financial Activity (RFA) Data. [Computer file.] Washington, DC: Federal Election Commission [producer]. Ann Arbor, MI: Inter-university Consortium for Political and Social Research [distributor].

Federal Election Commission. 1990. Campaign Expenditures in the United States, 1987-1988: Reports on Financial Activity (RFA) Data. [Computer file.] 2d release. Washington, DC: Federal Election Commission [producer]. Ann Arbor, MI: Inter-university Consortium for Political and Social Research [distributor].

Federal Election Commission. 1991. Campaign Expenditures in the United States, 1989-1990: Reports on Financial Activity (RFA) data [Computer file]. Washington, DC: Federal Election Commission [producer]. Ann Arbor, MI: Inter-university Consortium for Political and Social Research [distributor].

Federal Election Commission. 1994. Campaign Expenditures in the United States, 1991-1992: Reports on Financial Activity (RFA) Data [Computer file]. ICPSR version. Washington, DC: Federal Election Commission [producer]. Ann Arbor, MI: Inter-university Consortium for Political and Social Research [distributor].

Fenno, Richard F. 1973. *Congressmen in Committees.* Boston: Little, Brown.

Fenno, Richard F. 1978. *Home Style: House Members in Their Districts.* Boston: Little, Brown.

Fenno, Richard F. 1989. *The Making of a Senator: Dan Quayle.* Washington, DC: CQ Press.

Fenno, Richard F. 1991. *Learning to Legislate: The Senate Education of Arlen Specter.* Washington, DC: CQ Press.

Fenno, Richard F. 1997. *Learning to Govern: An Institutional View of the 104th Congress.* Washington, DC: Brookings Institution Press.

Ferejohn, John, and Charles Shipan. 1990. "Congressional Influence on the Bureaucracy." *Journal of Law, Economics, and Organization* 6:1–27.

Filson, Lawrence E. 1992. *The Legislative Drafter's Desk Reference.* Washington, DC: CQ Press.

Fiorina, Morris P. 1974. *Representatives, Roll Calls, and Constituencies.* Lexington, MA: Lexington Books.

Fiorina, Morris P. 1981a. *Retrospective Voting in American National Elections.* New Haven: Yale University Press.

Fiorina, Morris P. 1981b. "Some Problems in Studying the Effects of Resource Allocation in Congressional Elections." *American Journal of Political Science* 25:543–67.

Fiorina, Morris P. 1989. *Congress: Keystone of the Washington Establishment.* 2d ed. New Haven: Yale University Press.

Fiorina, Morris P., and Roger G. Noll. 1979. "Majority Rule Models and Legislative Elections." *Journal of Politics* 41:1081–104.

Fiorina, Morris P., and Kenneth A. Shepsle. 1989. "Formal Theories of Leadership: Agents, Agenda Setters, and Entrepreneurs." In *Leadership and Politics,* ed. Bryan D. Jones. Lawrence: University of Kansas Press.

Foerstel, Karen. 1994. "House Chairmen: Gingrich Flexes His Power in Picking Panel Chiefs." *Congressional Quarterly Weekly Report,* 19 November, 3326.

Foerstel, Karen, and Jackie Koszczuk. 1999. "Class of '94 Grapples with the Gavel." *Congressional Quarterly Weekly Report,* 19 June, 1424.

Fox, Harrison W., and Susan Webb Hammond. 1977. *Congressional Staffs.* New York: Free Press.

Frantzich, Stephen E. 1982. *Computers in Congress: The Politics of Information.* Beverly Hills: Sage Publications.

Freedman, Allen. 1996. "Returning Power to Chairmen." *Congressional Quarterly Weekly Report,* 23 November, 3300.

Frohlich, Norman, and Joe A. Oppenheimer. 1978. *Modern Political Economy.* Englewood Cliffs, NJ: Prentice-Hall.

Frohlich, Norman, Joe A. Oppenheimer, and Oran R. Young. 1971. *Political Leadership and Collective Goods.* Princeton: Princeton University Press.

Gettinger, Stephen. 1994. "Ghosts of Speakers Past and Yet to Come." *Congressional Quarterly Weekly Report,* 10 December, 3534.

Gibbons, Robert. 1997. "Incentives and Careers in Organizations." In *Advances in Economics and Econometrics: Theory and Applications,* ed. David Kreps and Kenneth Wallis. Cambridge: Cambridge University Press.

Gibbons, Robert, and Kevin J. Murphy. 1992. "Optimal Incentive Contracts in the Presence of Career Concerns: Theory and Evidence." *Journal of Political Economy* 100:468–505.

Gilligan, Thomas W., and Keith Krehbiel. 1987. "Collective Decisionmaking and Standing Committees: An Informational Rationale for Restrictive Amendment Procedures." *Journal of Law, Economics, and Organization* 3:287–335.

Gilligan, Thomas W., and Keith Krehbiel. 1989a. "Asymmetric Information and Legislative Rules with a Heterogeneous Committee." *American Journal of Political Science* 33:459–90.

Gilligan, Thomas W., and Keith Krehbiel. 1989b. "Collective Choice Without Procedural Commitment." In *Models of Strategic Choice in Politics,* ed. Peter C. Ordeshook. Ann Arbor: University of Michigan Press.

Gilligan, Thomas W., and Keith Krehbiel. 1990. "Organization of Informative Committees by a Rational Legislature." *American Journal of Political Science* 34:531–64.

Gilligan, Thomas W., and Keith Krehbiel. 1997. "Specialization Decisions within Committees." *Journal of Law, Economics, and Organization* 13: 366–86.

Grier, Kevin B., and Michael C. Munger. 1986. "The Impact of Legislator Attributes on Interest Group Campaign Contributions." *Journal of Labor Research* 7:349–61.

Grier, Kevin B., and Michael C. Munger. 1991. "Committee Assignments, Constituent Preferences, and Campaign Contributions." *Economic Inquiry* 29:24–43.

Groseclose, Timothy. 1996. "An Examination of the Market for Favors and Votes in Congress." *Economic Inquiry* 34:320–40.

Groseclose, Timothy, and Charles Stewart III. 1998. "The Value of Committee Seats in the House, 1947–1991." *American Journal of Political Science* 42:453–74.

Groseclose, Timothy, and Keith Krehbiel. 1994. "Golden Parachutes, Rubber Checks, and Strategic Retirements from the 102d House." *American Journal of Political Science* 38:75–99.

Hall, Richard L. 1987. "Participation and Purpose in Committee Decision Making." *American Political Science Review* 81:104–27.

Hall, Richard L. 1996. *Participation in Congress.* New Haven: Yale University Press.

Hall, Richard L., and Robert Van Houweling. 1995. "Avarice and Ambition in Congress: Representatives' Decisions to Run or Retire from the U.S. House." *American Political Science Review* 89:121–36.

Hall, Richard L., and Frank W. Wayman. 1990. "Buying Time: Moneyed Interests and the Mobilization of Bias in Congressional Committees." *American Political Science Review* 84:797–820.

Hausman, J. A. 1978. "Specification Tests in Econometrics." *Econometrica* 46:1251–71.

Hibbing, John R. 1991. *Congressional Careers: Contours of Life in the U.S. House of Representatives.* Chapel Hill: University of North Carolina Press.

Hibbing, John R., and Elizabeth Theiss-Morse. 1995. *Congress as Public Enemy: Public Attitudes toward American Political Institutions.* Cambridge: Cambridge University Press.

Holmström, Bengt. 1982a. "Managerial Incentives Schemes: A Dynamic Perspective." In *Essays in Economics and Management in Honour of Lars Wahlbeck.* Helsinki: Swenska Handelshogkolan.

Holmström, Bengt. 1982b. "Moral Hazard in Teams." *Bell Journal of Economics* 13:324–40.

Hook, Janet. 1985. "More Funding Urged for Vaccine Research." *Congressional Quarterly Weekly Report,* 16 March, 490.

Hook, Janet. 1989. "Leadership Races Intensify, Foley Ascension Nears." *Congressional Quarterly Weekly Report,* 3 June, 1296–97.

Hook, Janet. 1995. "GOP's Race to Move 'Contract' Hits a Few Bumps in Road." *Congressional Quarterly Weekly Report,* 14 January, 135–36.

Hosansky, David. 1994. "House Committees: Energy and Commerce." *Congressional Quarterly Weekly Report,* 12 November, 3260.

Hosansky, David. 1995. "Bliley Likely to Steer Panel Away from Activist Past." *Congressional Quarterly Weekly Report,* 7 January, 36–38.

"House GOP Offers Descriptions of Bills to Enact 'Contract.' " 1994. *Congressional Quarterly Weekly Report,* 19 November, 3366.

"House Votes $1.5 Billion Cut in Pentagon Spending." 1973. *Congressional Quarterly Weekly Report,* 4 August, 1973, 2176.

Huntington, Samuel P. 1973. "Congressional Responses to the Twentieth Century." In *The Congress and America's Future,* ed. David B. Truman. 2d ed. Englewood Cliffs, NJ: Prentice-Hall.

Inter-university Consortium for Political and Social Research, and Carroll McKibbin. 1993. Roster of United States Congressional Officeholders and Biographical Characteristics of Members of the United States Congress, 1789-1993: Merged Data. [Computer file]. 9th ICPSR ed. Ann Arbor, MI: Inter-university Consortium for Political and Social Research [producer and distributor].

Inter-university Consortium for Political and Social Research and Congressional Quarterly, Inc. 1997. United States Congressional Roll Call Voting Records, 1789-1994 [Computer file]. ICPSR ed. Ann Arbor, MI: Inter-university Consortium for Political and Social Research/Washington, DC: Congressional Quarterly, Inc. [producers]. Ann Arbor, MI: Inter-university Consortium for Political and Social Research [distributor].

Jacobson, Gary C. 1978. "The Effects of Campaign Spending in Congressional Elections." *American Political Science Review* 72:469–91.

Jacobson, Gary C. 1997. *The Politics of Congressional Elections.* 4th ed. New York: Addison-Wesley.

Jacobson, Gary C., and Samuel Kernell. 1983. *Strategy and Choice in Congressional Elections.* 2d ed. New Haven: Yale University Press.

Jacoby, Mary, and Gabriel Kahn. 1994. "The Future of 22 House Panels." *Roll Call,* 14 November.

Johannes, John R. 1983. "Explaining Congressional Casework Styles." *American Journal of Political Science* 27:530–47.

Johannes, John R., and John C. McAdams. 1981. "The Congressional Incumbency Effect: Is It Casework, Policy Compatibility, or Something Else?" *American Journal of Political Science* 25:512–42.

Kahn, Gabriel. 1994. "On House Panels, Challenges Galore." *Roll Call,* 10 November.

Kahn, Gabriel, and Timothy J. Burger. 1994. "Solomon, Livingston Win Chairs." *Roll Call,* 17 November, 1.

Kalb, Deborah. 1995. "The Official Gingrich Task Force List." *The Hill,* 29 March, 8.

Kaplan, Dave. 1994. "This Year, Republicans Gamble That All Politics Is National." *Congressional Quarterly Weekly Report,* 22 October, 3005–8.

Katz, Jeffrey L. 1998a. "Livingston Straddles Republican Fault Line as He

Hunts for Votes for Speaker's Job." *Congressional Quarterly Weekly Report,* 18 April, 979–84.

Katz, Jeffrey L. 1998b. "Shakeup in the House." *Congressional Quarterly Weekly Report,* 7 November, 2989–92.

Katz, Jeffrey L. 1998c. "GOP Must Decide How Much of Gingrich's Team to Keep." *Congressional Quarterly Weekly Report,* 14 November, 3057–61.

Katz, Jeffrey L. 1999. "House Opens a New Session with a Coach and a Prayer." *Congressional Quarterly Weekly Report,* 9 January, 57–59.

Kessler, Daniel and Keith Krehbiel. 1996. "Dynamics of Cosponsorship." *American Political Science Review* 90:555–66.

Kiewiet, D. Roderick. 1983. *Macroeconomics and Micropolitics.* Chicago: University of Chicago Press.

Kiewiet, D. Roderick, and Mathew D. McCubbins. 1991. *The Logic of Delegation: Congressional Parties and the Appropriations Process.* Chicago: University of Chicago Press.

Kiewiet, D. Roderick and Langche Zeng. 1993. "An Analysis of Congressional Career Decisions, 1947–1986." *American Political Science Review* 87:928–941.

Kingdon, John. 1984. *Agendas, Alternatives, and Public Policies.* Boston: Little, Brown.

Kirzner, Israel M. 1973. *Competition and Entrepreneurship.* Chicago: University of Chicago Press.

Knight, Frank H. 1921. *Risk, Uncertainty and Profit.* Boston: Houghton Mifflin.

Koszczuk, Jackie. 1994. "Gingrich's Handpicked Chairman Has Bipartisan Credentials." *Congressional Quarterly Weekly Report,* 19 November, 3350.

Koszczuk, Jackie. 1995a. "Freshmen: New, Powerful Voice." *Congressional Quarterly Weekly Report,* 28 October, 3251–54.

Koszczuk, Jackie. 1995b. "Gingrich Puts More Power into Speaker's Hands." *Congressional Quarterly Weekly Report,* 7 October, 3049–53.

Koszczuk, Jackie. 1995c. "'Train Wreck' Engineered by GOP Batters Party and House Speaker." *Congressional Quarterly Weekly Report,* 18 November, 3506.

Koszczuk, Jackie. 1996. "With Humor and Firm Hand, Armey Rules the House." *Congressional Quarterly Weekly Report,* 2 March, 523–28.

Koszczuk, Jackie. 1997a. "Concerned GOP Urges Gingrich: Settle Down to Housekeeping" *Congressional Quarterly Weekly Report,* 30 August, 2030–33.

Koszczuk, Jackie. 1997b. "With Tone, Tenor of First Session, It Seemed Like Old Times." *Congressional Quarterly Weekly Report,* 6 December, 2975.

Koszczuk, Jackie. 1997c. "Gingrich under Fire as Discord Simmers from Rank to Top." *Congressional Quarterly Weekly Report,* 21 June, 1415–18.

Koszczuk, Jackie. 1999. "Hastert Gently Gavels in an Era of 'Order' in the House." *Congressional Quarterly Weekly Report,* 27 February, 458–65.

Krehbiel, Keith. 1988. "Spatial Model of Legislative Choice." *Legislative Studies Quarterly* 13:259–319.

Krehbiel, Keith. 1991. *Information and Legislative Organization.* Ann Arbor: University of Michigan Press.

Krehbiel, Keith. 1993. "Where's the Party?" *British Journal of Political Science* 23:235–66.

Krehbiel, Keith. 1995. "Cosponsors and Wafflers from A to Z." *American Journal of Political Science* 39:906–23.

Krehbiel, Keith. 1997. "Restrictive Rules Reconsidered." *American Journal of Political Science* 41:919–44.

Krehbiel, Keith. 1998. *Pivotal Politics: A Theory of U.S. Lawmaking.* Chicago: University of Chicago Press.

Kuntz, Phil. 1992. "Crowning a Cannon." *Congressional Quarterly Weekly Report,* 12 December, 3782.

Lancaster, Tony. 1990. *The Econometric Analysis of Transition Data.* Cambridge: Cambridge University Press.

Langbein, Laura I., and Lee Sigelman. 1989. "Show Horses, Work Horses, and Dead Horses." *American Politics Quarterly* 17:80–95.

Loomis, Burdett A. 1988. *The New American Politician.* New York: Basic Books.

MacNeil, Neil. 1963. *Forge of Democracy: The House of Representatives.* New York: David McKay.

Maddala, G. S. 1983. *Limited-Dependent and Qualitative Variables in Econometrics.* Cambridge: Cambridge University Press.

"Majority Leader Fights for Post." 1998. *Washington Post,* 13 November, A25.

Malbin, Michael. 1981. "Delegation, Deliberation, and the New Role of Congressional Staff." In *The New Congress,* ed. Thomas Mann and Norman Ornstein. Washington, DC: American Enterprise Institute.

Martinez, Gebe. 1999. "Armey Finds Rehabilitation on the House Floor." *Congressional Quarterly Weekly Report,* 5 June, 1326–27.

Mayhew, David R. 1974. *Congress: The Electoral Connection.* New Haven: Yale University Press.

Mayhew, David R. 1991. *Divided We Govern: Party Control, Lawmaking, and Investigations, 1946–1990.* New Haven: Yale University Press.

McAdams, John C., and John R. Johannes. 1988. "Congressmen, Perquisites, and Elections." *Journal of Politics* 50:412–39.

McCarty, Nolan, and Lawrence S. Rothenberg. 1996. "Commitment and the Campaign Contract." *American Journal of Political Science* 40:872–904.

McKelvey, Richard D. 1976. "Intransitivities in Multidimensional Voting Models and Some Implications for Agenda Control." *Journal of Economic Theory* 2:472–82.

Meyer, Margaret A. 1995. "Cooperation and Competition in Organizations: A Dynamic Perspective." *European Economic Review* 39:709–22.

Miller, Gary J. 1992. *Managerial Dilemmas: The Political Economy of Hierarchy.* Cambridge: Cambridge University Press.

Miller, Warren E., and National Election Studies/Center for Political Studies. 1982. American National Election Study, 1980 [Computer file]. Conducted by University of Michigan, Center for Political Studies. ICPSR ed. Ann Arbor, MI: Inter-university Consortium for Political and Social Research [producer and distributor].

Miller, Warren E., and the National Election Studies/Center for Political Studies. 1983. American National Election Study, 1982: Post-Election Survey File [Computer file]. Conducted by University of Michigan, Center for Political Studies. ICPSR ed. Ann Arbor, MI: Inter-university Consortium for Political and Social Research [producer and distributor].

Miller, Warren E., and National Election Studies/Center for Political Studies. 1986. American National Election Study, 1984 [Computer file]. Conducted by University of Michigan, Center for Political Studies. 2d ICPSR ed. Ann Arbor, MI: Inter-university Consortium for Political and Social Research [producer and distributor].

Miller, Warren E., and National Election Studies/Center for Political Studies. 1987. American National Election Study, 1986 [Computer file]. Conducted by University of Michigan, Center for Political Studies. 2d ICPSR ed. Ann Arbor, MI: Inter-university Consortium for Political and Social Research [producer and distributor].

Miller, Warren E., and National Election Studies/Center for Political Studies. 1989. The American National Election Study, 1988:Pre- and Post-Election Survey [Computer file]. Ann Arbor, MI: Center for Political Studies, University of Michigan [original producer]. 2d ICPSR ed. Ann Arbor, MI: Inter-University Consortium for Political and Social Research [producer and distributor].

Miller, Warren E., Donald R. Kinder, Steven J. Rosenstone, and the National Election Studies. 1992. American National Election Study, 1990: Post-Election Survey [Computer file]. Conducted by University of Michigan, Center for Political Studies. 2d ICPSR ed. Ann Arbor, MI: Inter-university Consortium for Political and Social Research [producer and distributor].

Miller, Warren E., Donald R. Kinder, Steven J. Rosenstone, and the National

Election Studies. 1993. American National Election Study, 1992: Pre- and Post-Election Survey [Enhanced with 1990 and 1991 Data] [Computer file]. Conducted by University of Michigan, Center for Political Studies. ICPSR ed. Ann Arbor, MI: University of Michigan, Center for Political Studies, and Inter-university Consortium for Political and Social Research [producers]. Ann Arbor, MI: Inter-university Consortium for Political and Social Research [distributor].

Miller, Warren E., and Donald E. Stokes. 1963. "Constituency Influence in Congress." *American Political Science Review* 57:45–57.

Mills, Mike. 1988a. "Base-Closing Issue: Back to Drawing Board." *Congressional Quarterly Weekly Report,* 30 April, 1145.

Mills, Mike. 1988b. "Pentagon Calls Amendments 'Death by Pinpricks': Members Go on the Offensive to Defend Bases." *Congressional Quarterly Weekly Report,* 2 July, 1815.

"Modified Irrigation Plan Approved." 1986. *Congressional Quarterly Weekly Report,* 22 March, 676.

Morton, Rebecca, and Charles Cameron. 1992. "Elections and the Theory of Campaign Contributions: A Survey and Critical Analysis." *Economics and Politics* 4:79–108.

Munger, Michael C. 1988. "Allocation of Desirable Committee Assignments: Extended Queues versus Committee Expansion." *American Journal of Political Science* 32:317–44.

Nelson, Garrison. 1977. Partisan Patterns of House Leadership Change, 1789–1977. *American Political Science Review* 71:918–39.

Oleszek, Walter J. 1989. *Congressional Procedure and the Policy Process.* Washington, DC: CQ Press.

Ornstein, Norman J., Thomas E. Mann, and Michael J. Malbin. 1996. *Vital Statistics on Congress.* Washington, DC: American Enterprise Institute for Public Policy Research.

Peabody, Robert L. 1976. *Leadership in Congress: Stability, Succession, and Change.* Boston: Little, Brown.

Pinto-Duschinsky, Michael. 1981. *British Political Finance, 1830–1980.* Washington, DC: American Enterprise Institute for Public Policy Research.

Plott, Charles. 1967. "A Notion of Equilibrium and Its Possibility under Majority Rule." *American Economic Review* 57:787–806.

Polsby, Nelson W. 1968. "The Institutionalization of the U.S. House of Representatives." *American Political Science Review* 62:144–68.

Poole, Keith T., and Howard Rosenthal. 1997. *Congress: A Political-Economic History of Roll Call Voting.* Oxford: Oxford University Press.

Price, David E. 1972. *Who Makes the Laws? Creativity and Power in Senate Committees.* Cambridge, MA: Schenkman.

Price, David E. 1989. "From Outsider to Insider." In *Congress Reconsidered,* ed. Lawrence C. Dodd and Bruce I. Oppenheimer. 4th ed. Washington, DC: CQ Press.

Ragsdale, Lyn, and Timothy Cook. 1987. "Representatives' Actions and Challengers' Reactions: Limits to Candidate Connections in the House." *American Journal of Political Science* 31:45–81.

Reid, T. R. 1980. *Congressional Odyssey.* San Francisco: W. H. Freeman.

"Republicans' Initial Promise: 100-Day Debate on 'Contract.' " 1994. *Congressional Quarterly Weekly Report,* 12 November, 3216.

Rieselbach, Leroy N. 1986. *Congressional Reform.* Washington, DC: CQ Press.

Riker, William H. 1986. *The Art of Political Manipulation.* New Haven: Yale University Press.

Rohde, David W. 1979. "Risk-Bearing and Progressive Ambition: The Case of Members of the United States House of Representatives." *American Journal of Political Science* 23:1–26.

Rohde, David W. 1991. *Parties and Leaders in the Postreform House.* Chicago: University of Chicago Press.

Rohde, David W. 1994. "Parties and Committees in the House: Member Motivations, Issues, and Institutional Arrangements." *Legislative Studies Quarterly* 19:341–59.

Rohde, David W., and Kenneth A. Shepsle. 1973. "Democratic Committee Assignments in the House of Representatives: Strategic Aspects of a Social Choice Process." *American Political Science Review* 67:889–905.

Rovner, Julie. 1986a. "House Passes Vaccine-Injury Compensation Bill." *Congressional Quarterly Weekly Report,* 18 October, 2626.

Rovner, Julie. 1986b. "Major Provisions of Nine-Part Omnibus Health Bill." *Congressional Quarterly Weekly Report,* 22 November, 2952–54.

Salisbury, Robert H., and Kenneth A. Shepsle. 1981. "U.S. Congressman as Enterprise." *Legislative Studies Quarterly* 6:559–76.

"Scandal and Statecraft: 12 Who Made a Difference." 1998. *Congressional Quarterly Weekly Report,* 21 November, 3150.

Schiff, Steven H., and Steven S. Smith. 1983. "Generational Change and the Allocation of Staff in the U.S. Congress." *Legislative Studies Quarterly* 8:457–67.

Schiller, Wendy J. 1995. "Senators as Political Entrepreneurs: Using Bill Sponsorship to Shape Legislative Agendas." *American Journal of Political Science* 39:186–203.

Schlesinger, Joseph A. 1966. *Ambition and Politics.* Chicago: Rand McNally.

Schneider, Mark, and Paul Teske. 1992. "Toward a Theory of the Political Entrepreneur: Evidence from Local Government." *American Political Sci-*

ence Review 86:737–47.

Schneier, Edward V., and Bertram Gross. 1993. *Legislative Strategy: Shaping Public Policy.* New York: St. Martin's.

Shepsle, Kenneth A. 1978. *The Giant Jigsaw Puzzle.* Chicago: University of Chicago Press.

Shepsle, Kenneth A. 1979. "Institutional Arrangements and Equilibrium in Multidimensional Voting Models." *American Journal of Political Science* 23:27–59.

Shepsle, Kenneth A. 1989. "The Changing Textbook Congress." In *Can the Government Govern?* ed. John E. Chubb and Paul E. Peterson. Washington, DC: Brookings Institution.

Shepsle, Kenneth A., and Barry Nalebuff. 1990. "The Commitment to Seniority in Self-Governing Groups." *Journal of Law, Economics, and Organization* 6:45–72.

Shepsle, Kenneth A., and Barry R. Weingast. 1987. "The Institutional Foundations of Committee Power." *American Political Science Review* 81:85–104.

Shepsle, Kenneth A., and Barry R. Weingast. 1994. "Positive Theories of Congressional Institutions." *Legislative Studies Quarterly* 19:149–79.

Sinclair, Barbara. 1983. *Majority Leadership in the U.S. House.* Baltimore: Johns Hopkins University Press.

Sinclair, Barbara. 1995. *Legislators, Leaders, and Lawmaking: The U.S. House of Representatives in the Postreform Era.* Baltimore: Johns Hopkins University Press.

Sloss, Judith. 1973. "Stable Outcomes in Majority Rule Voting Games." *Public Choice* 15:19–48.

Smith, Steven S. 1989. *Call to Order: Floor Politics in the House and Senate.* Washington, DC: Brookings Institution.

Smith, Steven S. 1995. *The American Congress.* Boston: Houghton Mifflin.

Smith, Steven S., and Christopher J. Deering. 1984. *Committees in Congress.* Washington, DC: CQ Press.

Smith, Steven S., and Christopher J. Deering. 1990. *Committees in Congress.* 2d ed. Washington, DC: CQ Press.

Smith, Steven S., and Eric D. Lawrence. 1997. "Party Control of Committees in the Republican Congress." In *Congress Reconsidered,* ed. Lawrence C. Dodd and Bruce I. Oppenheimer. 6th ed. Washington, DC: CQ Press.

Smith, Steven S., and Bruce A. Ray. 1983. "The Impact of Congressional Reform: House Democratic Committee Assignments." *Congress and the Presidency* 10:219–40.

Snyder, James M. 1990. "Campaign Contributions as Investments: The U.S. House of Representatives, 1980–1986." *Journal of Political Economy*

98:1195–227.

Snyder, James M. 1991. "On Buying Legislatures." *Economics and Politics* 3:93–109.

Snyder, James M. 1992. "Long-Term Investment in Politicians, or, Give Early, Give Often." *Journal of Law and Economics* 35:15–43.

Sorenson, Aage B. 1977. "The Structure of Inequality and the Process of Attainment." *American Sociological Review* 42:965–78.

Spencer, David E., and Kenneth N. Berk. 1981. "A Limited Information Specification Test." *Econometrica* 49:1079–85.

Stewman, Shelby. 1986. "Demographic Models of Internal Labor Markets." *Administrative Science Quarterly* 31:212–47.

Stokes, Donald E., and Warren E. Miller. 1966. "Party Government and the Saliency of Congress." In *Elections and the Political Order,* ed. Angus Campbell, Philip E. Converse, Warren E. Miller, and Donald E. Stokes. New York: Wiley.

Stratman, Thomas. 1992. "Are Contributors Rational? Untangling Strategies of Political Action Committees." *Journal of Political Economy* 100:647–64.

Sundquist, James L. 1981. *The Decline and Resurgence of Congress.* Washington, DC: Brookings Institution.

Thomas, Scott, and Bernard Grofman. 1993. "The Effect of Congressional Rules about Bill Cosponsorship on Duplicate Bills: Changing Incentives for Credit Claiming." *Public Choice* 75:93–98.

Thurber, James. 1981. "The Evolving Role and Effectiveness of the Congressional Research Agencies." In *The House at Work,* ed. Joseph Cooper and G. Calvin Mackenzie. Austin: University of Texas Press.

Towell, Pat. 1985. "Aspin: A Coalition-Builder at Armed Services." *Congressional Quarterly Weekly Report,* 19 January, 99–102.

Tuma, Nancy Brandon, Michael T. Hannan, and Lyle P. Groeneveld. 1979. "Dynamic Analysis of Event Histories." *American Journal of Sociology* 84:820–54.

U.S. House. 1987. Committee on House Administration. *Contemporary Congressional Use of Information Technology.* Washington, DC: Government Printing Office. Report prepared for the Committee on House Administration.

U.S. House. 1989. *Preamble and Rules of the Democratic Caucus.* Washington, DC: Government Printing Office.

Weingast, Barry R., and William Marshall. 1988. "The Industrial Organization of Congress." *Journal of Political Economy* 96:132–63.

White, Harrison C. 1970. *Chains of Opportunity: System Models of Mobility in Organizations.* Cambridge: Harvard University Press.

Wilson, Rick K., and Cheryl D. Young. 1997. "Cosponsorship in the U.S. Congress." *Legislative Studies Quarterly* 22:25–43.

Wright, John R. 1985. "PACs, Contributions, and Roll Calls: An Organizational Perspective." *American Political Science Review* 79:400–414.

Index